SOFT CITY

JONATHAN RABAN was born in Norfolk in 1942. Before becoming a full-time writer in 1969, he was a university lecturer in English Literature. In addition to *Soft City* he has written three books of travel and autobiography – *Arabia, Old Glory*, which won the Royal Society of Literature's Heinemann Award and the Thomas Cook Award, and *Coasting* – a novel, *Foreign Land*, and most recently *For Love & Money*, part autobiography, part anthology of unpublished works. Jonathan Raban has also written plays for radio, television and the stage, and is a frequent broadcaster and reviewer.

very much love
to
from

Christmas 1991

Jonathan Raban

SOFT CITY

COLLINS HARVILL
8 Grafton Street, London W1
1988

COLLINS HARVILL
William Collins Sons and Co. Ltd
London · Glasgow · Sydney · Auckland
Toronto · Johannesburg

BRITISH LIBRARY CATALOGUING IN PUBLICATION DATA

Raban, Jonathan
Soft city.
1. Cities and towns
I. Title
307.7'64   HT151

ISBN 0-00-272778-1

First published by Hamish Hamilton 1974
This edition first published by Collins Harvill 1988
Reprinted 1988 (twice)
Reprinted 1990

© Jonathan Raban 1974

Printed and bound in Great Britain by
William Collins Sons and Co. Ltd, Glasgow

For Robert and Caroline Lowell

Contents

ONE

The Soft City

I come out of a formica kebab-house alone after lunch, my head prickly with retsina. The air outside is a sunny swirl of exhaust fumes; that faint, smoky-turquoise big city colour. I stand on the pavement waiting to cross at the lights. Suddenly I know that I don't know the direction of the traffic. Do cars here drive on the left or the right hand side of the road? A cluster of Italian au pair girls, their voices mellow and labial, like a chorus escaped from an opera, pass me; I hear, in the crowd, an adenoidal Nebraskan contralto, twangy as a jew's-harp. Turned to a dizzied tourist myself, forgetful and jet-shocked, I have to hunt in my head for the language spoken here.

But this is where you live; it's your city — London, or New York, or wherever — and its language is the language you've always known, the language from which *being you, being me,* are inseparable. In those dazed moments at stoplights, it's possible to be a stranger to yourself, to be so doubtful as to who you are that you have to check on things like the placards round the news-vendors' kiosks or the uniforms of the traffic policemen. You're a balloonist adrift, and you need anchors to tether you down.

A sociologist, I suppose, would see these as classic symptoms of alienation, more evidence to add to the already fat dossier on the evils of urban life. I feel more hospitable towards them. For at moments like this, the city goes soft; it awaits the imprint of an identity. For better or worse, it invites you to remake it, to consolidate it into a shape you can live in. You, too. Decide who you are, and the city will again assume a fixed form round you. Decide what it is, and your own identity will be revealed, like a position on a map fixed by triangulation. Cities, unlike villages and small towns, are plastic by nature. We mould them in our images: they, in their turn, shape us by the resistance they offer when we try to impose our own personal form on them. In this sense, it seems to me that living in cities is an art, and we need the vocabulary of art, of style, to describe the peculiar relationship between man and material that exists in the continual creative play of urban living. The city as we imagine it, the soft city of illusion, myth, aspiration, nightmare, is as real, maybe more real, than the hard city one can locate on maps in statistics, in monographs on urban sociology and demography and architecture.

Yet the hard facts of cities tend to be large, clear and brutal. A hundred years ago they were the facts of appalling poverty, grimly documented by outside observers like Henry Mayhew, Charles Booth, and, a little later in America, Jacob Riis. Today the overwhelming fact of life in New York, if not in London is the violence brewing in its streets. Indeed, poverty and violence are clearly related: both are primarily dependent on the attitudes people hold towards strangers. The indifference that generates the one, and the hatred that animates the other, stem from the same root feeling. If a city can estrange you from yourself, how much more powerfully can it detach you from the lives of other people, and how deeply immersed you may become in the inaccessibly private community of your own head.

In October 1972 when the evenings had begun to darken early in London, a 19-year-old boy stepped out of Nash house on the Mall, Decimus Burton's splendidly laid-out approach to Buckingham Palace. The boy had been watching a movie at the Institute for Contemporary Arts, was bored, and wanted a cigarette. Just outside the ICA is a wide flight of steps, scantily lit and shaded by trees. The boy came out here for his smoke. It was a warm, Indian-summery night, and the Mall was buzzing with strolling couples and tourists out after dinner from their hotels. When the movie ended, the crowd emerging from the ICA mistook the boy's body for a zonked junkie or a pavement drunk. It's the sort of thing you see often enough on Piccadilly; here it was misplaced, an incongruous touch of squalor on this much swept and tended triumphal avenue.

The boy will live, but he will be permanently paralysed. Two men, he has said, came at him from the side of the steps: one gagged him with his hand, the other got his arm round his neck and severed his spinal cord with a 2½ in blade of a penknife. The whole encounter had a ghastly surgical precision. Nothing was stolen; the men were total strangers.

There are rumours of a gang called the Envies. Their brutal, seemingly motiveless assaults on strangers go largely unreported by the press, apparently for fear of 'carbon copy' crimes. Who might not fall victim to the Envies? You have a car, a girl, a new suit, a cigarette, even a smile on your face, and they may come at you out of the dark. They choose the most elegant and unruffled parts of the city for their attacks. They act on appearances: on what looks like prosperity, or good luck, or happiness. Unlike most muggers, desperate for the price of a fix, they say nothing, take nothing except your right to live. Like a soldier in a war, you die or are maimed because you were wearing the wrong uniform. What was the boy's mistake? his clothes? his expression? his mere attendance at a rather snooty resort of the cultured middle classes? In the last few years, it's become plain that you are at your most vulnerable to the mugger in the 'play and entertainment' areas of the city. In New York, Broadway and the Plaza are notorious danger spots; in London, the district around Waterloo, enclosing both the South Bank arts complex and the Old Vic, has the highest record of unprovoked violent assault. The assumption is usually made that these are areas where people carry stuffed wallets and, softened on food and wine and theatre, are easy game for the thief. But another, more frightening explanation presents itself: that the victims were chosen simply because they seemed to be enjoying themselves, having a good time, and that envy is perhaps an even stronger motive for violence than greed. We have so separated ourselves, person from person and group from group, in the city, that we have made hatred a dreadfully easy emotion. It comes to us as lightly and insidiously as the symptoms of an unconsciously harboured disease.

Coming out of the London Underground at Oxford Circus one afternoon, I saw a man go berserk in the crowd on the stairs. 'You fucking . . . fucking bastards!' he shouted, and his words rolled round and round the lavatorial porcelain tube as we ploughed through. He was in a neat city suit, with a neat city paper neatly folded in a pink hand. His fingernails were clipped to the quick. What was surprising was that nobody showed surprise: a slight speeding-up in the pace of the crowd, a turned head or two, a quick grimace, but that was all. I think we all knew, could feel on our own pulses, the claustrophobia and the hostility that was eating away at the man who was cursing us. Inside, we were all cursing each other. Who feels love for his fellow-man at rush hour? Not me. I suspect that the best insurance against urban violence is the fact that most of us shrink from contact with strangers; we don't want to touch one anothe. or feel that close to the stink of someone else's life. The muggers and the men who feel-up girls on crowded subway trains are exceptions. But if our unexpressed loathing for strangers in a crowd were to break that barrier of physical inhibition, who knows what hell might be let loose on the streets and underground.

As I write, the Liquid Theatre is in performance under the arches of Charing Cross Station; a 'participatory' theatre of touch-and-feel, where the members of the audience are led through games in which they explore each other's bodies. It is a pleasurable, gentle, moderately inexpensive therapy for urban people, yet on the surface it seems a strange one. We spend so much of our time, after all, in crowds: our bodies are always colliding and rubbing, our hands brushing; our areas of privacy, in a society where land and space are constantly and dangerously rising in value, are being eroded. The modern city, of small apartments and densely occupied communications routes — trains, pavements, lifts, sup-

ermarket walkways—makes us live hugger-mugger, cheek to
cheek. We need, apparently. to relearn how to touch each
other amicably, and are prepared to spend money and a night
out (pushing past more people on subways en route to
Charing Cross) on that rather simple human exercise. Touch
without violence or revulsion—and without sexual passion,
too—has turned into a faculty threatened with extinction,
preserved, at least for the urban middle class, in the hothouse
conditions of encounter groups and experimental drama shows.
To do it at all, we have to put on masks, act it out, be wheedled
into it by psychiatric gurus or bare-chested, Afro-headed
actor-managers.

In cities, we have good reason to shrink from strangers.
High rates of murder and assault are not in themselves symptoms of urban congestion. A remote, low-density rural area
like Cardiganshire in West Wales can more than hold its
own against London in its per capita murder figures. But
in rural areas the majority of the victims of violent crime
know their assailants (indeed, are probably married to
them); in cities, the killer and the mugger come out of the
anonymous dark, their faces unrecognised, their motives
obscure. In a city, you can be known, envied, hated by
strangers. In your turn, you can feel the exaggerated, operatic
emotions that the city arouses in its inhabitants. The urban
terrorist, the footpad, the Envy, the Angry Brigader, the
Weatherman, is the final, ugly performer in greasepaint
and grandiloquent gesture, of a drama which is for most
of us, thankfully, a mental affair, a script in the head which
few of us are sufficiently mad or desperate to act out.

The house I live in in London is five storeys of solid, lavish,
battlements. It was built when the Victorian middle class
family was the strongest institution in the world, and when
its houses reflected the imperial wealth and grandeur (not to
mention the divine ordination) of its status. Space was used
with throwaway generosity: high ceilings, vast halls and
stairways, marble-pillared porches which could themselves
comfortably accommodate a modern self-contained flat. The
house was once a working community. There were front-

door callers, and tradesmen who tugged on the side-road bellpull that goes down to the basement. Like a model of Empire, the family lived on the labours of the servants who toiled and slept in the warren of rooms 'below stairs'. But the twentieth century, with its smaller families, its reduced opportunities for massive individual wealth, its increased premium on the value of space, and its vastly more expensive labour costs, has destroyed the house as an organic structure. It has been sliced, horizontally and vertically, into a higgledy-piggledy pile of chunks of living space, some of many rooms, some of only a bit of floor big enough to make a bed. None of us live to scale; we are all dwarfed by the baroque proportions of the halls and passageways. There are strangers, not on the street, or across the square, but in the very next room. (There may even be strangers in your own room.) The house is constructed around a well – a deep rectangular column of light and air which was supposed to work like a lung through which the building breathed its own enclosed atmosphere. Now all it does is to bring strangers into eerie juxtaposition with each other. It transmits unasked-for intimacies, private sights, private sounds, which fuel suspicion and embarrassment and resentment.

I am woken in the small hours by the sound of a girl achieving her climax; a deep shriek of pleasure that has nothing to do with me. I can hear her man sigh as close as if he and I were under the same sheet. On another night, a TV blares through an open window with a late-late show. On another, a woman is crying, a miserable train of broken hiccups. A man – I can hear his feet crackling on the bare boards – says: 'Shut up. Why don't you bloody well shut up?' Then there are nights of joke-hashing: someone mutters like a priest going quickly through a private office, followed by bursts of yelling adenoidal laughter. The routine is repeated, and repeated; I fall asleep, alone, with Australians in my ears.

The flat across the well is occupied by a gaggle of people, and most of them are passing through; they flit when it suits them. I can't fit their faces – let alone their names – to

these night noises. Letters come for them, and go soggy and
stale in the mailbox. We share a front door, nothing more.
Could that girl there, with the dough-pudding features
and the shabby twinset, be the same girl who was so rapturously fulfilled last night? Perhaps. For unlikeliness is the
key here: you play *heads-bodies-and-legs* with incongruous
fragments of other people's lives. It's only with consistent
behaviour, where all the details fit, that strangers become
knowable, that their lives take on a pattern you can sympa-
thise with and understand. As long as they remain like this,
inchoate and unplotted, they are spooks: the easiest thing
to do with them is to knit them into a paranoid fantasy. So
lonely old people – and not just in cities – conceive of the
active, fragmentary life around them as a concerted plot, full
of sinister coincidences.

To live in a city is to live in a community of people who
are strangers to each other. You have to act on hints and
fancies, for they are all that the mobile and cellular nature
of city life will allow you. You expose yourself in, and are
exposed to by others, fragments, isolated signals, bare disconnected gestures, jungle cries and whispers that resist all
your attempts to unravel their meaning, their consistency.
As urban dwellers, we live in a world marked by the people
at the next table ('Such a brute, that man. She went to the
Seychelles,' comes the sudden loud phrase, breaking out of
the confidential murmur), the man glimpsed in the street
with a bowler hat and a hacksaw and never seen again, the
girl engrossed in her orgasm across the air-well. So much
takes place in the head, so little is known and fixed. Signals,
styles, systems of rapid, highly-conventionalised communication, are the lifeblood of the big city. It is when these
systems break down – when we lose our grasp on the grammar
of urban life – that the Envies take over. The city, our great
modern form, is soft, amenable to a dazzling and libidinous
variety of lives, dreams, interpretations. But the very plastic
qualities which makes the city the great liberator of human
identity also cause it to be especially vulnerable to psychosis
and totalitarian nightmare. If it can, in the Platonic ideal,

be the highest expression of man's reason and sense of his
own community with other men, the city can also be a violent,
sub-realist, expression of his panic, his envy, his hatred of
strangers, his callousness. It's easy to 'drop' people in the
city, where size and anonymity and the absence of clear
communal sanctions license the kind of behaviour that any
village would stamp out at birth. Just as the city is the place
where you can choose your society, so it is also the place
where you can 'drop' discarded friends, old lovers, the duller
members of your family : you can, too, 'drop' the poor, the
minorities, the immigrants, everyone, in fact, who isn't to
your taste or of your class. The mugger can step out of the
shadows to drop a victim who has been singled out by the
dimly seen cut of his clothes. In the city we can change our
identities at will, as Dickens-triumphantly proved over and
over again in his fiction; its discontinuity favours both instant-
villains and instant-heroes impartially. The gaudy, theatrical
nature of city life tends constantly to melodrama. My own
aim here is to investigate the plot, and its implications for
the nature of character, of the modern city, in the hope that
we may better understand what it is that cities do to us, and
how they change our styles of living and thinking and feeling.

TWO

The City as Melodrama

What did these vain and presumptuous men intend? How did they expect to raise this lofty mass against God, when they had built it above all the mountains and clouds of the earth's atmosphere?
Saint Augustine on Babylon, *City of God*, Bk XV.

The city has always been an embodiment of hope and a source of festering guilt: a dream pursued, and found vain, wanting, and destructive. Our current mood of revulsion against cities is not new; we have grown used to looking for Utopia only to discover that we have created Hell. We are accustomed to gazing at America to make out our future, and in America the city is widely regarded as the sack of excrement which the country has to carry on its back to atone for its sins. Radio, television, magazines, colleges mount ritual talk-ins in which the word 'urban', pronounced in the hushed and contrite tone of a *mea culpa*, is monotonously followed by the two predicates, 'problems' and 'renewal'. On these joyless occasions, it is made clear that the problems have no real solutions, and that the notion of rehabilitation is a piece of empty piety, a necessary fiction in which no-one really believes. When Mayor Lindsay of New York made his abortive bid for the Democratic Presidential nomination in 1972, the only tangible result of his campaign was a flood of sick jokes about the garbage in his streets, animal, vegetable, and mineral. It further became apparent that nobody in the United States wanted a big-city president: better to look to Maine, Alabama, South Dakota, California, whose native sons would not be polluted by the stench of those cities where most of America's domestic troubles are located.

A middle-sized American city at 7 p.m., after the commuters have taken to their cars and the too-bright sodium
lights show through the quickening dusk (I am thinking of
Worcester, Hartford, Springfield Mass.), feels like a burnt-
out dream. No-one is about, bar a dusting of blacks, Puerto
Ricans, Chicanos, and they have the furtive air of people
habituated to being always suspected of being up to something. The white-domed Statehouse, memorial of a gran-
diose colonial conception of civic order, looks a tartarous
yellow. A hundred years ago, people put up portly brown-
stone houses along wide wooded avenues. Their architecture
is proud, but one can almost smell the rot in the stone, rank
and soggy with inattention. In the hallways, you catch a
whiff of bacon-fat and Lysol. Each apartment door has a
winking spyhole cut into the wood, and people live behind
chains and double-locks, with mail-order .38 revolvers tucked
handily into a drawer along with the napery. The humans
most in evidence are the policemen. Their car headlights
rake housefronts for junkies, and you can hear their klaxons
screaming, always a block or two away, like invisibly ominous
owls. After midnight, in the neon-blaze of the Dunkin' Donut
shop you can see them, a line of broad bums stretched over
red plastic stools, their pistols hanging out on straps like
monstrous genital accessories.

Or there is the dismal story of Bixby Hill on the outskirts
of Los Angeles. There nice people have erected their $150,000
homes inside a fortified stockade, eight feet high, patrolled by
heavily armed security guards, with an electronic communication system installed in every house. In a TV programme about
this armour-plated ghetto, a shrill housewife, surrounded by
hardware and alarm-buttons, said, 'We are trying to preserve
values and morals here that are decaying on the outside.' And
her husband, a comfortable Babbitty figure, told the reporter:
'When I pass by the guard in the evening, I'm safe, I'm home,
it's just a lovely feeling, it really is.' When they talked of the
city beyond the walls, they conjured a vision of Gomorrah
where the respectable and the innocent are clubbed, butchered,
burglarised, where every patch of shadow has its resident

badman with a knife, a gleam in his eye, and a line of punctures up his forearm.

Perhaps the original dream of the American city, with its plazas, squares, avenues, and Washingtonian circles, was too optimistic and elevated for reality. On Chestnut Street and Elm Street, the trees languished. But the present disreputable state of *civitas* in the United States is the product of an exaggeratedly Calvinist sense of sin. Finding the city irredeemable is only the other side of the coin to expecting it to be Paradise : utopias and dystopias go, of necessity, hand in hand. Disillusion is a vital part of the process of dreaming — and may, one suspects, prove almost as enjoyable. When New Yorkers tell one about the dangers of their city, the muggings, the dinner parties to which no-one turns up for fear of being attacked on the way, the traffic snarl-ups, the bland indifference of the city cops, they are unmistakably bragging. Living in Greenwich Village is almost as exciting as war-service, and beneath the veneer of concerned moralism it is not hard to detect a vein of scoutlike enthusiasm for adventure. The New Yorker, echoing Whitman, is a proud participant in the decadence which has made his city even more world-famous than it was before : he is the man, he suffers, he is there.

His nightmare city is simply an ideal city in reverse, just as the great ideal cities in history, from Plato's Republic to Le Corbusier's Radiant City, have been constructed in protest against the uninspiring conditions of cities as they actually were and are. The failures and imperfections of Athens, Rome, London, New York, Paris, have given rise to towns in books which in their architecture, their social and political life, would express man's highest aspirations to perfectibility. The very existence of the city, with its peculiar personal freedoms and possibilities, has acted as a licence for sermons and dreams. Here society might be arranged for man's greatest good; here, all too often, it has seemed a sink of vice and failure. Nor has this melodramatic moralistic view of city life been the exclusive province of philosophers and theologians; political bosses, architects, town planners, even those professionally tweedy sceptics, sociologists, have happily connived at the idea of the city as a controllable option between heaven and hell. Bits and pieces of ideal cities have been incorporated into real ones; traffic projects and rehousing schemes are habitually introduced by their sponsors as at least preliminary steps to paradise. The ideal city gives us the authority to castigate the real one; while the sore itch of real cities goads us into creating ideal ones.

Saint Augustine wrote *The City of God* in a state of sorrowful contemplation of a succession of earthly cities. A modern ecologist looking at the effects of megalopolis could hardly have more cause for despair than Augustine staring at the mark of Cain on every city in history. Babylon, Troy, Athens, Rome, Syracuse, had all fallen : Carthage itself was sacked on the morning of Augustine's death. There was a good reason for Cain, the first murderer, to found the first city. Ancient cities were, before all else, fortifications against hostile strangers; their architecture, like that of Bixby Hill, began not with the life of the community inside the walls but with defence against the marauders outside. So slaughter, pestilence, siege, sacking, plunder, and burning – to use Augustine's own words – were the city's inevitable fate. If, by some accident, the city survived sacking by foreigners, there were many precedents for the citizens to occasion their own ruin by shiftless self-indulgence. Byzantium failed to maintain its huge population (at its height, it had 500,000 inhabitants). There are desolate accounts of sheep grazing within the city walls, nibbling among the stumps of deserted dwellings. The medieval city, under constant threat of under-population, feared paganism and homosexuality for practical as well as moral reasons. The Christian cult of the family was the cornerstone of the expanding and prosperous city.

The economics of city life have always enabled an entertainment-industry to take root in a large town. The citizen has more money and more leisure than his country cousin, more opportunities to spoil himself at the circus, the theatre, the whore-house. Augustine, grimly observing these antics, addressed himself to the crowd as they swarmed into the 'scenic games, exhibitions of folly and licence':

> Oh infatuated man, what is this blindness, or rather
> madness, which possesses you? How is it that while, as
> we hear, even the eastern nations are bewailing your ruin,
> and while powerful states in the most remote parts of the
> earth are mourning your fall as a public calamity, ye
> yourselves should be crowding to the theatres, should
> be pouring into them and filling them, and, in short, be
> playing a madder part now than ever before? This was the
> foul plague-spot, this the wreck of virtue and honour
> that Scipio sought to preserve you from when he prohibited
> the construction of theatres; this was his reason for desiring
> that you might still have an enemy to fear, seeing as he
> did how easily prosperity would corrupt and destroy you.
> He did not consider that republic flourishing whose walls
> stand, but whose morals are in ruins.

It is the very success of the city as an economic unit which
causes its downfall as a spiritual republic, and that paradox
is the hardest of all truths for Augustine to bear. The city of
man ought to be a harmonious reflection of the city of God;
in actuality, it is vulgar, lazy and corrupt, a place so brutish
that it lacks even the dignity of the Satanic. Better the besieged
city than the corpulent city, better poverty than wealth;
for whatever nourishes the city chokes it too.

This is a diatribe that has gone soft with repeated use.
William Cobbett saw London as 'the great Wen' and de-
manded that it be 'dismantled' in order that civilisation might
have a second chance. William Booth wrote of it as 'The
Slough of Despond'; for Jack London it was 'the abyss',
for George Gissing, 'the nether world'. Behind all of these
dystopian metaphors lies an anguished charge of disappointment, a sense of what the city might have been, *if only* . . .
The theatres, strip-joints, brothels, slums, traffic jams are not
simply bad in themselves; they are reminders that once we
dreamed of something so much greater, a paradise on earth,
and it has come to this. The man nearest in spirit to Saint

Augustine today, Lewis Mumford, has devoted most of his
life to a tireless explication of where we went wrong, how
we might set it right. His histories, plans, critiques never
falter from that vision of human perfectibility. In the idea of
the new town, pioneered by Patrick Geddes and Ebenezer
Howard, the real city was entirely abandoned to the corrupted troglodytes and all hope vested in what Howard
called 'the garden cities of tomorrow'. They are with us today :
Crawley and Welwyn, and they are hardly any nearer to
Paradise than Wardour Street and Shaftesbury Avenue.

But Mumford, Geddes and Howard, though perhaps inspired by a measure of the same moral feeling as Saint
Augustine, broke with him in one major and calamitous
respect. They shifted the emphasis from the inner to the
outer man, from the spiritual to the technical. Augustine's
vision of the twin cities of God and Man was wonderfully
and delicately balanced; his writing exhibits a constant wonder
at the sheer inventive fecundity of human civilisation, from
the divine gift of reason to such obscure talents as that of
the man who could fart in time to music. The tragedy of
the secular city, as far as Augustine was concerned, was its
failure to embody the good in man, its inherent susceptibility
to the cruelty and violence of Cain. It was in the spirit of man,
the capacity for good in the individual consciousness, that the
salvation of the human city lay. But for Geddes and Mumford, the answer was to be found in *techniques*; and they
coined a quasi-evolutionist vocabulary for technology . . .
'eotechnic', 'paleotechnic', 'neotechnic'. Individual reason and
love had failed the city, so they resorted to a home-made
stew of science, sociology, and bureaucratic administration.
It was called, innocuously enough, town-planning; and it
sought to revive the old dream of an ideal city, a Jerusalem
The Golden, by means of faith, not in man himself, but in
his structures.

They had some inauspicious precedents. Thomas Campanella was a Hermetic theologian and fashionable magus who
was flung into prison and tortured by the Spanish Inquisition.
In jail Campanella dreamed of a City of the Sun, whose

nobility and enlightenment would shame the corrupt and fallen civics of Rome, Naples (where he spent his sentence), and Madrid. His *Civitas Solis* (1623) is lifeless: a representation of worthy hopes which is sadly innocent of imagination. But its broad outline is interesting, and both its aspirations and its failures of vision are not unconnected, I think, with those of much twentieth-century town-planning.

Campanella starts with architecture, and to begin with he shows us a city without people, or, at least, with only the wispiest of sketch-figures, of the kind that architects like to put (merely as indications of relative scale) walking outside projected factories and town halls. It consists of seven concentric fortified circles, named after the planets, and four streets following the points of the compass. At the centre is the Temple of Knowledge and Metaphysics, an awesome and uncomfortable place which sounds darkly like the Royal Festival Hall. Each of the seven city walls is painted with representations of various aspects of human knowledge — maths, geometry, botany, physics, folklore, geology, medicine, engineering, and so on — so that living in the city would be like inhabiting a symmetrical three-dimensional encyclopedia. Like the timid sculptures and murals which the Greater London Council dots about its prizewinning housing estates, these educational decorations were supposed to keep you in a continuous state of uplift and learning. It does not sound very joyful.

When Campanella eventually reaches the laws and customs of the citizens, he sketches the life of a puritanical, ecologically sound kibbutz. The community is run by observing the laws of nature and share-and-share alike. Prohibition is effective; speakeasies wouldn't have occurred to Campanella. Work means either agriculture or cottage craft-industries like weaving, ornament making, and carpentry. Gold and silver have no special value beyond their intrinsic prettiness. Women wear make-up and high-heeled shoes on pain of death.

It all has a drearily familiar ring to it. We need to be reminded that rural nostalgia is not by any means a post-

nineteenth century phenomenon. The trade economy of the
city, with its merchants and entrepreneurs, its delegations of
labour and responsibility, has always been treated by those
who dislike cities as an unnatural practice, a perversion of
the 'natural' life of an agricultural economy. An 'ideal city'
would live to the simple, seasonal rhythms of a rural village.
But, as Jane Jacobs showed brilliantly in *The Economy of
Cities* (1969), the myth of agricultural primacy has no foundation in either archaeology or economics. Cities do not necessarily grow out of the excess production of their pre-existing
rural hinterlands; as often as not, it is the city which enables
the spread of farming on its outskirts. Yet the myth has
been used repeatedly to browbeat the city, and it is wielded
with no more prescience by Lewis Mumford than it was by
Campanella.

The City of the Sun, like so many ideal cities, wasn't a
city at all. It lacked an urban social and economic structure,
just as it lacked a genuinely urban architecture. The only
thing which distinguished it from a village was its dogged
high-mindedness, its air of being at two removes from real
life. It was an anti-city; a reflection perhaps, of Campanella's resentment of cities as they were, as well as of a
romantic innocence about the life of the country which he
sought to use as a salve for the diseases of urban society.
He was not so far from the architects and renewers of today,
who love green space, rapid exit routes, convenience shopping areas which cut down on in-city movement and street life.
They achieve a terrible parody of rural simplicity by bull-
dozing down the old, intricate structures and replacing them
with massive slabs of pale concrete. Somewhere at the
bottom of every planner's mind must be a dream like Campanella's: a dream of glass and grass and concrete, where a
handful of watercolour humans, tapering from the shoulders
down, flit their spidery way through an architecture so
simple and gigantic that they cannot corrupt it.

So Le Corbusier laid down his fourteen cardinal principles
in *La Ville Radieuse* (1935):

The Plan: totalitarian

The death of the street

Classification of simple speeds and complex speeds

Arrangements made to come to an agreement on imminent
LAWS of machine civilisation, laws which can halt the
menace of modern times

The mobilisation of the soil, in both cities and rural areas

Housing considered as an extension of the public services

The green city

The civilisation of the road replacing the civilisation of the
railway

Landscaping the countryside

The radiant city

The radiant country

The twilight of money

The essential joys, satisfaction of psycho-physiological needs,
collective participation, and individual liberty

The renaissance of the human body

This document deserves a close scrutiny, for it enshrines
some of the most hallowed modern principles on which
planners in London and New York are still acting to
change our lives. It is both as conservative and as thinly
idealistic as Campanella's totalitarian plan, as if the only
thing which divided the twentieth century from the seventeenth was the invention of the motor car. Again the
myth of agricultural primacy is presented as axiomatic:
La Ville Radieuse is founded on 'the release of the soil' —
courgettes and petits pois sprouting greenly between tower-
blocks. There is the same undercurrent of hatred for the
money economy of the city. The 'essential joys' are named
and listed in such a way as to make us instantly wish not to
have them. 'Les temps modernes' are linked to 'la menace'
as surely as winter follows autumn, and architectural dic-
tatorship, those grimly capitalised LAWS, must be immediately granted by society if the menace is to be fought off.
As happens so often in the manifestoes of modernism, what
looks, at first sight, a brave and energetic release from

slavery of old habits of thought, reveals itself to be in fact a shrilly puritanical backlash.

Corbusier clearly thought that the people were getting away with something, and must be stopped. His second principle, 'le mort de la rue', is the most radical and frightening of all. Take away the street, and one cuts out the heart of cities as they are actually used and lived in. Corbusier wanted a city of high-rise tower-blocks, and it is in that proposal that his profound conservatism is most evident. One can see why by looking at the very fair stab at a Radiant City which was made by Southampton City Council in the late nineteen-fifties and early 'sixties.

Four miles to the west of Southampton city centre, they built a housing estate called Millbrook, a vast, cheap storage unit for nearly 20,000 people. Laid out on a sloping plain, it has fifty acres of grassland at its centre, a great, useless, balding greenspace of sickly turf and purely symbolic value. What one sees first are the tower-blocks, twenty-four storeys high, of pre-stressed concrete and glass, known, I am told, as 'slab block/scissors-type', should anyone order more. The roads are service roads; they loop purposelessly around the estate in broad curves that conform to no contours. There is no street life on them: an occasional pram pushed by a wind-blown mother, a motorbiking yobbo or two, a dismal row of parked Ford Anglias, an ice-cream van playing 'Greensleeves' at half-tempo, a mongrel snapping at its tail. The acres of greensward sweep monotonously between the blocks, patrolled by gangs of sub-teenage youths and the occasional indecent-exposure freak. Church halls have been allocated by proportional representation, and a mathematical genius has worked out diametrical sites for the shopping plazas, with vandalised launderettes and 'Joyce: Ladies Hairdresser' offering cheap perms to pensioners on Thursdays.

A few years ago, I interviewed fifty of the tower-block residents. Most of them had been uprooted from slum areas in the city centre, from the rows of terraces and back-to-backs where social life happens on the street and in the corner shop. In Millbrook they had cramped lifts (out of order as often as not) and concrete staircases instead of the street, and they were poor substitutes. Most of the people I spoke to complained of theft and vandalism: you could never leave your shopping with the pram, never hang clothes in the communal drying areas. A surprising number did not know any of their neighbours. The thin walls, and the 'scissors design' which makes every bedroom back on to a corridor, meant that people's most frequent contact with their neighbours was having their sleep disturbed by next door's brawling children. The petty larceny of stolen milk, and, worse, milk-money, bred an incipient paranoia about the malevolent habits of the people across the corridor.

Here social worlds were shrinking: often the most common contact with someone outside the flat was the weekly visit to or from a mother or father in the city centre. Church groups in Millbrook hardly begin to dent the neurotic privacy behind which so many of the place's inhabitants have taken to hiding. The stay-at-home mother in a tower-block flat can be as alone as an astronaut marooned in space: indeed, the sociological space in which she moves is almost as uncharted.

The densely interwoven street-life of the traditional city (or the life of the Italian piazza, really the living-room of the apartments around the square) has always been feared by the middle classes: who knows what unpleasant radical ideas might not be brewed up in those hugger-mugger enclaves of the proletariat? Tower-block planning, by driving people into disconnected private cells, reliably insures against mass insurrections. Bad neighbours make for a certain kind of social security; Millbrook breeds vandals, but not revolutionaries.

The Sun City and Radiant City — really the same place — are both expressions of apprehension, disgust, and despair, and we should not fall for the assumption that utopias are usually the work of optimists. Far more often they are thinly-veiled cries of rage and disappointment. Millbrook is, of course, something less — an expression of funk, piety, and the exercise of a deficient imagination. Were one to read the place as a novel, one might say that the author had read and copied all the fashionable books without understanding them, and had produced a typical minor work in which all the passions and prejudices of the current masterpieces were unconsciously and artlessly reflected. It is full of heartless innocence, a terrible place to live precisely because none of its effects are truly willed.

But it does piously reflect the moral extremes, the melo-drama, which has so afflicted modern town-planning. A city is a very bad place which one might convert into a very good place, a dangerous place to be made safe, a black place to be coloured green. The answer to the terraced, two-up, two-down house is a grey skyscraper with its head lost in the clouds; to the crowded street, a stretch of unbroken grass big enough to fight a war on; to the corner grocer's, a yawning shopping plaza. Behind all these strategies lies a savage contempt for the city and an arrogant desire to refashion human society into almost any shape other than the one we have at present.

The planners have grasped a single truth. They have recog-nised that in the city they are dealing with some hugely enlarged frame for human behaviour in which moral extremes are likely to be the norm. The city, they sense, is the province of rogues and angels, and a style of building, or a traffic scheme, might tip it conclusively in one or the other direc-tion. More to the point, it is a place where individuals are so little known that they can be conveniently transmuted into moral ciphers. A man who designs a farm has to know a little about the farmer – whether he has cows, or pigs, or grain. He has to know the pattern of his day, his movements from one building to another. He has to understand the living require-ments of different species of animals. But a man who designs a city can make up his people as arbitrarily as a novelist in identical batches of thousands at a time. And if he works in the service of the state or the local authority, he tends to create his characters in the images of insensible oafs, inspired by indifference, softened by chronic inactivity. His architecture is supposed to anaesthetise or ameliorate these glibly imagined moral characteristics. If people stick cautiously to the edges of the shopping plaza and never use the paved space provided at the centre, or if they prefer a bus ride and a real city supermarket to the overpriced minimarket he has allocated them, then they are at fault – they have not learned to live in a city that ought, for them, to be ideal.

If architects tend to see us as opaque wisps or rude diagrams, they are, perhaps, doing no more than falling into a characteristically urban habit of mind, a way of thinking and feeling about other people which the conditions of the city make particularly easy. Finding the city a bad place, and suspiciously viewing its citizens as potential wastrels and villains, are responses which proceed out of a basic and widespread nervousness about the kind of moral drama which the city forces us to participate in.

For in a community of strangers, we need a quick, easy-to-use set of stereotypes, cartoon outlines, with which to classify the people we encounter. In a village, most of the people you deal with have been known to you (or to someone in your family circle) for a long time; they have matured subtly and slowly as characters, and are painted in varying shades of grey. You will probably have seen them in more than one role: the milkman or the postman is not just the man who delivers milk or mail, he is known too for a variety of off-duty interests and occupations. He is, you happen to know, a keen gardener; his marriage is reputed to be rocky; he is just out of hospital after an operation. My city milkman, though, happens. fully fledged: a uniform hat, a smudge of moustache, a rounding belly . . . I have no more to go on. Most of the time I need no more: the city is a great deadener of curiosity. But if, for instance, I am thinking of buying something from one of these patchy strangers, I have to guess at his history, try instantly to gauge his moral and emotional qualities. All I have to help me is my subjective knowledge of accents, clothes, brands of car, my reactions to endomorphic or ectomorphic figures: external signs and signals from which I construct the character with whom I am going to deal. Is he good or bad? A truth-teller or a liar? Lecherous or chaste? An actor, a bookie, a clerk, a dimwit, an enemy . . .?

People who live in cities become expert at making these rapid, subconscious decisions. At any large party, one can see people 'reading' strangers with the abstracted speed of a blind man tracing over a book in Braille. Mechanical aids to such character-reading are at a premium in cities. The rise of the industrial city in the nineteenth century coincided with the craze for phrenology and palmistry. At any bookstall today one can find several cheap pamphlets on graphology and quasi-scientific disquisitions on the relationship between body-shape and moral character. There is a vast market for cranky guides to person-spotting, guides that correspond, worryingly closely, to those charts designed for idle children showing the silhouettes of every aeroplane in the world. Judgments have to be made fast, and almost any judgment will do. The riot of amateur astrology we have suffered from recently is one of the more annoying expressions of this city hunger for quick ways of classifying people.

'What are you?' says the girl in the caftan, then, impatiently, 'No, I mean what's your *sign*?'

Gemini, Taurus, Aries, Libra . . . a character synopsis for everyone. Margot has initiative and tact, a strong sense of loyalty and a need to conform; Derek is creative, ambitious, and self-confident, seeks harmony in personal relationships, but needs help in money matters.

The great urban visual art is the cartoon. In Gillray, Hogarth, Rowlandson and Cruikshank, the people of the city are portrayed with exactly that physical and moral exaggeration which girls who are 'into' astrology endow the men they meet at parties. They are very thin or very fat, giants or dwarfs, excessively angelic or excessively corrupted. Emblems tell everything: Hogarth's idle apprentice, for example, is known by his clay pipe, his open collar, the jug of ale on his loom, and the page from *Moll Flanders* pinned up over his head. These public signs compose all that we need to know of his character.

In Dickens, our greatest urban novelist, the physical shape of someone is a continuing part of his personality. People appear in his novels as they might appear on a street or in a party, equipped with a set of dimensions and a name which we learn later. In *Our Mutual Friend*, Bradley Headstone is huge, coarse and slablike; Jenny Wren is a tiny cripple; Rumty Wilfer is pink and roly-poly. And, however much the characters change and emerge during the course of the novel, we are constantly reminded of these initial cartoon images. They carry their personal stereotypes with them like grotesque, gaily-painted husks – even when, morally, they have outgrown them. How different this is from a novelist like Jane Austen, in whose work the closer you get to a character, the less visible is his external, easy-to-spot carapace. Most writers use caricature for their background characters : Dickens foregrounds the technique, and makes caricature something which the characters themselves have to lug, often unhappily, through the plot. R. Wilfer wishes he wasn't so infuriatingly round, pink, and ineffectual; Bradley Headstone rages against being so damningly associated with graveyards and dark, thickset emotions. Yet that is how people in cities are recognised again and again by every new acquaintance, by every observer of the crowd; and Dickens's characters simply have to put up with their dwarfishness, their wooden legs, and their toppling craggy heights. To be merely grey, especially subtly grey, in a city, is not to be seen at all.

Both cities themselves and the people who live in them are subject to this convenient distortion and exaggeration. Both fall easy prey to that impulse, which besets almost everyone who writes about urban life, to find a fixing synecdoche, to substitute a simple lurid part for a bafflingly complex whole. In a world of crowds and strangers, where things happen at speed, are glimpsed and cannot be recalled – a world, in short which is simply too big to be held at one time in one's imagination – synecdoche is much more than a rhetorical figure, it is a means of survival.

To call a city a slough of despond, or a great wen, or a cesspool, is to give it a functional identity, to fix it in the mind as surely as Bradley Headstone is fixed in Dickens's novel. The city, like the people in it, lends itself to this sort of moral abstraction. Oddly enough, cities, for all their bigness and complexity, get tagged with hard-edged images much more readily than small towns. What mental picture is conjured by, say, Chicago or Sheffield? Isn't it more definite, more dominant, than that of Banbury? A line of cattle trucks, a lamplit street, a waterfront of cranes, are emblematic substitutes for the contrary lines of millions of individual lives. Moral fervour – seeing a particular city as especially evil, a sink of quite unprecedented iniquity – may be a simple convenience, a way of glueing together those visual fragments that compose the city in our head. The sheer imaginative cumbersomeness of the city makes us frequently incapable of distinguishing its parts from its whole; and moral synecdoche, the utopia/dystopia syndrome, is part of our essential habit of mind when we think about it. One might add that, in England, the single feature of the city which has adhered most strongly to writers' minds is its dirt, and dirt is one of the few objects whose moral connotation is as definite and public as its physical characteristics. The presence of dirt provides us with the elusive key we have been seeking, and the English have been quick to seize on dirt as the single defining quality of the big city. Charles Kingsley, who was no slouch on inner cleanliness, wrote in 1857:

> The social state of a city depends directly on its moral state, and – I fear dissenting voices, but I must say what I believe to be truth – that the moral state of a city depends – how far I know not, but frightfully, to an extent uncalculated, and perhaps uncalculable – on the physical state of that city; on the food, water, air, and lodging of its inhabitants.

Kingsley wrote a series of bad novels in which he explored the filth and disease of London and, by way of contrast, sketchily adumbrated the alternative kingdom of sweetness and light. The original metaphor was Augustine's, but Kingsley worked at it with fanatical literal-mindedness. Fogs, smogs, stinks, suppurations, chimneys (swept by consumptively angelic little boys), stains, lumps of raw sewage . . . this was London, and very convenient it was too. Seeing the city in its turds was the simple synecdoche of a simple moralist, and Kingsley throve on it hysterically. (The most vivid, and clearly most enjoyably written, chapter of *Alton Locke* concerns a delirious victim of cholera sitting by the side of a reeking open sewer and talking of the rats which have grossly disfigured the bodies of his wife and children.)

People with more elaborate minds have been more inventive with the form. Dickens loves and exploits synecdoche, and identifies it especially with the new energetic middle class who were making over the industrial city for their own ends. They were – and are – the people quickest to label others simply by their functions, who saw that the city offered a ready-made theatre for fast, opportunistic self-aggrandisement. These people could capitalise on the speed and superficiality of London's social and business life; people who acted on appearances, who, to all intents and purposes, *were* appearances. Dickens called these 'bran-new' people the Veneerings, nicely linking them with that other Victorian craze for marquetry.

Mr and Mrs Veneering were bran-new people in a bran-new house in a bran-new quarter of London. Everything about the Veneerings was spick and span new. All their furniture was new, all their friends were new, all their servants were new, their plate was new, their carriage was new, their harness was new, they themselves were new, they were as newly married as was lawfully compatible with their having a bran-new baby, and if they had set up a great-grandfather, he would have come home in matting from the Pantechnicon, without a scratch on him, French-polished to the crown of his head.

When the Veneerings give a dinner party, they do not invite people: rather, they acquire, 'an innocent piece of dinner furniture' called Twemlow, 'a Member, an Engineer, a Payer-off of the National Debt, a Poem on Shakespeare, a Grievance, and a Public Office.' How simplified does society thus become, its members concisely labelled by the single role you want them to play and which, hopefully, you may exploit. Here Dickens is satirising a whole way of seeing and acting in the city: we pick someone out from the crowd because they possess one significant functional quality. This feature turns into all the person is: it turns him into a living Rowlandson grotesque — a walking nose, a pair of sated bulbous lips let out on their own, while their parent mind and body stay home minding the dog.

It is no coincidence that synecdoche provides the basis of the moral melodrama — the play in which Envy, Sloth, Anger, Lust, Pride, Virtue, and Heroism compete for the soul of Everyman. Once we treat people, morally and functionally, in terms of single synecdochal roles, we turn both our lives and theirs into a formal drama. The city itself becomes an allegorical backdrop, painted with symbols of the very good and the very evil. The characters who strut before it similarly take on exaggerated colourings. Isolated from their personal histories, glaringly illuminated by the concentrated light of a single defining concern, under constant interrogation from their fellows, these urban people turn, unwittingly, into actors. They saw the air, their faces are thick in greasepaint, they live the disembodied stage-life of pierrots — who knows or cares where they sleep or eat? Their reality lies solely in their performance. When Saint Augustine castigated the Romans for going to the theatre, he accused them of 'playing a madder part now than ever before', as if a double theatre was involved — as if the audience at the circus was itself enacting a riotous drama. The dutch-picture recedes into infinitude: actors applaud actors applauding actors . . .

It is surely in recognition of this intrinsic theatricality of city life that public places in the city so often resemble lit stages awaiting a scenario. At dinner time in London, people strip off their working clothes and uniforms, and put on the costumes that go with being a character. Out come bangles, neckerchiefs, broad-brimmed hats, wild coloured jackets with jackboots to match. In any restaurant, one can find people taking to self-expression with histrionic fervour, giving themselves over to monologues and dramatic scenes which, to judge by their volume, seem to be intended not for their immediate companions at all, but for the city at large — that uncountable audience of strangers.

I have in mind an expensive mock-up of an Italian *trattoria* in South Kensington : low-slung lighting, strings of empty Chianti bottles, bread-sticks in tumblers, and conically folded napkins of unearthly whiteness and rigidity. Although the tables are arranged in a maze of low, white-wood cubicles with potted ferns growing out of ice buckets, this is not at all a private place. The fanciful cubicles rather enhance the atmosphere of a public spectacle, like chalk marks on a stage showing where separate blocks or groups of actors ought to stand. Everyone is visible and within earshot of everybody else. To enter, one has to be checked in by a florid waiter at the desk, one's way barred by a sumptuously scrolled hatstand. Thus newcomers are subjected to a ritual which calls everyone's attention to the arrival of these new characters in the drama; and the cross-talk of the waiters — delivered in a style of gamey operatic *recitatif* — makes the waiting group an embarrassed centre of disturbance.

At one table, I am sitting with a girl; in the cubicle across the narrow aisle, a middle-aged couple are with a younger woman; they're in their trim early fifties, scented, polished and silver grey, she is in her thirties, tangled, nervous, chain-smoking. At my side glance, her voice pauses, then intensifies in volume and expression.

'My thing was self-absorption. Eric couldn't take it.' The couple with her look across at us, a little abashed. But the woman is set for her aria, and the addition of an audience of strangers turns the story of her divorce into a vibrant, plotted skein, a work of dramatic self-exposure.

'. . . a twenty-two year old acid freak who'd gone through a whole shipful of sailors between Algiers and Southampton!'

The man comes in, lugubriously jovial, trying his voice out for pitch: 'Ghastly. Oh, ghastly. But what exactly did you do about the bottle of rose hip syrup?'

'. . . I wouldn't have minded so awfully if he hadn't sneaked off in the Cortina. I'd got everything at Sainsbury's that morning, and the bastard didn't even take the shopping out of the boot.'

My friend picks sourly at her cocktail. The middle-aged woman across the way finds something to hunt for in her handbag. But the man, the divorcée and I are set for a three-act meal. Everybody's voice rises. I start telling a boring restaurant story to my companion, but I can feel it growing loud and contrived, intended for public consumption. My friend responds with an exaggeratedly intimate whisper so that I have to bend to her face to listen. The younger woman does a proficient travesty of her husband's hippie mistress, loose-mouthed, blurry-eyed. The man, a little uneasy now at the extravagance of his friend's display, turns to his wife and tries to involve her in the conversation, but she won't be drawn. At a particularly juicy moment in the divorce story, his eyes flick up to my friend, who registers him with a tight smile. At another juncture the woman is apparently delivering her monologue for me alone, and I grin cautiously.

This particular dinner ended with a suitably outrageous symbol. The waiter had brought round a plate of those Italian bon-bons wrapped in patterned rice-paper. The divorcée wanted to watch her paper burn. She smoothed it out, folded it into a squat cylinder, and stood it on end in a saucer. The waiter lit it. It was a piece of pure ritual: the paper flared green and blue, then flounced into the air, hovering for a moment between the two tables in the dark space above the hanging lamps. The divorcée laughed, the man laughed, his wife pulled a polite grimace, I laughed, my friend smiled in complicity with the wife. The waiter (an expert stage-manager, tipped heavily for his collusion in the show) stood tolerantly by. It was a burst of rigged applause at the end of a performance.

Such improvised, crass theatre could only have happened amongst strangers. Like real theatre, it broke with social conventions, allowed the participants to communicate things to each other which are not licit in normal circumstances. But a city, judged in terms of our social behaviour inside it, is not a normal circumstance; and its public arenas – restaurants, late-night tube trains, certain streets and squares, like Piccadilly Circus in London – are licensed for a degree of theatrical abnormality.

In cities, people are given to acting, putting on a show of themselves. And it was in recognition of this fact that Plato saw imitation as a major vice to be stamped out from the city. He was convinced that drama, spontaneous or rehearsed, corrupts the actor. The role you play, he argued, too easily turns into all you are. In Book Three of *The Republic*, Socrates says: 'Did you never observe how imitations, beginning in early youth and continuing far into life, at length grow into habits and become a second nature, affecting body, voice, and mind?' He goes on to describe the lowest sort of actor, the man who will accept any part he is offered:

Nothing will be too bad for him: and he will be ready to imitate anything, in right good earnest, and before a large company. As I was just now saying, he will attempt to represent the roll of thunder, the noise of wind and hail, or the creaking of wheels and pulleys, and the various sounds of flutes, pipes, trumpets, and all sorts of instruments: he will bark like a dog, bleat like a sheep, or crow like a cock; his entire art will consist of imitation of voice and gesture, or will be but slightly blended with narration.

The condition of chronic impersonation portrayed by Plato has always afflicted the city. As we try to grasp it as an imaginative whole, we endow it with exaggerated, Manichean qualities of unique goodness and unique evil. Our own characters distort; we grow in size, but the growth is of a single feature. At any one time, we are likely to perform

like the gross types of a comedy of humours: Lechery now,
tomorrow Wit, or Sentiment, or Melancholy. The newcomer to the city has to learn to live on a perpetually inflated scale, to adapt himself to these highly-coloured pro-
jections of spontaneous melodrama.

THREE

Greenhorns

The steamer is at rest, the captain awaits the visit of the Custom House officials. All eyes are strained, searching through the shifting mist and dense forest of masts for the first glimpse of the eagerly hoped-for relations and friends, for the first sight of the long-dreamt-of city of freedom and prosperity. Presently a boat rows briskly to the side of the vessel; seated in it a young woman with mock seal-skin coat, vandyke hat slashed up with blue satin, and surmounted with a yellow ostrich feather, and long six-buttoned gloves. She is chaffing the boatman in broken English, and shouts words of welcome and encouragement to the simple bewildered peasant who peers over the side of the vessel with two little ones clasped in either hand. Yes! That smartly dressed young lady is her daughter.

Beatrice Potter on the arrival of Jewish immigrants to London, in Charles Booth's *Life and Labour of the People in London,* 1897.

I was all in a flutter at having at last got to the place which I was so madly fond of.

James Boswell, *London Journal,* 19th November 1762.

When I finally arrived in London to stay, I felt twice life size. To be an immigrant is to play one's first and key role in the drama of city life. You are part of a mythology. The Jewish refugee, at the end of the three-week voyage in steerage from Bremerhaven, kisses the stones of the dock at Ellis Island, thankfully fingers his phylacteries, and gazes, stunned, at the buildings of Manhattan, so tall that they are as high as the sky. Dick Whittington turns again on High-gate Hill, summoned across the valley to the city by the

bells of Bow . . . For every immigrant, the city is a different
dream. He comes to it in flight – from persecution, from
economic drought, from the stifling tittle-tattle of the home
town – and enters it in wonder and hope. Even his fear and
bewilderment at the massive scale on which it all works,
at the impersonality with which he is treated by strangers in
the custom hall or café, contribute to his excitement. The
entry to a new city, even when it's made in the internation-
alised tedium of an airport lounge, is a dramatically heightened
occasion. Everything seems bigger, more blatant than its
familiar photographed images; a giant labyrinth of un-
measured hopes and threats and possibilities.

Today, we come to the metropolis more often from
suburbs or other cities than from villages. Our sense of shock
is less intense. The culture of the big city spreads a long
way beyond its ring-roads, and the newcomer to London, off
the train from Norwich or West Hartlepool, is likely to feel
that he has come home. This is the source of so much of the
gossip and fashion with which he has been living at third
hand. Provincial cities now tend to subsist like dogs, on the
scraps dropped from the metropolitan table. One waits for
the new films, new clothes, new slang, to get around to the
local Odeon and the Gay Birds boutique, and by the time
they arrive they seem already staled. In London, everything
is fresh; the ink is hardly dry on the reviews, and the latest
thing in clothes still has the air of a violent departure –
in a few weeks, it will have been absorbed into cliché as
magazines and advertisements reproduce and flatten it; but
for now, on the King's Road, it is stunning, lurid, shock-
ingly new.

This continuous freshness of the city composes most of
what is left of the city's power to persuade the immigrant
that he has crossed a frontier into a new world. The slovenly
drift of urbanisation, a process which combines all that is
most lifeless in both the city and the country, has desensi-
tised us to the dramatic contrasts between the nature of the
village and the nature of the metropolis which so preoccupied nineteenth-century writers. A British sociologist,

R. E. Pahl, recently remarked, 'In an urbanised society, "urban" is everywhere and nowhere; the city cannot be defined.' If that is true, the truth seems a little dim and wet; and it smacks of a certain academic blindness to a very real imaginative experience – the knowledge that in Paris, London, New York (in the metropolis, if not just in 'the city') one is in a realm of thought and action quite different from that of the suburb, the small town, the provincial city.

The difference is easier to symbolise than to describe, and the architects of the city in the nineteenth century instinctively grasped its importance. They filled the outskirt areas of great cities with grandiloquent gestures and promises, signs, notices, and monuments, whose extravagant tone was in keeping with the heightened, self-mythologising emotional state of the newcomer. They announced that here was a territory of unprecedentedly expanded experience; a stage for human activity which was bigger, freer, more conducive to dramatic success or spectacular tragedy, than anything you had ever known before. As the steamer from Europe sails through the straits between Brooklyn and Staten Island, Manhattan is paged by the Statue of Liberty and its inscribed poem by Emma Lazarus:

> Give me your tired, your poor,
> Your huddled masses yearning to be free:
> The wretched refuse of your teeming shore,
> Send these, the homeless, tempest-tossed to me.

In Jewish American novels, for which the experience of coming new to the city has been a particularly rich thematic source, the halo of Liberty's head is characteristically seen silhouetted against a setting western sun; it is at once welcoming and sinister, a generous promise and an omen of disillusion. In his superb and only novel, *Call It Sleep* (1934), Henry Roth began with the figures of a mother and child standing on the deck of an incoming steamer as it nosed into New York:

Behind the ship the white wake that stretched to Ellis
Island grew longer, raveling wanly into melon-green. On
one side curved the low, drab New Jersey coastline, the
spars and masts on the waterfront fringing the sky; on
the other side was Brooklyn, flat, water-towered; the
horns of the harbor. And before them, rising on her high
pedestal from the scaling swarmy brilliance of sunlit
water to the west, Liberty. The spinning disk of the
late afternoon sun slanted behind her, and to those on
board who gazed, her features were charred with shadow,
her depths exhausted, her masses ironed out to a single
plane. Against the luminous sky the rays of her halo were
spikes of darkness roweling the air; shadow flattened
the torch she bore to a black cross against flawless light
– the blackened hilt of a broken sword. Liberty. The child
and his mother stared again at the massive figure in
wonder.

The statue stands, synechdochally, for the whole city; and
written on it, for those who can see, is their future history.
It is a melodramatic vision, but its most magniloquent or
nightmarish features can hardly hope to match the amazing
range and change of the city itself. Nothing could be too
dazzling or black for that.

Even the bourgeois piety of the East Anglians relents
at that moment of ring-road grandiosity, in the shy boast:
WELCOME TO NORWICH – A FINE CITY. Approach
roads and waterways are sites for architectural extravaganzas,
bursts of civic definition and ambition. The western entry
to London has astonishing feats of gothic whimsy, built in
brick of inky scarlet, crowding behind giant signboards
on which airlines promise you that the earth is yours. BOAC
TAKES GOOD CARE OF YOU sprouts in front of a castle
of pinnacles and leaded windows. The stretch of road from
Chiswick to Earl's Court, where, by the 1880s, London
really began, is an anthology of inspirational monuments. Here
more than anywhere else in the city, one feels an exotic
spirit of architectural licence. Indeed, what better function

for the late gothic style could be imagined, than to adorn
the entrance to a dream. Gross marble pillars are pushed up
against slit-eyed chambers; mock-Tudor beams are worked in
stone; flying buttresses fly free, supporting nothing; slender
blackened pinnacles spike the low industrial sky. And if you
come to London from the north, there is the heady, baroque
span of Archway Bridge on the scarp-face of Highgate Hill
and Hampstead Heath – the 'northern heights' as they were
grandly known in the nineteenth century. The Archway has the
best view of London as it drops down to the Thames, five
miles south. It is also the best place to commit suicide; and
nearly every week someone takes that plunge into the swirl of
container trucks below, and Archway Road is noisy with
klaxons of ambulances and fire engines – a macabre living
theatre of urban promise, urban disillusion.

But in London, the most splendid boasts and promises
are made in the architecture of its railway stations. When
they were built, you arrived in the city at rococo palaces
of steel and glass, trellised with curving girders and brilliant with sunlight on the hanging, forsythia coils of smoke.
Designers like Sir Gilbert Scott turned the Victorian railway
termini into technological wonderlands, half giant mock-
medieval castles, half working exhibitions of the peculiarly
Victorian science of engineering. Until 1964, when it was
knocked down in typical access of official vandalism, you left
Euston Station through a massive, triumphal Doric arch.
The city lay before you like an anticipated victory, celebrated
before it had been won.

Every big city has a particular entrance, a route inwards
which is established by mythology, a point of focus which
endows the whole complex with a clear shape and pattern.
Cities built on the sea have a special advantage: New York
needs to be approached from the Atlantic, not through the
suburban grizzle along the Merritt Parkway, Route 15, and
its slow trail through half-built overpasses and the waste-
land of the Bronx. In New York, as once in Venice and
Amsterdam, the city grows out of the water all around you,
turned twice as tall by its own reflection, a perpendicular

city on a horizontal sea. One should enter London from the
north, either through one of the great stations – Euston,
King's Cross or St Pancras – or down the ragged, gouged-
out crevasse of the Great North Road. Then the heart of the
city becomes the cluster of buildings ranged against the north
bank of the Thames, in a line from St Paul's to the Houses of
Parliament. As you descend into the valley and across the plain,
the metropolis gradually intensifies; it grows taller, grander,
more thickly populated, until, at the riverside, it suddenly
reveals itself, and one understands the disorder one has
travelled through as a pattern, marked out and bounded by
monuments. Such entrances owe their origins to economic usage
– but they have been substantiated by that sense of dramatic
occasion which always enlivens the best urban architecture.
Once established, they are adhered to superstitiously; for
they offer us the beginnings of an understanding of the city,
the first inkling of scale and direction in the maze. Further-
more, they assure us that the city really is a new and different
place, and that the ceremony of entrance leads us across the
threshold of a new life with its own rules and possibilities.

The 'greenhorn' is the central character in this mythology
of initiation to the city; he is the prototypical stranger, the
raw innocent. He is the shy figure on the dockside, with his
money sewn into his underclothes and his docketed cardboard luggage roped with frayed manila. He wears the wrong
clothes, he speaks the wrong language, he comes from a
village or *shtetl*, expert at some craft – shoemaking, tailoring,
ploughing – which, if it is practised at all in the city, is to
be found only in the mass-production methods of the factory
assembly-line. Myths are attempts to explain contradictions
in nature. The myth of the greenhorn tries to reassure us
that, despite all appearances to the contrary, there is a real
continuity between the culture of the country and the culture
of the town – between, in effect, our rural past and our
urban future. The greenhorn at the dockside, like the grandiloquent architectural slogans at city entries, marks a boundary which is as historically and biographically important as
it is geographically. Where does (or did) the country end

and the city begin? The most important and most ordinary city miracle is its capacity to transform the greenhorn into just another face in the crowd. He will learn the language, make his way, become a citizen. The very hay-chewing oddity of his appearance at the outset is a tribute to the city's power to change us all.

The greenhorn has everything to lose: his phylacteries, his innate convictions about the nature of human community, even the language in which he thinks and feels. We relish his loss, his poignant sense of displacement. For he is the past we have somehow survived: and he may tell us, in innocence or naive imitation, who we are now, because our present is his future. So city writing lavishes attention on the newcomer at that point of entrance: the greenhorn, at once the city's hero and its most vulnerable victim, is urban man at the crucial stage of emergence and transformation.

Waves of urban immigration have happened at times when the country as a way of life has let people down badly, when 'the land', with its associations of primal, organic community, has been seen to fail. The Irish potato famine of 1847-48 led a vast, destitute army of smallholders and agricultural labourers to the steamers that sailed from Cork to London. They paid five shillings for a deck passage, and settled in a widening circle round the Irish lodging houses of Rosemary Lane, a few steps from the jetty where the Cork Packet tied up. London was the place where you could get, according to one of Henry Mayhew's respondents, 'plenty of taties – plenty of mate – plenty of porruk'. In Eastern Europe, as the Pale of Settlement closed in a tightening net around the Jewish villages, and as more and more occupations were closed to Jews by Tsarist statute, the Jews fled to Bremen, Hamburg and Bremerhaven, en route for New York and London. By 1890 there were 135,000 Jewish refugees congregated in Brooklyn's Lower East Side alone; a community of victims, united by the Yiddish language and a common history of persecution. Between the two world wars, American Negroes, exhausted and bitter at their servile state in the hands of southern landowners, and made redundant by technological changes in the cotton industry, trekked north to the big cities; up the Mississippi to Detroit and Chicago, across the Alleghenies to Washington, Boston, and New York. From the cantankerous dust-bowl of Oklahoma, poor whites set off with their possessions piled on the roof-racks of clanking Model T's bound for Los Angeles and San Francisco, where you were supposed to awake to a dawn of citrus groves and plenty, but found yourself in a growing, smoggy megalopolis of heavy industry. For all these greenhorns, the soil had refused them a living; in a massive reverse of the Renaissance thirst for virgin land, the last hundred and thirty years or so have seen a great migration of the poor, the disenfranchised and the hopeful to the big cities. It is now the prerogative of the rich to move to the country; the metropolitan immigrant is likely to be hard-up to the point of defeat, cheated by nature or by labour-saving mechanical inventions of the right to live in his birth-place.

The new arrival is always shown in a stunned state: wide eyed, guileless, reduced to bafflement and incompetence by the strange rules of city behaviour. Louis Adamic, a Slovenian 'Bohunk' who arrived in New York at the age of 14, later described his first day in the city in *Laughing In The Jungle: The Autobiography of an Immigrant in America* (1932):

> For minutes at a time, walking . . . through the deep canyon of downtown Broadway, I hardly felt, saw, heard or thought anything. I was a blank. The sensation of being in New York, in the midst of America's tallest buildings, with trains thundering under my feet, was so overwhelming.

It is in the nature of the experience that the response to it should be inadequate. Language codifies an order, a hierarchy, a stable view of the world, which is grossly exceeded by the reality of the modern city: and the arrival of the immigrant propels him into abstractions and the contemplation

of his own internal state of mind. It is a source of transformations and distortions of scale which can only be received
with dumb wonder. In American fiction and autobiography,
the townscape of New York is turned into a giant perceptual
conundrum, as if it has been deliberately designed as a monstrous challenge to eyes and ears accustomed to the human
proportions of village and small-town architecture. (Le Corbusier's Modulor principle was based on a unitary measure-
ment of 6 ft – the height of the policemen in the English
detective stories to which he was addicted.) The gigantism
of the Statue of Liberty, with her 4 ft 6 in. nose, her 3 ft
mouth and her 42 ft long right arm sets the scale for the
Woolworth Building and Brooklyn Bridge, whose vast and
sturdy span might reasonably connect two of Plato's spheres,
and on which an evening spill-out of Liberty-sized commuters
would not look inappropriate. Like Gulliver in Brobdingnag,
the immigrant suddenly finds himself to be a mini-man. If the
city is normal, then he is a dwarf; if he is normal, then the
city must be some sort of concrete optical illusion, for what
perspective or grammar exists in which such breathtaking
heights and breadths are possible? Shifting in size, at once
dwarfed and elevated by these amazing confusions of scale,
the greenhorn lurches forward into his myopic destiny.

City architecture is an eloquent proclamation of the absolute strangeness of city life, a reminder that here you
must abandon hope of holding on to your old values, your
old language. Wordsworth, who, not surprisingly, was rather
bad at living in cities, tries and fails to comprehend London
in the seventh book of the *Prelude*. He begins bravely with a
fighting, Cobbett-like image, calling the city, a monstrous
ant-hill on the plain of a too-busy world'. But as he proceeds
to catalogue the streets and faces of London, one can feel
him unwillingly succumbing to that numbed giddiness of the
immigrant at the first stage of his initiation. It is all too
huge and too prolific for Wordsworth's elephantine Cumbrian
sensitivities to take hold of, and, having visited Bartholomew
Fair – an event which, for Ben Jonson two hundred years
before, had triggered off a spectacularly complete urban drama

– he resigns himself to a state of orgiastic inebriation at the
mind-blowing awfulness of it all :

> Oh, blank confusion! true epitome
> Of what the mighty city is herself,
> To thousands upon thousands of her sons,
> Living amid the same perpetual whirl
> Of trivial objects, melted and reduced
> To one identity, by differences
> That have no law, no meaning, and no end –

Here the inner and the outer worlds have got hopelessly
mixed up : the only way Wordsworth can describe London
is by rendering the confusion of his own hyperactive brain,
and the city itself seems to drain clean out of the verse. A
couple of lines later, he is pulling himself together :

> Though the picture weary out the eye,
> By nature an unmanageable sight,
> It is not wholly so to him who looks
> In steadiness, who hath among least things
> An under-sense of greatest; sees the parts
> As parts, but with a feeling of the whole.

It isn't very convincing. If you are used to teasing out the
nature of the world from a single stone, or a tree, or an old
Cumberland beggar, the city offers an unparalleled resistance
to your habits of mind. One sympathises with Wordsworth's
bafflement and feels vicarious relief for him when he returns
to Helvellyn. (The much more successful 'Sonnet Composed
on Westminster Bridge' manages to deal with London by
appropriating it for nature, by looking to the horizon beyond
the city, and by viewing it in the depopulated and silent
light of dawn. It is a hard-won celebration of all the un-
urban qualities of the city, caught in an uncharacteristic
hushed moment.)

But Wordsworth does convey the amazement and the
incipient terror of the newcomer to the city: his dazed

mental abstraction, his sense of loss, his vain attempts to
find forms and precedents for an experience that seems to
go far beyond his capacity to respond sensibly to it. Experienced city dwellers have always delighted in rubbing the
nose of the greenhorn in his own inadequacy. To be initiated,
the newcomer must first be stripped of his past; he has to
become a child again, innocent of everything except a
humbling consciousness of his own innocence and vulner-
ability.

In 1912, the Connecticut Daughters of the American Revolution commissioned a pamphlet guide to the United States for
the Jewish immigrant. It was printed in Yiddish, and dis-
tributed amongst the steerage passengers on the Atlantic
steamers. Imagine how, propped on one's bed-roll, one
might have responded to this first paragraph, under the
heading 'Special Advice to the Immigrant':

BEWARE of swindling expressmen, cabmen, guides, agents
of steamships and hotels, solicitors, porters, men who
say they are journalists or lawyers. BEWARE of loan
sharks and usurers.

The New York which rises from the pages of the pamphlet
is a nightmare-city; a place of strangers where every stranger
is to be distrusted ('BEWARE of people whose friendship
is too easily made'), where the penalties of innocence are
injury or worse:

Every year hundreds of immigrants are hurt or killed in
America, because they do not understand the shout of
warning, or do not know how to read danger signals,
when a few English words might have saved their lives.

The immigrant is told that the currency of the new country
may be counterfeit, that men who propose to girls are
probably swindlers, that he must bathe daily or die of
pneumonia or consumption, that he is likely to lose himself
in the subway system, that in America Jews who have

divorced and remarried may be regarded as criminal bigamists, that lawyers and real estate agents are frequently crooked, and that Jews are best advised (against all actual immigration patterns) to go off to the Midwest and become farmers. So much for the Promised City. By this stage, the prospective citizen would not have been surprised to learn that :

A great many immigrants who have been strong and well on their arrival in this country have died from tuberculosis within three years of their coming.

The city enchants, baffles, and kills. Burdened with all these warnings, the greenhorn still, somehow, has to make his way, serve his apprenticeship as a city-dweller.

He finds himself in a world of symbols and signals, every one arcane. Adamic tells of his first friend in America, another Bohunk called Steve, who spent his first day in New York still wearing his peasant clogs :

All morning he walked in the streets of Brooklyn, not a little confused by the traffic and turmoil. His wooden shoes clattering on the pavement added to the noise, and passers-by, amused, paused to grin at him. This suffused him with a pleasant glow. People seemed very kind in America.

Your clothes, never thought of till now, your accent, the way you do your hair (one of the first stages of the Jew's assimilation was the loss of his earlocks), turn suddenly and alarmingly into advertisements for yourself. You become a walking legible code, to be read, and as often misinterpreted, by strangers. You are frighteningly exposed. You walk the streets in innocence, and people mistake you for a clown. The freezing self-consciousness which is liable to grip the urban immigrant is, like Adam's shame, the first intimation of urban knowledge.

But if the immigrant himself finds that he has been transformed willy-nilly into a coatstand of symbols, how much more puzzling is the elaborate code by which the inhabitants

of the city communicate with each other. Billboards pass, a
maze of exhortations and obscure references. (Adamic taught
himself English by studying them, and the Connecticut Daughters of the Revolution advise their readers to do the same.)
The simplest of actions – buying a ticket on the underground,
catching a bus, locating an address – become complex rituals
to be shyly and awkwardly imitated. Not long ago, London
Transport installed automatic ticket machines at entry and
exit points on tube stations. They are minefields for strangers
to the city, who can be watched going through balletic routines
with the machines, of slow encounter, and rejection, and
entrapment.

On the streets, people wear strange clothes and cosmetics.
On my own first morning in Manhattan, I was astonished by
the made-up faces of expensively dressed black women.
Every feature was exaggerated : lips of lurid ultra-violet,
scarlet tinted cheekbones, turquoise eye sockets . . . bright
and electronic as the illuminated headboards of pinball
machines. They were faces designed for long-range action;
close-to, they had the same unnaturalness as actors glimpsed
in a theatre bar still in their greasepaint. The proper way of
seeing these women would have been through the window of
a speeding car : they left a vivid after-image, like an un-
peeled Polaroid colour print with its violent blues. But, like
all newcomers, I was in the wrong place, didn't know where
to stand to get the correct perspective. As it was, I walked
among so many gargoyles, and felt my own dim pallor was
a dishonourable badge of my blistering newness in the city.
My pace was different, my English clothes were all wrong
for February in New York, my focus was too haphazard, too
promiscuously inclusive, to adjust to the narrow, known routes
and angles of a genuine inhabitant. Warned of muggers,
I kept my head swivelling on my shoulders, hawking for
figures in doorways. Had any Puerto Rican junkie, desperate
for his next fix, been in my vicinity, he could hardly have
asked for a riper victim. I was transmitting signals as un-
mistakable as the bleeps from a bugging device. If the black
whores, with their hipswinging walk and their Greek-mask

faces, belonged there, then I was in clogs and earlocks, green as a comic-strip Martian.

In novels and autobiographies, the first positive move that the immigrant makes towards assimilation is to buy himself a suit of city clothes. Before anything else, he must dress the part. The city is a world of bewildering surfaces, and it is in surfaces that he must learn to be an artist. (The process works both ways. When weekending Londoners, randy for Tudor beams and flagstone floors, descended on the Hampshire village where I grew up, their first rural gesture was to rig themselves out in ghastly pepper-and-salt tweeds. We regarded these sportive costumes with considerable contempt. Uniforms aren't important in villages; and they are seen as the mark of irredeemable townees, signs of an obsession with symbols which the countryman finds incomprehensible and absurd.)

So the Slovenian peasants in New York in 1913 'developed a taste for striped shirts and fancy ties, the kind that they saw the swells wear in the movies. They wanted to lose no time in getting Americanised, and thought that to dress in the American fashion was the initial and most important step in that direction.' It was no coincidence that one of New York's great economic growth-industries in the nineteenth century had been the garment manufacturing business. What Jane Jacobs has called 'differentiated production' (in *The Economy of Cities*) – the output of cheap, mass-produced, yet fashion-styled clothes – made a variety of inexpensive, glossy identities available to the immigrant. For $15.00, a greenhorn peasant just off the boat could transform himself into a city slicker, in a gangster suit, a snap-brim hat and a loud tie. It was the first proof of the miracle of the American experience. The New York garment industry, writes Jacobs:

> . . . used to amaze visiting Europeans; they took back the extraordinary news that even shopgirls and factory girls in the United States were fashionably clothed in a dazzling variety of dresses. Europeans now use this kind of manufacturing themselves. In America it is this manufacturing

that renders the poor deceptively invisible,. as Michael Harrington has pointed out. They do not wear a uniform of the poor, nor do they dress in rags. Because of their clothes they look more prosperous than they are.

Indeed, the garment industry fed as well as clothed many of the immigrants to the city. Thousands of Jews who had had their own tailor's shops in Europe took jobs on the assembly lines, as machine-operators, cutting and sewing. All over the Lower East Side, people set up small sweat-shops in tenement buildings. As the city itself fattened on successive waves of immigration, the garment industry ab-sorbed many of the newcomers it was clothing. It mass-produced symbols, badges of rank and affiliation. This was a time when educational hucksters were making an easy living by running back-room classes in civics for immigrants (in preparation for the naturalisation exam); the garment industry, in a more practical and immediate fashion, American-ised a generation of European peasants, turning them, in a single fast deal, into New Yorkers and Chicagoans. To the eye, at least, they were indistinguishable from the rest of the citizenry – an amazing achievement, when one considers that the Jews especially had been accustomed to centuries of stigmatisation, and had been the most involuntarily visible of peoples.

In London in the 1950s and 1960s, a new class of urban immigrant created a parallel boom in the cheap fashion industry. As wages for very young workers rose, and parental restraints eased, boys and girls in their teens migrated to the city, filling bedsitters several to a room, and spending more on clothes than on any other single item. A rash of boutiques, loud with pop music, crammed with mock-gilt mirrors and day-glo colours, spread outwards from the King's Road and Carnaby Street towards the squally suburbs.

In the early 1950s when the post-war squeeze relaxed under the Conservative government, the 'teddy-boys' had created a market for that curious style which was half-Edwardian, half Edward G. Robinson: drainpipe trousers, velveteenlapelled jackets which came down to the knee, bootlace ties, and shirts like lacy meringues. Ten years later, the 'mods' established Carnaby Street as their fashion centre. They wore dapper Italianate suits and short haircuts, and looked like chocolate soldiers wrapped in tinfoil. Just as the Jewish immigrants to New York found a welcome invisibility in their new flashy city clothes, so these English working class children abandoned, symbolically at least, the stratified system of class deference into which they had been born. Their folk heroes, on whom they modelled their own style of dress, were pop singers and photographers—people like David Bailey and the Beatles, who had used the city as an escalator, rising into a glamorous, classless stratosphere, a publicity-world of images and trends, where money was extravagantly spent rather than accumulated. Their clothes reflected this casual, ironic stance towards established social values; they were parodies—of a period, as in the teddy-boy look, or of the fashions of another country, as in the craze for Italian, and later Indian and Moroccan clothes.

In the last ten years, following the rise and decline of Carnaby Street, the clothes business has erupted in a splatter of camp irony, romantic nostalgia, and outright grotes-querie. Motheaten furs from the Oxfam shop, 'granny' glasses, sailor trousers, Dr Zhivago boots, clown suits, co-respondent shoes, trailing gowns, ponchos, caftans, floppy hats, suits with Union Jacks all over them, and other emblems of imperial decline . . . each one a uniform, freed from its strict function, available, at low cost, to enhance an identity, give life to a dream of achieved selfhood. The dullest youth in the city can buy himself the trappings of a mincing gigolo, a 'thirties gangster or a frock-coated, ginger-whiskered Victorian rake.

The newcomer to the city finds that, though uniform is of central importance in city life, its nature is bafflingly diverse. Your new city clothes are quite unlike the occupational, regional or class uniforms of the countryside and small town. They aren't at all like peasant costumes, butcher's aprons or the flannel trousers hitched about the knee of the agricultural labourer in cartoons in old volumes of *Punch*. Nor are they like the commuter's pinstripe suit, bowler, and umbrella, the school-teacher's leather-elbowed Harris Tweed jacket, or the duffel-coat and long sweater which was the universal uniform of the university student when I was an undergraduate. All these sets of clothes are geared to a known function, to one's place in a hierarchy which is thoroughly and instinctively understood. In many areas of the city, of course, the hierarchy still holds good : the lawyer, the broker on the Stock Exchange, the gentleman-publisher, wear rigid uniforms which announce their adherence to a firm tradition which yet survives in a naughty fluid world. But for the young without a profession, without precedents, the clothes they wear register the city's immense and arbitrary range of choice. They announce simply that you have chosen, made your personal bid for a fantasy. Adamic and his friends turned themselves into fifteen-dollar movie swells; on the King's Road, the bright young things of the 1970s (the grandchildren, perhaps, of the domestic servants of Evelyn Waugh's original Mayfair set) transform themselves into witty parodies of the nineteenth-century upper class or the Hindoo peasantry. They are whimsical make-believe aristocrats and make-believe slaves; not long ago, there was a brisk trade in old policemen's uniforms . . . anything goes. As I write, it is fashionable to clump like a Bohunk through the streets of London on brightly enamelled clogs – but only because there is no likelihood of anyone mistaking the smart secretaries who do so for real Slovenian peasants.

The urban uniform, whose sole function is differentiation and arbitrary variety, is an important symptom of that condition of seemingly meaningless flux which Wordsworth diagnosed as the great disease of the city – 'differences that have no law, no meaning, and no end'. Certainly their law, meaning, and end were not – could not be – apparent to someone equipped with the social logic of Cumberland and the romantic doctrine of Nature. In Cumberland's, and Nature's, terms such gratuitous diversity makes no sense at all : but in the city it may be the most important way of making possible the individual life, the personal identity. Such manic plurality may not be necessary in the single-industry city, but in the metropolis it is essential. The problem of the greenhorn is to make that leap, from a society in which each person and thing has its own set place, to a society which is in essence unfixed, plastic, and amenable — a society on which you are called to impose your choice, rather than a society which imposes its historical and customary order upon you. The greenhorn is the mythical figure who proves that it is possible to move from one state to the other; who, in effect, demonstrates that the laws and meanings of city life can be learned and understood just as thoroughly as those of the country. His ventures into role-playing and fashion attest to the intrinsic *differentness* of the metropolis; and in a world where the word 'urban' is becoming an umbrella of ever-increasing spread, his function is surely more not less crucial, for he explains by example why social life in Hull is so different from that of London.

Yet there is something inherently puzzling and squashy about the initiation rites which attend the immigrant's entry to the society of the city. In institutions and other small closed societies, such rites are organised by the elders, who then confer badges of identity on the successful entrant. (One thinks of degree-giving ceremonies, or the ritual 'blooding' of children that used, until recently, to go on at hunts.) Indeed, this was the function of the city guild, the Free-masons' Lodge, and the gentleman's club in St James. But the non-professional city immigrant has to make up his own tests and design his own badges. Society at large leaves him in no doubt that he is an initiate; he is deluged with jokes, stories, and warnings that perpetually remind him of his unblooded status. But where is the test, and how can he know that he has passed it? Distinguished strangers are granted the Freedom of the City as an ancient civic honour, but how does the ordinary citizen set about obtaining this most ordinary of rights?

Like so many things in cities, the test, and the subsequent granting of honours, happen inside the head. Some urban immigrants, with the mentality of the ghetto ingrained into them, never take it, never pass; they live in the city, decade after decade, nourishing the culture of the home-country in the unlikely soil of a cold-water flat in a tenement block. Like Yeats creating the Lake Isle of Innisfree out of the autochthonous rumble of Charing Cross, they press the soft city into the rural mould of a nostalgic dream life. Right under Piccadilly Circus, there is the yellow cavern of Ward's Irish House, and it is full of people who had never thought to be greenhorns. In the slop of Guinness and Jameson's they drink and talk in Ireland not in London; but one feels that this too is peculiar to the life of a metropolis, an expression of a freedom which any smaller city would curtail. By contrast, Adamic and the Jewish immigrants of American fact and fiction turn into urban aficionados within hours of stepping off the boat. For them, the real greenhorns, the city offers a destiny and identity that have lain chrysalid-like in the heart, waiting for that sudden blast of heat and light and change of scale to set them free.

When I came to London, I took a room in a friend's flat in Highgate, a few steps from the spectacular wrought-iron Archway Bridge which carries a sedate Edwardian avenue high over the ravine of the A1. Up on the crest of the hill, one is in the world of the forever fading glory of sober, middle-class prosperity. Down in the thick chemical air of the ravine, one is in the quick-penny land of used-car dealers, betting shops, grave Irish bar-loungers, and men who stop you in the street with offers of second-hand shirts. I lived for a few months midway between the two; it was perfect territory for an immigrant, a place at once inside and out of the city, a hill with a view.

From Archway Bridge, London in summer looks like a primitive lake-city on stilts: only the top storeys of the new tower blocks stick out from the turquoise mirror of exhaust fumes – the pre-1960 city, in which St Paul's was the dominant architectural landmark, is completely submerged. Human life down there is mysterious, subaqueous; the traffic disappears down into the blue, rippling and steaming as it goes. It was from this hill that Whittington turned again (a pub and a milestone mark the spot), and a mile to the west Guy Fawkes's fellow conspirators sat it out on Parliament Hill Fields, waiting for the brilliant splash on the sky that never came. They must have seen it in their heads again and again, painfully slow, a dream sequence in a movie cranked at half speed. The city itself is a mirage from here: one might see or hear anything – promises, revolutions, ancestral phantoms – in that immense, ambiguous ripple of population and power.

For me, it promised release and a libidinous surge of adrenalin. I wanted London as I'd once lain awake wanting a glassy, enamelled split-cane trout rod . . . both took one to dark pools and the grey silhouetted backs of fish too big to catch. I was shy, vain and bristling: I was writing for the television and books came to review in thick wadded parcels. I had left my job at a provincial university, and it was as if school was out, and there were days of truancy and fishing ahead. I sent my phone number and new London address to every literary editor I'd heard of, bought a velvet suit at the cheap end of the King's Road, and swapped a district-nurse-style Wolseley for a worn out Sunbeam Alpine whose resprayed cream paint fizzed on the bonnet. The phone rang, infrequently, but just often enough to keep my euphoria on the boil. A radio programme sent me off with free tickets to theatres. From the rim of Highgate Hill, I could cast into the city and wait for my float to bob under, for the long rolling pull of the fish under the mirage.

For the first time in my life I felt I was in tune; following through the coils of a myth, happily in flight from the institutional paranoia of university corridors and grim sniping parties. London was pure make-believe, a city I could belong to because I could invent it. And in Highgate, I was in the company of people whose lives seemed as theatrical and dreamlike as my own, a whole society of truant players and fishermen. Some were acting out a pastoral comedy,

others a self-projecting *bildungsroman* or thievish picaresque
novel.

On the clear windy top of Highgate Hill there is a community of ardent villagers. They wear country clothes —
riding macs and headscarves, tweeds and Wellington boots
— and talk in gentry voices, braying bravely over the tops of
taxis. They have their church, their teashop, their family
grocer, their village green, three village pubs, and the Highgate Society with its coffee-mornings, its knighted president
and its evening lectures delivered by distinguished FRS's. By
the standards of a real village, their style of life has the
exaggerated quaintness of one of those 1930s family comedies
beloved of amateur dramatic societies — *George and Margaret,*
ferociously hammed through by the rector, the retired colonel
and the lady of independent means from the WVS. They
are not less but more of a village because of their beleaguered
position in a suburb of one of the world's largest cities.
Where real villagers drift away to the towns, and are forcibly
cosmopolitanised by the culture of juke-box and TV, the
Highgate villagers have frozen a version of village life into
the sepia tints of an Edwardian postcard; as embarrassed,
exaggerated and sentimental as 'There'll always be an England'.
In Highgate there is honey still for tea, though its price has
vastly inflated. Villaging is a recreation for the very rich
indeed; if you can buy a house with trellis and cottage-garden
in Highgate Village, you could probably afford Cannes and
polo ponies too.

I had thought it natural to be on the run from villages;
the real ones where I had grown up had been close and sticky
places, reservoirs of prejudice and refined malice. The quasi-
gentry of the private bar, sheltering behind wet dogs and
shaggy pipes, had been loud and philistine. The dog was
called Ajax, and its owner was himself a kind of muddy-
booted Greek, standing the verger drinks and roaring through
the fog. Yet the Highgate villagers made this despised life
precious; they were pickling it with the same wonder that
I reserved for the Dickensian labyrinth of colour and coincidence. If I was unable to respond to the style itself, at least

I could recognise the yearning and affection which went into its making.

Nosing about in my new urban uniform of crushed velvet and clotted-cream Alpine, an apprentice to the city, I found other aspirants, more to my taste. On the lee of the hill there were eager fashionables, avid for the demi-monde. They had David Hockney prints in their halls; they experimented with batik and oxblood paint on the walls of their living-rooms; they cooked out of raggy Elizabeth David Penguins; they hung huge Japanese paper lampshades from their ceilings, and squatted on brilliant polystyrene-chipping sag-bags. Angela, Liz, Janey, Michael, Robert, Ann, Joyce . . . names of people born in the dimmer parts of Surrey and the Home Counties in the late 1930s and early 1940s, who had come to the city from university. They worked in journalism, publishing, TV; they did whatever management consultants do; they were into anti-psychiatry, smoked pot at weekends, and talked in jangling voices which at dinner time carried all the way down to Crouch End, and floated across, like scraps of burnt paper, to Muswell Hill. A frantic, christian-naming talk, anxiously knowing, painfully vulnerable to the least breath of satire. In it, newspaper columnists and TV personalities lived like spooks, their familiar diminutives trotting in and out like lazy susans, there to furnish an identity not their own.

Janine, who'd been at Oxford and wrote feature articles for a tabloid paper; earnest, prickly, divorced . . . she glowed in amazement at the glamour of her life, and as quickly subsided into dramatic desperation. For her the city was a rollercoaster: one moment up with names famous enough to be embalmed with the dead, the next sunk in the immense, untravelable distance between her station and theirs. She wanted to be gay, in a swizzle-stick, Café Royal, champagne and midnight swims in Highgate Ponds way; then to be fierce, bespectacled and serious, a Simone de Beauvoir for our times; to be a mother; to be a mistress, heading for Rome in a silver Trident; to retire to a cottage in the country; to write a novel about the plight of Woman; to collect

Persian carpets, to not live on an overdraft, to go on television, to work for the Labour Party, to be gay . . . This
cycle of conflicting spiritual necessities kept her in a state of
continuous brilliance. Even her depressions were exciting. She
gasped at her own enormity : reading a bank statement, she
thrilled to its impossibility, and for the next three weeks
trailed in penance every Saturday by taxi to a distant supermarket reputed to be fractionally cheaper than everywhere
else. She was a democrat : for her the city was a source
of such amazing booms and reversals of fortune, of identity-
changes, coincidence and mad twists in the plot, that she
assumed surprise as a norm. You could not rely on the milkman
not turning out to be a genius; in this world of fable, he
might write the greatest novel of the mid-century, or be
invited by London Weekend Television to host a late-night
chat-show (distinctions between the two activities had long
since ceased to be visible).

Janine embraced the Wordsworth urban flux with a generous
passion; like all her affairs, it kept her in an electric trance
of bliss and despair. She flowered on it : her voice gathered
in edge and resonance, her cheekbones grew more prominent,
her eyes larger. On the phone, she carolled, full of wonder,
and sent flowers to everyone by puzzled messenger boys.
She was the immigrant as heroine, and had succeeded in
transforming her life into a spectacular drama, to which all
her friends were invited as honoured witnesses.

Her friends in their turn aspired to a style of bland
insouciance; they knew everybody, from promising undis-
covered painters to recently deposed cabinet ministers. This
gave them a curious geriatric air; they had foresuffered all,
nothing could surprise them. To have accused them of
naivete would have been the most cutting imaginable slight,
and they loved Janine's constant theatrical wonder because,
perhaps, it distanced them from their own innocent appren-
ticeships to the city. A consistent feature of the urban autobiography is its synthetically historical tone : Adamic wrote
Laughing In The Jungle only sixteen years after he first
arrived in America, when he was thirty; yet the boy in the

book might be half a century or more away from the tough experienced reporter who chronicles his initiation. So, at Highgate dinner parties, I often felt amazed and incompetent in the presence of these immensely elderly young people – they had been born in much the same year as I, but they had acquired an unruffled blasé that turned me into a gulping greenhorn, perpetually out of the know. We were peculiarly essential to each other.

Both the villagers and the media sophisticates watched themselves living: they were all actors, and their performances were subject to a continual, wry critical scrutiny. The studied gesture, the hand cupped round the igniting tip of the cigarette, the flounce of a caftan, the muddy stride across the Green, these were part of a calculated repertoire. To be part of the city, you needed a city style – an economic grammar of identity through which you could project yourself. Clearly this was something to be learned; an expertise, a code with clear conventions. If you could not get the surface right, what hope was there of expressing whatever lay beneath it? This language which extended from living-room decor to the furniture of the imagination and the intellect – preoccupied the society I lived in at Highgate. Some people dealt so finely in its niceties that they lived out a kind of vulgar poetry. (Who's in, who's out . . . the latest fashionable idea, from eco-systems and zoological notions of human aggression, through participatory politics to the merits of Acapulco Gold and concrete verse . . .)

It may sound fraudulent and blatant, this fragile theatre of surfaces. Yet, like all rituals, it enshrines a body of unexposed feelings that are neither superficial nor dishonourable. The newcomer to the city is beset by a terror of not belonging, of being left out alone on the hill. All round him, he sees evidence of failure and rejection. On the tube, the ads for computer-dating agencies: they mix an unnaturally jolly, keep-your-pecker-up tone with a salt-in-the-wound probe into the most lonely and anxious corners of the heart. One displays a pencil sketch of a crowd, with two people widely separated within it drawn in more detail; their faces, male

and female, wear brave smiles that look as if they have been
pasted on. Without a computer, they'll never reach each other
through the crush. American singles bars, packed with deodor-
ised divorcées . . . the personal columns, with their plaintive
appeals, as lacking in human detail as a radar scanner . . .
isolated people in the fluorescent brightness of a late-night
launderette . . . the urban flat, empty except for the flicker of
the TV screen . . . the suicide, careering from the smugly
gothic railing of the Archway bridge . . . the bum on methyl-
ated spirits, picking his way through garbage bins like a
lumbering racoon . . . everywhere there are people who have
failed to belong; severed from their families, without sexual
partners, lacking a tribe to identify with, or a style in which
to consummate a shared culture. These are the greenhorns who
never found the right uniform to wear, for whom the promised
freedom of the city turned bitterly cold and sour.

The gossip, the fashionability, the studied play-acting and
the arch cosiness of the Highgate I have tried to describe
are the inevitable responses of strangers and newcomers
who have felt that possibility of being left in the cold. Most
of my acquaintances there had no real precedents for the
life they were leading; they wanted to be 'in London' without knowing where London really was. And so they con-
spired to build a metropolis as glamorous, witty, and up-
to-date as the place they'd imagined as sixth formers in
some small town or suburb in the bleak 1950s.

It had not worked out quite the way they had planned.
They seemed to have arrived too early or too late. They
found that they were on their own. And the immigrant, unlike
the city-bred who have been able to take friends and community for granted, never forgets that the city has the capacity
to isolate and belittle him. In his anxiety he builds up a
community in words and symbols; he peoples his own tribe.
He knows that if he can't keep out the cold with these stylistic
acrobatics, there are plenty of basement rooms with rising
damp and rotting net curtains, and a score of dubious computer-dating schemes, waiting to give him an icy welcome.

FOUR

The Emporium of Styles

In the city, we are barraged with images of the people we might become. Identity is presented as plastic, a matter of possessions and appearances; and a very large proportion of the urban landscape is taken up by slogans, advertisements, flatly photographed images of folk heroes – the man who turned into a sophisticated dandy overnight by drinking a particular brand of vodka, the girl who transformed herself into a latter day Mata Hari with a squirt of cheap scent. The tone of the wording of these advertisements is usually pert and facetious, comically drowning in its own hyperbole. But the photographs (and photography has largely replaced drawing in this business of image-projection) are brutally exact: they reproduce every detail of a style of life, down to the brand of cigarette-lighter, the stone in the ring, and the economic row of books on the shelf. Yet, if one studies a line of ads across from where one is sitting in a tube train, these images radically conflict with each other. Swap the details about between the pictures, and they are instantly made illegible. If the characters they represent really are heroes, then they clearly have no individual claim to speak for society as a whole. The clean-cut and the shaggy, rakes, innocents, brutes, home-lovers, adventurers, clowns, all compete for our attention and invite emulation. As a gallery, they do provide a glossy mirror of the aspirations of a representative city crowd; but it is exceedingly hard to discern a single dominant style, an image of how most people would like to see themselves.

Even in the business of the mass-production of images of identity, this shift from the general to the diverse and particular is quite recent. Consider another line of stills: the back-lit, soft-focus portraits of Valentino, Navarro, Garbo, Gable, Cooper, Lamarr, Colbert, Tracy, Ladd . . . the first and second generations of great movie stars. There is a degree of romantic unparticularity in the face of each one, as if they were communal dream-projections of society at large. Only in the specialised genres of westerns, farces and gangster movies were stars allowed to have odd, knobbly, cadaverous faces. The hero as loner belonged to history or the underworld: he spoke from the perimeter of society, reminding us of its dangerous edges.

The stars of the last decade have looked quite different. Soft-focus photography has gone, to be replaced by a style which searches out warts and bumps, emphasises the uniqueness not the generality of the face. Voices, too, are strenuously idiosyncratic; whines, stammers and low rumbles are exploited as features of 'star quality'. Instead of romantic heroes and heroines, we have Waifs, Drop-Outs, Queens, Dandies, Lowering Sadists. Robert Redford, Dustin Hoffman, Jean-Paul Belmondo, Jean-Louis Trintignant, Mia Farrow, Faye Dunaway, Jeanne Moreau, Jon Voigt, Oliver Reed, Jack Nicholson . . . each one a name for a brutalist, hard-edged style in which isolation and egotism are assumed as natural social conditions.

In the movies, as in the city, the sense of a stable hierarchy has become increasingly exhausted; we no longer live in a world where we can all share the same values, the same heroes. (It is doubtful whether this world, so beloved of nostalgic moralists, ever existed; but lip-service was paid to it, the pretence, at least, was kept up.) The isolate and the eccentric push towards the centre of the stage; their fashions and mannerisms are presented as having as good a claim to the limelight and the future as those of anyone else. In the crowd on the underground platform, one may observe a honeycomb of fully-worked-out worlds, each private, exclusive, bearing little comparison with its nearest neighbour. What is prized in one is despised in another. There are no clear rules about how one is supposed to manage one's body, dress, talk, or think. Though there are elaborate protocols and etiquettes among particular cults and groups within the city, they subscribe to no common standard.

For the new arrival, this disordered abundance is the city's most evident and alarming quality. He feels as if he has parachuted into a funfair of contradictory imperatives. There are so many people he might become, and a suit of clothes, a make of car, a brand of cigarettes, will go some way towards turning him into a *personage* even before he has discovered who that personage is. Personal identity has always been deeply rooted in property, but hitherto the relationship has been a simple one – a question of buying what you could afford, and leaving your wealth to announce your status. In the modern city, there are so many things to buy, such a quantity of different kinds of status, that the choice and its attendant anxieties have created a new pornography of taste. The leisure pages of the Sunday newspapers, fashion magazines, TV plays, popular novels, cookbooks, window displays all nag at the nerve of our uncertainty and snobbery. Should we like American cars, hard-rock hamburger joints, Bauhaus chairs . . .? Literature and art are promoted as personal accessories: the paintings of Mondrian or the novels of Samuel Beckett 'go' with certain styles like matching handbags. There is in the city a creeping imperialism of taste, in which more and more commodities are made over to being mere expressions of personal identity. The piece of furniture, the pair of shoes, the book, the film, are important not so much in themselves but for what they communicate about their owners; and ownership is stretched to include what one likes or believes in as well as what one can buy.

This is one of the most important ways in which the city becomes legible. To the newcomer who has not learned its language, a large city is a chaos of details, a vast Woolworths-store of differently coloured, similarly priced objects. Yet, just as there are consecrated routes through its labyrinth of streets, so the welter of commodities is ordered by patterns of human usage. They are arranged in clusters around particular personalities; a velvet suit, a string of beads, a furled umbrella, a watch-chain, a caftan, an ivory cigarette-holder, each belongs to a conventionally established 'character', and the adept city-dweller is engaged in the constant manipulation of these stylistic quantities, continuously relating his self-presentation to his audience through the medium of such expressive objects.

When Louis Adamic arrived in New York in 1913, his choice of urban identity was clearcut: he would dress like a 'movie swell'. When I came to London, there was no such dominant single style to follow. Even in the restricted circle of my acquaintances, almost everyone seemed to talk and dress in a different idiom. One man who worked on a literary magazine had the flowing hair and loose colourful clothes of a sedated pop star; another preserved the leather-elbowed jackets, Paisley ties and close-barbered hair of the Oxford and BBC generation of the 1940s. Janine dressed, thanks to the fashion department of her newspaper, in the icy glamour of the current collections; another woman of the same age wore a succession of trouser suits that looked like the discarded wardrobe of a seaside pierrot. A TV producer dressed up as a gangster; the director who worked under him tried to look like a country antique dealer, with splashy cavalry twill trousers, brogues and neckerchief. A poet-critic lived entirely in black, like Olivier's Hamlet; a radio producer wore electric blue American suits, while a writer on ballet went about encased in a squeaking chrysalis of pink patent leather. With the clothes came appropriate voices and manners, from mincing camp to laconic Bogartese.

But one could not rely on the consistency of any of these guises. The next month, or at another time of day, they might be quite different. Hair and beards shrank and grew waywardly . . . significations, certainly, but of what it was impossible to say. The techniques of differentiated production described by Jane Jacobs have taken a large and important sector of city social life into the realm of fantasy and disguise: boutiques, hairdressers and photographers are the court-magicians of the city, experts at changing identity at a stroke. (The photographs of David Bailey are a case in

point: his model-girls are used like plasticine, worked by the
lens of the camera and the studio lighting into angular
symbols, simultaneously much more and much less expressive
than real people, converted into dehumanised diagrams of
shape and shadow.) These facetious transformations are acted-
out proofs of the hypothesis that in the city personal identity
has been rendered soft, fluid, endlessly open to the exercise
of the will and the imagination.

Accustomed as we are to an instinctive, convenient belief
in a mild social determinism, such arbitrary characterisations
and appearances are very worrying. They are so casual, so
irresponsibly free, so deliberately superficial, as to be insult-
ing: in an impertinent thumb-nose fashion, they mock the
ancient reverences of society for continuity, permanence, and
controlled change. They wilfully flout our sense of social
reason.

Mary Douglas, the British anthropologist, has written
about the way in which cosmologies find expression at
every level, from the control of society, through the
structure of its rituals and customs, to the control and
management of the body, clothes, and hair. She argues (in
Natural Symbols, 1970) that social constraint and bodily
control are necessarily linked: that, for example, a loosely
organised nomadic society is likely to favour long hair, loose
clothes, fuzzy metaphysics and a religion of spontaneous
ecstasy. Conversely, a tightly-knit society produces short
hair-styles, rigid body controls, a condensed symbolic system,
and a reverence for ritual and magic. These cosmological
patterns are reflected in society's art and intellectual life;
and Dr Douglas shows how all our activities are shaped
by the pressure towards consonance – everything must fit,
from beliefs and ideas, to fashions, manners, and the restraint
or release of our bodily orifices. Dr Douglas's basic frame-
work, which is elaborated with great detail and subtlety,
is highly relevant to my purpose here. But it seems pointedly
and dramatically inapplicable to modern metropolitan life.
If it is to work, then any one member of a particular society
should have relatively few options open to him. We might

expect a big city to display the characteristics of several
societies gathered together in one place, but it would be unreasonable to predict a state of promiscuous swapping around,
in which people exhibited the signs of two or three separate
cosmologies during the course of a year, or a week, or a day.
(Indeed, Dr Douglas conspicuously refuses to confine her
analysis to small tribal societies, and brings it to the centre
of London, where she finds long hair and loose clothes performing their classical expressive role. Had she watched long
enough, she might have observed the same people shearing
their hair and converting to Roman Catholicism, and, by so
doing, communicating exactly the same unconstrained freedom.) It is a characteristic of the city that two or more opposed
cosmological sets can grow out of the same social earth : lax
and hairy Rockers used to emerge from neighbouring doors
in the East End to trim and finicky Mods, as did Hell's Angels
and Skinheads. Sociologists have usually tried to explain these
seeming-contradictions by unearthing smaller and smaller
levels and distinctions in the internal stratification of the
working class. It is an unfortunate assumption that wherever
the city evades the rhetoric of- class-analysis, then it must be
the details, not the nature, of the rhetoric which is at fault.
For class-determinism simply does not help us very much
when we confront the random and wilful patterns of personal
style and behaviour in the city. One is always in the position
of stating categorically that people ought to be living in one
way, and discovering that in fact they are living in quite another.

Sociology and anthropology are not disciplines which take
easily to situations where people are able to live out
their fantasies, not just in the symbolic action of ritual, but
in the concrete theatre of society at large. The city is one
such situation. Its conditions effectively break down many
of the conventional distinctions between dream life and real
life; the city inside the head can be transformed, with the aid
of the technology of style, into the city on the streets. To a
very large degree, people can create their cosmologies at
will, liberating themselves from the deterministic schemes

which ought to have led them into a wholly different style
of life. To have a platonic conception of oneself, and to make
it spring forth, fully clothed, out of one's head, is one of
the most dangerous and essential city freedoms, and it is a
freedom which has been ignored and underestimated by
almost everyone except novelists.

In a brilliant essay written in 1958, Robert Warshow
described the movie gangster as a contemporary urban tragic
hero :

> The gangster is the man of the city, with the city's language
> and knowledge, with its queer and dishonest skills and its
> terrible daring, carrying his life in his hands like a
> placard, like a club. For everyone else, there is at least
> the theoretical possibility of another world – in that happier
> American culture which the gangster denies, the city does
> not really exist; it is only a more crowded and brightly lit
> country – but for the gangster there is only the city;
> he must inhabit it in order to personify it : not the
> real city, but that dangerous and sad city of the imagination
> which is so much more important, which is the modern
> world. And the gangster – though there are real gangsters
> – is also, and primarily, a creature of the imagination. The
> real city, one might say, produces only criminals; the
> imaginary city produces the gangster; he is what we want
> to be and what we are afraid we may become.

This seems to me to be an inspired analysis of the Bogartian hero; but in the last two sentences the moralist and
the rationalist in Warshow get the better of him. His
distinction between the 'real' and the 'imaginary' cities
funks the important truth that the city we actually live in
lends itself to displays of lurid artistry – flesh and blood
'criminals' can, all too easily, turn themselves into 'gangsters', living out the Bogartian fantasy in real bullets, real
knowledge. The city as a form is uniquely prone to erode
that boundary between the province of the imagination and
the province of fact.

During the 1960s, the twins Reggie and Ronnie Kray dominated the London underworld until their trial in 1968, when they were brought down in an extended public ritual and sent to prison for thirty years. Their biographer John Pearson, who was initially commissioned to write about them by the twins themselves, has produced a quantity of fascinating evidence about the way in which they managed their careers in his book, *The Profession of Violence* (1972). I want to concentrate on the dimmer of the two, Ronnie Kray; a man whose grasp on reality was so slight and pathologically deranged that he was able to live out a crude, primary coloured fiction, twisting the city into the shape of a bad thriller. His story is an urban morality tale, and to understand it is to understand one of the deepest of all the wellsprings of city life: he shows how a style, cheaply come by in the emporium of the city, may completely supplant every forecastable reality, every determinable social pattern. He is city man as wilful artist; and those of us who live in cities are perhaps a good deal closer to him than we like to think.

He grew up in Vallance Road, Bethnal Green, one of a close tangle of working-class streets in the East End, where, before high-rise rehousing projects broke it up during the 1960s, there was a tightly loyal, if sometimes violent, community life. Ronnie's mother dominated the family, dressing the twins in matching angora woollen hats and coats on the money which his father raised as a minor baron of the street markets. Ronnie was slower than Reggie, but he did learn to read; in his teens he pored over books about Lawrence of Arabia and Orde Wingate, and got into street-fights. He collected a library of biographies of Al Capone and stories of gang warfare in Chicago in the 'twenties. Equipped merely with a low IQ and the background of Vallance Road, he might have become a seedy small-time protection thug; as it was, he was determined to make his story books come alive and, amazingly, for a remarkably long time, he succeeded.

At twenty-one, he was still living with his mother, cos-

seted, homosexual, given to fits of savage petulance. He
was comfortably off, on a steady dribble of protection
money and the profits of various street-market fiddles; and
he rigged himself out in gangster style clothes – dark double-
breasted suits, tightly knotted ties and shoulder-padded
overcoats. He had a large gold ring, a thick gold wrist-
watch and diamond cufflinks; it was a classic uniform, and
he followed the books slavishly. When he learned that
Chicago mobsters had their own barbers, he arranged for
an East End hairdresser to turn up at Vallance Road every
morning. He ordered shirts and shoes over the telephone,
practised yoga, and tried living on a diet of raw eggs.
He bought a dog, and started a collection of guns. Whenever he went out, he had a swordstick and a .32 Biretta.

When the twins took control of a local billiard hall
which they used as their headquarters, Ronnie made himself
responsible for the atmosphere. He turned it into a pool-
room out of an American novel, with low lights and swirl-
ing cigar smoke (assiduously blown about the place by
Ronnie before it opened). By this time they had become
successful racketeers. Reggie bought a Mercedes – symbol
of a rather conventional kind of middle-class affluence –
while Ronnie bought a series of American cars, Buicks
and Pontiacs, low-slung, bulbous, bemedalled in chrome.
Reggie stuck to the East End, Ronnie moved around the
city, first to Chelsea (to a flat he won in a gambling game),
later to a luxury flat in Walthamstow. John Pearson describes its glories:

The decor was cockney Moroccan: rugs, leathercraft, silk
hangings, brass trays had all been purchased on a recent
visit to North Africa. Some of the rooms were without
curtains or carpets, but in the living-room there was a
large screen television, several big bright-flowered china
vases, gilt mirrors, a yard-long plaster figure of a re-
cumbent alsatian and an oil painting of a naked boy in
a Victorian gold frame.

'I feel happy,' he told people, 'now I've got a place of my own.'

Ronnie's trigger-happy over-enthusiasm brought him a jail sentence from which he was soon sprung by his twin. Prison psychiatrists found him, variously, educationally subnormal, psychopathic, schizophrenic, and insane. Photographs show his face to be as heavy as an Easter Island sculpture, with the cruel soft mouth of the sentimental bully. No-one in his right mind would trust him, one would think. But one would be wrong. Outside of prison clothes, able to afford the costumes for his roles, he was brilliantly plausible.

Local papers portrayed him as a benevolent businessman, always the first to give colour TV sets to children's charities; he liked to be seen (and reported in gossip columns) in the company of well-known actors and politicians. He lunched at the House of Commons dining-room, courted Tom Driberg, MP, and made a thoroughly favourable impression on Emanuel Shinwell, who arranged for him to make a V.I.P. trip to Nigeria, where he was going to help finance the building of a new city. A famous photograph showed him sitting side by side with Lord Boothby on a sofa; and in a letter to *The Times* designed to squash the scandal which had bloomed round the photo, Boothby described Ronnie as the 'gentleman who came to see me, accompanied by two friends, in order to ask me to take an active part in a business venture which seemed to me of interest and importance'. When Ronnie went into hiding in a flat on the Edgware Road, he solaced himself with long-playing records of Churchill's wartime speeches. His two favourite books of this period were both archly sentimental : *Boys' Town* and Steinbeck's *Of Mice and Men*. He wept over Charlton Heston's film portrayal of Gordon of Khartoum.

But, depressed at the failure of his scheme to build the Nigerian city, Ronnie knifed a black boxer in a Fulham Road drinking club, before being driven out to dinner by his chauffeur. The man was said to have 'half his face beside him on the floor', needed seventy stitches, and got nicknamed 'Tramlines'.

Ronnie's behaviour was gloriously inconsistent. He was a thug, a respectable businessman, a philanthropist, a socialite, a mother's boy, a patriot, a strong-man-with-a-heart-of-marsh-mallow, a gunman, an animal lover, a queen, at the end, a tweedy country squire with his own estate in Suffolk. Caught at any one moment, his identity had a perverse dramatic perfection. An astonishing number of people never doubted that he was what he seemed. For every audience, he had a different voice and face, and people who saw him performing in one role did not guess the existence of others. His repertoire would have been the envy of many versatile professional actors, and he could effortlessly slip from part to part during the course of a single day. The secret lay in keeping his audiences separated; it was only when he was in the dock that they came together, and then it was to destroy him. Yet neither of the twins seems to have grasped at the time that their art was essentially illusionism; that, once the strings and connections had been exposed only contempt, ridicule and revenge could lie ahead. Pearson writes of their showing in court:

> The twins seemed far more concerned with the appearance they made than with mere details of defence. Since they believed the outcome was now more or less decided, they would concentrate on the impression they would leave posterity. This was the moment when they sealed their myth. What they wanted was to be remembered as the great undefeated heavyweights of crime.

In the words of the prosecuting counsel, there was 'a terrifying effrontery' in the twins' deeds: they had made an ass of society, and in the dead factuality of the courtroom, society would get its own back. The trial did not 'seal the myth' of the Krays; rather, it broke it down into a long rehearsal of sordid facts. The dream smashed up, the daring impersonation turned into the mere lie, and society gave Ronnie only one identity in exchange for the many he had invented to exploit and puncture it. There is no elasticity in the part of a convicted murderer.

By all conventional standards, Ronnie Kray was an extremely stupid man. Yet in the lucky disconnections of the city, he was able to turn his infantile fantasies into realities which, for many years, were unquestioned, even seriously respected, by the most worthy of establishment greybeards. It would be silly to say that people like Shinwell and Boothby should have had more sense when they took Ronnie at his face value. In the world of business and affairs, most things have to be done on the strength of appearances: the problem is that in the city—unlike a village, a club, or a Rotarian fraternity—appearances are easy to come by, and very hard to test for authenticity. For any one citizen, outside the immediate community of his work and family, the city is nearly all dark: moments of exposure are bright and fleeting . . . a face here, a handshake there, a glimpse of the cut of a suit, the loudness of a tie, the sound of an accent, a quick association between the make of a car and its corresponding social type. The city is a natural territory for a psychopath with histrionic gifts. Closed societies live on history and continuity; reputation there comes hard and slowly. But the life of a city happens in discontinuous moments, its continuity is a continuity of appearances, of style. And style, in this sense, is quite neutral, equally at the command of the intelligent and the stupid, the upright and the vicious. Since the Kray trial, a special police detachment has been working to ensure that never again will such large-scale criminal enterprises flourish in the gang-land of the East End. (Actually, the Krays' major offence appears to be that they did not confine themselves to that quarter, but moved 'out west' into Mayfair and Soho. They wanted more of the city than the police were prepared to recognise as their due.) If the police are really serious in their intentions, they will probably have to begin by demolishing London.

Ronnie Kray, precisely because he possessed the psychopath's freedom from the usual constraints of consonance and continuity which afflict most of us, was able to shop wantonly around in the emporium, choosing whatever stylistic attributes took his fancy at that moment. He thrived on mobility, changing roles, locales, social groups, boyfriends, with unflustered, bullish energy. Endlessly on the move, he never stayed long enough for his roles to catch up with him and bog him down. When he was forcibly kept in one place — once in prison, twice when he was hiding out from the police — he fell into a state of acute, maudlin, paranoid depression.

When the black hero of Ralph Ellison's novel, *Invisible Man* (1952), migrates from the South to New York, he finds himself repeatedly mistaken for a contrary and ubiquitous character called Rinehart. This other invisible man seems to the narrator to embody all the baffling characteristics of the city itself :

> Can it be, I thought, can it actually be? And I knew that it was. I had heard of it before but I'd never come so close. Still, could he be all of them : Rine the Runner and Rine the gambler and Rine the briber and Rine the lover and Rinehart the Reverend? Could he himself be both rind and heart? What is real anyway? But how could I doubt it? He was a broad man, a man of parts who got around. Rinehart the rounder. It was true as I was true. His world was possibility and he knew it. He was years ahead of me and I was a fool. I must have been crazy and blind. The world in which we lived was without boundaries. A vast seething, hot world of fluidity, and Rine the Rascal was at home. Perhaps *only* Rine the rascal was at home in it. It was unbelievable, but perhaps only the unbelievable could be believed. Perhaps the truth was always a lie.

Of course we are disturbed when the city throws up a Rinehart or a Ronnie Kray as its corrupted hero. We are shocked that such men are possible; worse, we see that they are the people who make most use of the intrinsic possibilities of the city. 'London', said Henry James, 'is, on the whole, the most possible form of life;' but, while it is possible for the reclusive novelist, how much more possible is it for the enterprising con-man who is able to exploit the gullible innocence of society with more flair and cold cheek than James ever dared to endow his own urban villains with.

The Krays and Rineharts are extreme examples: they belong as spectacular textbook cases in the psychopathology of city life, living out a full arc of possibility which few of us begin to scale. Thankfully, our dreams are meaner, more cautious and constrained. With my two suits and gulping manner, I'm in no sort of competition with these adroit tricksters. Yet the vivid flashes of their careers – each time they fire, they burn another colour – light up the smaller, more abashed and secretive details of our own lives.

During the course of a day, one passes from identity to identity. These roles are nothing like as glamorous and deliberate as Ronnie Kray's, but they do compare with his in number and variety. I have contact with perhaps thirty people every day, and I lead a sedentary and relatively isolated life. Some are just voices over the phone, some are casual strangers (cab drivers, shop assistants), some distant acquaintances, some close friends. In addition, there are the crowds one passes through: faces across the carriage of a tube train, bodies moving in a street. Some of these anonymous figures will become suddenly and temporarily sharp; they will take on a fleeting, partial personality – a look of complicity or interrogation, a sly shove, moments in which identity is asserted then as quickly withdrawn. Even of my basic thirty people, I may see or talk to only fifteen ever again. In the city, nearly everyone disappears into the dark, and to emerge again is to participate in that peculiarly urban trick of coincidence.

Yet in every contact with every stranger, the self is projected and exhibited – or, at least, a version of the self, a convenient mask which can be looked at and listened to, quickly comprehended, easily forgotten. My first morning phone call is from my agent; I try to sound a man of business, and not to spill my coffee on the floor. I talk fees and reminder letters, and slide into gossip. Then the absent-minded euphoria

of work, when one hardly seems to be anyone at all, just a
hand moving, eyes following print, dead from below the
shoulder. A phone call from a friend, gushing and over-
sprightly for my dim morning mood; a letter written, 'Dear
Sir, With reference to . . .'; then, stiff suited, I take a tube
for lunch at a club. In transit, a brown girl and I eye each
other and read the titles of each other's closed books on our
knees . . . an anaemic Don Juan on an empty stomach. Suddenly, through the swing door of the club, I am a Gentleman; I have things I had forgotten . . . an old school, an
awkward nodding bonhomie, the gentleman's ducklike walk,
waddling over swathes of maroon carpeting. There are other
parts to come: one shifts from dullard to smoothie, from
customer to salesman, from high-minded speculator to fryer-up
of mince and onions. And between all these lie stretches of
unbeing, minutes out of time, out of character, periods in
which it seems as if you are simply waiting for the next
script to be delivered, the next performance to begin. Hypo-
chondria brings one back to oneself; the tug at the throat,
the twist of pain in a knee-joint . . . symptoms to remind
one that one is alive. Always it feels possible that these dead
patches of ennui might be arbitrarily protracted into whole
days or weeks of empty rolelessness. Sometimes I gawp mind-
lessly at afternoon TV programmes, just waiting to become
someone again, and envying that sense of vulgar destiny
which possessed Ronnie Kray.

Everyone has his own rhythm, and I don't know how
representative is my own chronic cycle of performances interspersed with stretches of near-complete vacancy. But it does
seem to me to be a logical product of the way in which cities
make us live in them, of the urban necessity of playing many
parts to a succession of short-order audiences. The twin components of the cycle have the effect of illuminating and exaggerating one another: by contrast, the vacancies seem overwhelmingly blank, the performances florid and strident. The
invisible man's awful suspicion that, beneath the disguises,
there may be nothing there at all, a rind without a heart, a
reality of lies, is one that comes disturbingly easily and often

to the city dweller.

The city has shaken our confidence in reality. As a result we have tended to become excessively knowing and breezy about role playing and sham. (One copy of the *Times Literary Supplement* yields five examples of the phrase 'not spurious' to describe books admired by their reviewers – as if it was a generally acknowledged fact that most books are spurious . . . which, if true, ought to shock the writers out of the coolly complacent tone of their reviews.) The junkie's habitual question about anyone who behaves differently from himself – 'What's he *on*?' – is bandied about in society at large. 'Isn't everyone in on some sort of act . . . what part is *he* playing?' People readily label others as 'pseudos', and the metropolis is habitually presented as a place full of cut-out cardboard humans jigging about to the call of some bland synthetic puppeteer.

Such gestures proceed out of a genuinely felt anxiety that the city may have made human identity mechanical and crude, an artifact not a product of nature. It is significant that the *Yellow Book* 'decadents' of the 1890s – perhaps the most self-consciously urban group of artists in our history – should have elevated that anxiety into a style. In the drawings of Beardsley, the writing of Wilde, and the clothes and ironic self-projection of Max Beerbohm, the lie became an art form : its elaborate stylisation; its capacity to make fantasies come true, its preference for the plausible over the truthful, led the decadent movement into a rapturous embrace of the spurious. In architecture, the grotesque affectation of Pont Street Dutch . . . or the joyous parodies of horse-and-trap combinations which were executed by the early designers of automobiles . . . For the first, euphoric burst of urban technological development, such fanciful impersonations and departures from the truth were gestures of liberation. The artistic extravaganzas of the late nineteenth century suggested that city life might be a gravity-defying dance against nature. The fashion, the role, the lie, the daring fantasy, were assertions of the human – living proofs that in a world of machines and city streets the machine could be man's toy not his master, and that the street, far from being a jungle of anonymity, could be the stage for a uniquely personal performance. If the gangster represents one side of the peculiar knowledge of the city, the dandy stands for another, just as important; with his silver-handled cane, silk hat and ruffled lace, he shows us that it is possible to survive – lazily, gorgeously and eloquently – on the very lip of the abyss.

But now the point seems fudged. Far from proving that we can deny nature, we are frightened that somewhere – on the street . . . in some dark labyrinth of technology . . . in our own over-fertile reproductive system . . . – we may have lost nature altogether. The dandy-gangsters of the King's Road and Greenwich Village do not strike most of us as optimistic symbols. The garish goods on sale at the emporium weigh us down as heavily as if they had themselves replaced the burden of nature and its attendant constraints. We are overloaded with their intrusions, sick of their gleaming surfaces. The opportunities for fakery and versatile impersonation which the city affords are, we suspect, more likely to favour a Ronnie Kray than an Incomparable Max.

Techniques of mass production, mass communication and rapid movement from one part of the city to another have made it very easy for us to drift into being dandies and gangsters. The price of maintaining an identity is cheap; appearances come ready-made and packaged, do-it-yourself kits. It sometimes seems as if one might flip over the edge into a deliriously fragmented confusion of postures and roles. In this maelstrom of possibilities, it is a pressing problem merely to find out who one is – to tease out at least the semblance of a nature from this heap of masks and rejected scraps of artifice.

Beneath the old uniforms, old voices and expressions, last year's poster hero, last month's craze in chic baubles or party line in ideology . . . a shrivelled self, raw, barely recognisable, like the hideous dwarf king stripped of his finery in the famous revolutionary cartoon, 'Le roi . . . soleil'. Techniques of self-determination have themselves turned into fashionable crazes: astrology, acid, casting sticks for the *I-Ching* . . . the inspirational and non-rational have been hawked about as spy-glasses through which the elusive self might be discerned. Nature, sincerity, self-expression are all words we have seen over-used at a time when nature and the self have been leading a conspicuously dubious and diminished existence. The more we try to reject machine-turned styles and rhetorical embellishments, the more firmly trapped in their grasp we seem to get.

It was not always so. The trade in purchasable identities absorbed Dickens in *Our Mutual Friend*; yet, by modern standards, the industry is primitive and circumscribed— hardly even the germ of the situation we have today. Dickens, like Marx, was fascinated by the power of money, its move-ments, its accumulation, its capacity to change and determine the lives of the people who are touched by it. Throughout the novel, Dickens acts as a shady banker towards his characters, parcelling the stuff out, then arbitrarily withdrawing it, scrutin-ising its effects on those who lose and receive it. Legacies real and bogus, deals, secrets, impersonations, hidden treasure, usury, speculation . . . the whole book reverberates with the chink of coinage and the rustle of transferred shares. At the centre is the miraculous transformation of Mr and Mrs Boffin, the 'Golden Dustman' and his wife. On their sudden rise, from being servants to being plutocrats, the rest of the characters hang like leeches, watching, waiting, begging, embezzling, cantankerously eager to see whether their riches will 'spoil' the Boffins.

When the legacy comes to them, the first question to which the Boffins apply themselves in their parlour is whether or not to 'have a go-in for Fashion'. Set free into a dizzying world of total choice, they decide in the course of a single page how they will live, who they are going to be. Having a go-in for Fashion means, simply, a carriage, a move from grimly genteel Holloway to dashing Mayfair, a quick course in literacy (provided by Silas Wegg declaiming selected passages from Gibbon's *Decline and Fall of the Roman Empire*), more velvet and feathers for Mrs Boffin, a pile of copperplate visiting cards on the hall table, and a monstrous amount of paperwork. 'We have come into a great fortune,' says Mrs Boffin, 'And we must do what's right by our fortune; we must act up to it.' Much later in the book, she is to accuse Mr Boffin of not being his old self, and Mr Boffin is to reply :

> 'Our old selves wouldn't do here, old lady. Haven't you found that out yet? Our old selves would be fit for nothing here but to be robbed and imposed upon. Our old selves weren't people of fortune; our new selves are; it's a great difference.'

Indeed, all Dickens's people of insecure fortune have this habit of talking about their *selves* as if they were determined by the capricious appearance and disappearance of their money. The novel is a satire of genius on the way in which the Victorian middle class equated property and character; and Dickens achieves his boldest and most brilliant effects when he forces his own vision of the stubborn permanency of identity, good and bad, against the quicksilver life of radical change and reversal which the characters themselves believe that they are leading.

Yet in Dickens there is really only one style on sale in the emporium, and it is the style of wealth. When people buy it on credit, or steal it, we know that they will eventually get their come-uppance. They may borrow it temporarily, they can succeed to it rightfully, it may be blown away from them in an unpredictable gust of wind from the stock market; but every movement of money serves only to reinforce that basic, two-tier distinction, between showy affluence and cringing poverty. Poverty is not a style; affluence can be. To live honourably in a Dickens novel, one must reject style except as a decoration; the good character is the man who can use style as a disguise, who can move through society wearing an appropriate mask at every level, but who still knows his

essential self, and can listen more closely to his heart than
to the call of his possessions. In matters of style, he must
never forget that he is an actor, that these are only parts –
costumes to be worn and discarded. He may delude the reader
– he often seems to delude Dickens – but he must never
delude himself.

It sounds a wise and timely counsel for our plight today.
But I suspect that it only serves to underline the difference
between Dickens's city and our own. All round us there are
signs that people are trying to reject style, to live as openly
and directly as they can without the masks and mannerisms
which the city forces on them. In *Writing Degree Zero*
Roland Barthes argued that the central movement of modern
literature has been the abandonment of 'style' in its bourgeois decorative sense. One solution to the problem of dis-
engaging literary language from the ideological burdens laid
on it by the accretions of historical usage is, Barthes says:
'to create a colourless writing, freed from all bondage to a
preordained state of language . . . This transparent form of
speech . . . achieves a style of absence which is almost an
ideal absence of style.' This is the degree zero, the point of
utterly divested confrontation between the self and the world.
Barthes discovers this 'ideal absence of style' in, amongst
many other examples, the narration of Camus's *Outsider*. In
England, we have less gallically theoretical equivalents. We
have watched the work of George Orwell grow steadily in
stature and importance since his death; and it is primarily
valued for its tone of flat honesty and unfrilled, seriousness
– its style of tough unstylishness. We have had enough of
dandies (is it possible to imagine Waugh, let alone Firbank,
beginning his career in England today?); seriousness is the
order of the day, and, dismally often, it is a routine sluggish
seriousness, as mannered in its way as the overheated or facetious prose for which it is intended as a corrective. Like
Richard Hoggart's Reith Lectures, it is earnest, bare, complacent in its conspicuous lack of flash and posing. We have
taken to according it an undeserved quantity of respect.

This concern for unclothed honesty in writing is part of a

wider revolt against style, a search for something like
Barthes's degree zero in life as well as in art, a quest for the
kind of uncompromising seriousness which the city threatens
to deny. Already this movement has had an able resident
satirist, in Mark Boxer, who for several years drew a weekly
strip cartoon for *The Listener* called 'Life and Times in
NW1'. His characters, the Stringalongs and Touch-Paceys, were
drawn libellously-closely from the life: sceptical, middle-class
liberal intellectuals with jobs in journalism and television.
who subscribed to strenuously advanced views on politics, art,
psychology and education. They were ardent campaigners for
ever kind of Liberation, they belonged to the intellectual left
wing of the Labour Party, they discussed the population
problem and the novels of Beckett, they appeared on late-
night discussion programmes as spokesmen for the new enlightenment. Their private life was represented as a continuous, intense bespectacled debate, an orgy of scrupulous self-
questioning. They inspected each other for signs of corruption (acquired in their rapid accumulation of mild wealth and
respectable fame), and made ritual trips to university socialist
groups to lecture on the prograess of the revolution (an
eminently rational and unbloody affair, necessary but rather
distant). The cartoon was vastly successful. At the time, it
seemed to encapsulate the follies of a new and speedily growing class of British intelligentsia – a class that was trying, and
failing, to redeem its ancestral sins of swagger, show, conspicuous consumption and extravagant fashionability. Boxer's
point was that such a denial of style constituted a ripe style
itself, although many of his audience, I suspect, took the cartoon rather differently, and were simply anxious to keep up
with the Stringalongs. Certainly the weekly goings-on at the
Crescent found a surprisingly quick echo in the party and
dinner-time life of the university town in which I was living
at the time.

The cartoon has stopped (although some of its individual
characters still turn up in Boxer's drawings for *The Times*);
the style goes on blithely unchecked. Its most eloquent
practitioners have been drawn from the young hereditary

middle class; people who have assumed the right and necessity of owning property as an automatic reflex. We may
imagine that they grew up in rather grand houses with gravel
drives, comfortably distant from the steamy life of their
nearest working-class neighbours. As adults, they turned
guiltily on the boldly bourgeois ethos of their parents. Not
for them the vulgar exhibition of wealth, or the unthinking
defensive conservatism which their income and capital might
have led them unthinkingly towards, a generation or two
ago. Their professions are vaguely, entrepreneurially 'cultural'; academics, journalists of a literary turn, television
directors and producers, actors, copywriters, publishers, agents,
with a few lawyers, accountants and business executives.
For them the purchase of a house has become an act of
conscience; and they have left the old strongholds of their
class behind (believing that their education and judiciously
left politics have declassed them anyway), and searched
out 'unspoiled' areas in the city, where they can live conspicuously cheek-by-jowl with the polyglot poor. They have
rejected the suburbs, and found parts near the centre of the
city which had been rendered invisible to the bourgeois eye
by a century of railway engineering, immigration, and pro-
gressive dilapidation. In the blackened, small-windowed brick
terraces (built for better-off artisans and the shabbier members of the lower middle class in the late eighteenth and
early nineteenth century), they have seen an honest unpre-
tension which fits very well their conception of themselves.
For they are much shrewder, less driven by illusions, more
veiled in their ambition and wholly uninfatuated with the
city, than the anxious immigrants on Highgate Hill.

Perhaps Orwell himself was the first of these people,
when he moved to Islington in the 1940s (though Canonbury Square, where he took a house, has always remained
expensively sedate and leafy despite the fluctuations of the
neighbourhood around it). The movement really started in
London in the late 1950s and early 1960s, with the colonisa-
tion of the western side of Camden Town (the 'NW1' of
Boxer's cartoon), between Regents Park and the Roundhouse,

a great locomotive shed which has since been converted into
a vast draughty theatre. Then they went steadily eastwards;
across Camden, into Islington, Lower Holloway and Barnsbury; now they are working in a pincer movement south of
the Thames, through New Cross, Camberwell, Clapham and
Battersea.

This burrowing out of new postal districts inside the city
is like a drive into a new frontier. Like a frontier, it produces edgy and painful encounters with the indigenous
population (the sitting tenants, some of whom are immigrants, some Cockneys), who are alternately harassed with
eviction notices and raised rents, and romanticised, like
Fenimore Cooper Indians, as 'real' people. Like a frontier,
it offers ennobling privations: few restaurants, poor recreation areas, no delicatessens or antique shops. Like the telegraph and the barber's saloon, these first signs of civilisation follow a year or two after the establishment of a new
township, when property prices have already begun to rise
steeply. Like a frontier, this move is at once a dramatic rejection of an old soft world, and an embrace of an idealised
future. Its inconveniences are proudly worn as badges. Its
new perspectives alert the frontiersmen to sights they have
been blind to for decades. Enervated Georgian architecture
suddenly becomes beautiful, after every architectural writer
since their erection has glossed over them with a yawn.
(Pevsner, writing about Islington in the *London* volume of
the Penguin *Buildings of England,* sounds antedeluvian today;
he is *bored* by the most lovely and desirable squares in the
whole city . . .) The Victorian public lavatory, the horseshoe
pub bar, the railed verandah, the Edwardian gilt shop sign,
the heavy portico, even sheet-metal advertisements for cocoa
and cigarettes, turn into prized antiques at the same time
as they are being torn down or covered over as vulgar
objects in other quarters of the city. The frontiersmen want
to conserve the working class past at the very moment when
the working class themselves are trying to escape it. The
frontiersmen's own future, spiritedly anti-bourgeois, at least
in the parental sense, lies in the recreation of a pastoral world

in which the trappings of the industrial revolution (for whose attendant miseries many of their own ancestors have been immediately responsible) can be hung as ironic ornaments. The pocky *Gold Flake* advertisement hangs in the hall, grandly outdoing the framed Whistler reproduction and the 1908 Variety Theatre playbill.

But decoration is the least important part of the style, and it is done with caution and embarrassment. Its dominant features are bare rectangles and circles, *natural* materials, a colour scheme in white paint and unstained wood surfaces, a lust for light and air, and a horror of fuss, embellishment and chi-chi. A house converted on these principles has an atmosphere of passionate neutrality; it is a controlled projection of negative attitudes – idealistic, spartan, scrupulous to the point of vulgarity. Destruction is its whole point. The first stage of conversion is 'knocking-through'; tearing down internal walls so that each room is turned into an extended patio, hardly a room at all, except insofar as it is protected (by double-glazed picture windows) from the weather. Out come staircases and balustrades; in go feathery key-hole steps in white wrought-iron. Wallpaper is stripped and replaced by white paint. The floorboards are sanded free of varnish, then sealed and left uncarpeted, save for the odd goatskin rug. Tasselled and richly coloured lampshades are thrown out, and vast Japanese plain paper globes are hung up in their stead.

The furniture is stripped-pine; tables are sheets of smoky glass supported on bare wooden legs and frames; hessian sag-bags are scattered on the floor instead of armchairs. Bedspreads are Indian prints or Moroccan weaves, echoing some distant peasant culture, like the pottery, rough under a thick glaze, looking and feeling like the warty skin of a toad. In a period when technology has been capable of unprecedented, euphoric flights from the structural limitations of natural forms of materials, a period of day-glo defiant fantasy, here is a style which seeks to reproduce the do-it-yourself, Woodcraft-and-Survival air of a boy scouts' summer camp.

The clothes favoured by these new frontiersmen are oddly

outdoor, more suited to a desert tribe than to the tight spaces
of a modern city. They are loose and flowing . . . smocks,
caftans, ponchos . . . or exaggeratedly functional (but for
what function?) . . . denims, jeans, corduroys. Their cars
are grimly economic and ecological, as near to bicycles as
four wheels and the internal combustion engine will allow
– the Deux Chevaux, the Renault 4L, the baby Fiat and the
Volkswagen. Here children play with chunky all-wood Abbatt
toys; here girl-wives grill anaemic escalopes of veal; everyone takes the *Guardian*; everywhere one senses that continuous, mild ironic encounter between the preserved self
and the excesses of the loud carnival beyond the white-painted
housefront.

This style is a strategy of urban disengagement; it is a
deliberate renunciation of almost every possibility afforded
by the city. At the same time it is a wholly urban phenomenon, a case of city people exercising a series of negative
options which are options only because they exist in the city.
The fluid movement of city life is rejected in favour of the
firm anchorage of property, of the house as a machine for
believing in. (Significantly, London is unique amongst capital
cities in that its middle class regard it as a right to live in
a whole house and not in an apartment.) The card-deck of
roles and identities exploited by the Krays, the Beerbohms,
the Rineharts, is held in fear and contempt, as the frontiersmen stubbornly substitute a single style of back-to-first-prin-
ciples honesty. Here people try to live like Orwell writes :
bluntly, earnestly, truthfully. Their style is hatched in anxiety
and elaborated in scruples. Its first obvious sign – white paint
– stands as a symbol for the rest : white is not a colour, can't
be in bad taste; white is the hue of minimum risk, as near to
being discreetly transparent as solid objects can become.

If the style itself is anxiously regressive, its means of production are emphatically urban and industrial. The demand
for plain wood furniture and glass and paper accessories has
led to a small revolution in the furnishing industry. Large
stores are being outnumbered by furniture boutiques which,
like their counterparts in clothing, offer a range of designs

within a single broad style. Shops like Habitat, Casa Pupo,
and David Bagott Design sell home-made-looking tables and
chairs in bulky stripped pine which are actually mass produced and mass-marketed. All over Kensington, Primrose
Hill, and Islington, there are small 'craftsmen's' shops
selling roughly identical lines in clear-varnished wood.
Stereo units which, a decade ago, used to be displayed in all
their technological glory of gunmetal and knurled silver
knobs, now go into grainy deal cabinets; and I have seen a
stripped-pine fridge, mutedly humming in its mesalliance
between nature and culture. Such gestures of simplicity
come very expensive; it is only the affluent who can afford
to be so loudly inconspicuous. In the unconverted houses
down the street or across the square, the working class have
to manage as best they can, lumbered with boastful gew-gaws
and the arrogantly, complacently *de luxe*.

It is a determinedly monist way of living in a city, this
style of minimum inflection and display. In a situation where
discontinuity is an automatic condition of existence, these
are people who have chosen to assert continuity in the face
of all forces to the contrary and their attempt has some of
the strained air of a moral exemplum. In Boxer's strip-cartoon,
one of the central charms of life in NW1 was its back-door
and back-garden neighbourliness, and this has a real basis
in social fact — even though, as long ago as 1821, Pierce
Egan was able to write, in his *Life in London*, 'The next
door neighbour of a man in London is generally as great a
stranger to him as if he lived at the distance of York.'
Such exaggerated estrangement was confined to the middle
and upper classes; but our contemporary stripped-pine
pioneers have recreated a pattern of street life that originally
belonged to the old working-class East End, before tower
blocks and rehousing tore out its heart. Their crescents and
squares are turning into one-class communities of neighbours. (In an updated version of nipping next door for a
twist of sugar and a spoonful of flour, people borrow each
other's secretaries in Gloucester Crescent, the real-life stamp-
ing ground of the Stringalongs and Touch-Paceys.) In a city,

there is always the opportunity given money and property, to create your own society, to choose a locality and turn it into a village of friends. Inevitably, that is the prerogative only of the wealthy, as estate agents have been quick to see. The easiest way of making house prices soar is for two people to move into a decrepit square and paint their facades white. The point should be taken within a few weeks, when these ghost pioneers should then be able to re-sell their houses at an amazing profit. But the serious point is that working class life itself has become much too expensive for the working class to live : all over London, they are being ousted from their close-knit networks of terraced houses by well-heeled people who are buying neighbourliness as part of the property. Community is becoming an increasingly expensive commodity.

Back to nature . . . back, with love, to the proletariat . . . away from the gross comfort and flash of the old bourgeoisie . . . these are all aims which seem to honourably reject style. They have been carried through with great conviction, too, by people acting on the highest motives, in genuine guilt and hope. And they have changed the face of residential London in the last ten years, given it as piously honest an air as the 'styleless' writing of recent English and French literature. Yet this changed face bears all the hallmarks of style in its most showy connotations : it has led to the involuntary displacement of a poorer class, it has added to the vast inflation of the property market, it has been at the core of the cyclone of new ancillary industries which manufacture and distribute all the details of a concrete cosmology – the furniture, the decor, the small scrupulous restaurants, the little foreign cars, the bookshops, the delicatessens, the baby-boutiques. Later in the book I want to discuss the impact of the pioneers on one London square. It is enough to say here that, for a way of life which aspires to transparency, this one is extraordinarily colourful. It also, I think, suggests something larger about our involvement in style in general : that we are, in fact, as style-bound as traditional sociologists have found us class-bound. Righteous disdain for show and imposture tends only to lead us to new and more subtle forms of stylistic self-advertisement, and there may well be something spurious about facile condemnations of the metropolis as a temple of spuriousness. We still find it very hard to face the elementary truth of life in big cities: that in them we are necessarily dependent on surfaces and appearances a great deal of the time, and that it is to surfaces that we must learn to attend with greater sympathy and seriousness.

FIVE

The Moroccan Birdcage

The Metropolis is a complete CYCLOPEDIA, where every man of the most religious or moral habits, attached to any sect, may find something to please his palate, regulate his taste, suit his pocket, enlarge his mind, and make himself happy and comfortable.

Pierce Egan, *Life in London*, 1821

One indication of the intense difficulty we experience when we try to perceive the city is the way in which it irritates us into metaphor. I have already noticed some of the Manichean metaphors which writers in the nineteenth century tried to apply to the city – seeing it as a pustular disease, a giant dirt trap, an embodiment of original sin, or a reincarnation of primeval chaos. These are romantic images, and they stem from the passionate English discovery of an idea of Nature which led the most articulate and outspoken members of Victorian society to reject the city at the very time when cities were growing faster and bigger than ever before. It was an unfortunate coincidence, and we are still suffering from its consequences. It is especially ironic, when we remember the temperate affection for and understanding of city life displayed by eighteenth century writers. Boswell, for instance, remarks in his *Life of Johnson*:

I have often amused myself with thinking how different a place London is to different people. They, whose narrow minds are contracted to the consideration of some one particular pursuit, view it only through that medium. A politician thinks of it merely as the seat of government in its different departments; a grazier as a vast market for cattle; a mercantile man, as a place where a prodigious deal of business is done upon 'Change; a dramatick enthusiast, as the grand scene of theatrical entertainments; a man of pleasure, as an assemblage of taverns, and the great emporium for ladies of easy virtue. But the intellectual man is struck with it, as comprehending the whole of human life in all its variety, the contemplation of which is inexhaustible.

Pierce Egan's *Life in London,* a civilised romp through the streets in the company of Tom and Jerry, two gentlemen of leisure, was far behind its times. It is an expression of an eighteenth century sensibility which happened to be published in the nineteenth century; and Egan's image of the city as an encyclopedia was already overshadowed by darker, direr notions. In Cruikshank's illustrations to the book, the foregrounds, depicting scenes from high and low life, are determinedly jolly; but in the background of the sketches we glimpse a dim grey life of poverty and corruption, as if the tenements behind were pressing to have their portraits painted. The book is a nostalgic tribute to an age of the city which was already passing.

Yet the idea of the city as encyclopedia or emporium is a useful one, and it might have helped the planners, philanthropists and journalists who, during the course of the nineteenth century, resorted to more and more totalitarian metaphors to describe this impossible unnatural entity of metropolitan life. The image of the encyclopedia suggests the special randomness of the city's diversity; it hints that, compared with other books or communities, the logic of the city is not of the kind which lends itself to straightforward narration or to continuous page-by-page reading. At the same time, it does imply that the city is a repository of knowledge, although no single reader or citizen can command the whole of that knowledge. His reading, his living, are necessarily selective and exclusive: it is in the uniquely personal combination of entries with which he alone is familiar that his expertise, his grasp of the larger impersonal wisdom of the encyclopedia or the city is vested. One man's city is the sum of all the routes he takes through it, a spoor as unique as a finger-print.

I think this goes some way towards explaining many of the problems we have had when we have tried to under-stand the structure of the city. It is not continuous, it does not conform to the shape of smaller, more comprehensible models (New York and London are not simply vast multi-plication sums of Middletown and Banbury); the closer we look, the more impenetrable and unprecedented it all seems. We are tempted into extreme metaphors, or, like Words-worth, into helpless ejaculations (the *Residence in London* section of *The Prelude* is a long drawn out cry of frustration at the delirious chaos which the city creates in the poet's head); or we come to realise, numbly, that the social systems we know are of little use when it comes to decoding the city, and we go off to exotic foreign parts in search of systems which seem to make a better fit.

This is just what Mayhew does in his preface to *London Labour and the London Poor* (1851), a part of the book which most modern readers skip, to get to the brilliant documen-tary portraiture in the middle. The theories which Mayhew expounded in his preface, which were intended as a serious contribution to anthropological science, now sound a little dotty, but they are worth looking at. Whatever their intrinsic worth, they formed the conceptual scaffolding of Mayhew's survey, and enabled him to write the classic book about the city at a time when most observers were only able to work themselves into fits of apoplectic statistics punctuated by intervals of hellfire rhetoric.

When Mayhew looked at the swarming street-life of nine-teenth century London, he saw that it eluded all traditional western classifications of society. It was not a proletarian 'mass' (even Frederick Engels, in *The Condition of the Working Class in England in 1844*, failed to make the idea of the 'mass' convincing—his cities are populated by con-ditions rather than people); there were far too many evident distinctions of status and style for that. Nor was it a tidal accumulation of members of the working class, in any sense of the expression which would have been meaningful to, say, George Eliot, Mrs Gaskell or Charles Kingsley: the people Mayhew saw were invincibly alien – untempted by the charms of evening institutes, self-help, union organisation, or edifying talks with missionary clergymen. They were pagan, superstitious, hostile, and fatalist. They spoke in a thieves' slang which sounded frighteningly like the beginning of some primitive foreign language. They lived, apparently quite contentedly, in areas of the city which were disgusting and taboo to decent people; they collected dogs' dung off the pavements and tramped in thigh-boots up evil-smelling sewers. They were feckless, without religion, they had lost large parts of their families, they seemed dangerously indifferent to the systems of deference and order by which English society had been traditionally maintained. If the image of the native in the Africa of Empire was of a grinning black simpleton whose worst faults were his laziness and stupidity – or of a crazed Hottentot brandishing a wooden spear – the street people of London presented a face that was more inscrutably foreign, more complex, ultimately more menacing. To talk of 'Darkest London' (a phrase used thirty years after Mayhew's survey) as if it was like an African jungle, was more of an understatement than an exaggeration. London was, in many ways, a far darker continent.

Mayhew opened it up with a stunningly simple distinction borrowed from anthropology. He divided the race of man into two groups of tribes, each distinguished by their physiognomic characteristics. These were the Settlers and the Wanderers. Settlers had big heads; Wanderers had big jawbones. Civilised people settled (so, eventually and with help, did the George Eliot-Charles Kingsley members of the radicalised working class); uncivilised people wandered. It was as satisfactory and watertight a scheme as a Calvinist's vision of the elect and the damned – and it had the enormous advantage of cutting straight through the conventional class hierarchy. Most important of all, it offered an eloquent, pseudo-scientific justification for the baffling sense of alienation which people from the middle class felt when they contemplated the astonishing lives of their poorer brethren. They had guessed it all along . . . two tribes was an even more convincing statement of the difference than Disraeli's analogy of the two nations.

When Mayhew measured the features of the industrial working class, he found himself confronting Caliban. The nomad, he wrote:

> is distinguished from the civilised man by his repugnance to regular and continuous labour – by his want of providence in laying up a store for the future – by his inability to perceive consequences ever so slightly removed from immediate apprehension – by his passion for stupefying herbs and roots, and, when possible, for intoxicating fermented liquors – by his extraordinary powers of enduring privation – by his comparative insensibility to pain – by an immoderate love of gaming, frequently risking his own personal liberty upon a single cast – by his love of libidinous dances – by the pleasure he experiences in witnessing the suffering of sentient creatures – by his delight in warfare and all perilous sports – by his desire for vengeance – by the looseness of his notions as to property – by the absence of chastity among his women, and his disregard of female honour – and lastly, by his vague sense of religion – his rude idea of a Creator, and utter absence of all appreciation of the mercy of the Divine Spirit.

Such painstakingly detached and quirky generalising is Mayhew's unlikely prologue to a spectacularly imaginative and sympathetic investigation of the personal lives of these ignoble savages. Perhaps he needed this self-conscious distance from his material in order to exercise his warmth of feeling and avid curiosity upon it. Certainly he tends to sound, in his preface, like a collector of fossils – or, rather, he shared, with Darwin and Linnaeus, the passion for systematic inventories, ways of discovering the world by cataloguing it:

Those who obtain their living in the streets of the metropolis are a very large and varied class; indeed, the means resorted to in order to 'pick up a crust', as the people call it, in the public thoroughfares (and such in many instances it *literally* is,) are so multifarious that the mind is long baffled in its attempts to reduce them to scientific order or classification.

But reduce them Mayhew did: he found six general classes of occupation – sellers, buyers, finders, performers, artisans, and labourers. He then subdivided each group according to the materials they handled, from fresh eatables down to dog dung and cigar butts. In other words, he classified this outcast tribe in terms of taboo, by the classes of objects which they were allowed to touch.

This was a radically new technique to apply to English society. It was generally known that social ranking in the caste system in India depended on the relationship between people and touchable objects; but in a democratic capitalist system it was an essential part of the unstated creed that a person's position in society was to be measured in terms of his relationships, not with objects, but with his fellow men. On this assumption rested the whole edifice of Victorian morality and the righteous pursuance of a social policy of *laissez faire*. Implicit in Mayhew's theory of classification was the suggestion that the industrial city might resemble a caste system (with all the inequalities and superstitious boundaries which are necessarily entailed) much more than a class system. In the East End of London, Mayhew discovered a honeycomb of caste groups, each one circumscribed by the commodities in which it dealt, living in a state of thievish animosity towards a society of hostile others.

The moral and political implications of Mayhew's argument have never been considered with the seriousness of attention which they deserve. The tone of his preface is too eccentric and inconclusive. But the practical results were immediate. By associating people and things in this way, Mayhew was able to discover an order where other people had only seen a colourful chaos: the mass became suddenly, and subtly, articulated – its strange hierarchy was revealed to be as intricate in its way as the English class system, though its laws appeared primitive, foreign and cabalistic. Mayhew rendered the dark side of the city legible, and at the same time he explained to his readers why they had been unable to see before – they had peered at it through the wrong glasses, expecting it to be a familiar English kind of society when in reality it was quite another.

The perceptual problems which the city presents today are substantially different from those which engrossed Mayhew: most important, it is not the poor we find so puzzling, but the young, the thriftless middle class, the temporary and mobile, the cult camp-followers, the stylists. It is these people from the economic centre of things whose diversity seems so random and illogical, who, like the street arabs of the nineteenth century, might have come from another continent for all the nonsense they appear to make of our conventional class categories. A *Cosmopolitan* reader moving in a diaphanous sheen under her turquoise 'fun fur', bedraggledly svelte; another girl with an Afro frizz and a copy of *One Dimensional Man*; a close-cropped Primrose Hill boylette; a car-customiser rigged out in a parody of 1950s teddy-boy gear; a flipped-out King's Road dandy; a puddingy Promenade Concerteer; one boy dressed like a Red Indian, another looking like a Mexican bandit; a middle-aged man in full drag; a glimpse of tinted spectacles, leather jacket and signet ring . . . the different house fronts, the assorted styles purveyed by individual boutiques, the savagely diverse tastes in furniture, in books, in music and painting and eccentric religions . . . the way in which established national politics provoke an increasing uninterest and inertia at a time when ideologies, of a more private and local kind, seem to be taking demoniacal possession of more and more members and groups within society. I think we find these things as baffling, intractable, and ultimately invisible in their detail, as Mayhew's contemporaries found the poor. Like the poor, they defeat by their sheer numbers. Like the poor, they are a by-product of a city life whose workings have persistently defeated our attempts to explain them. Like the poor, they are liable to strike us in the mass as the very type of what is alien and nasty. We had better heed Mayhew's method, and recognise that we may need some outlandish scheme of classification, a suitably exotic hypothesis, if we are to understand them.

One needs to look first at some of the specific ways in which conventional hierarchies fail to apply to the modern city. We are encouraged to think of capitalist societies as pyramids, and to assume that within the pyramid status and power continuously dilute towards the broad, pale working-class base. Energy is generated in the system by what letter-writers to *The Times* like to call 'incentives' — bribes to persuade everyone to strive to move further up into the narrowing cone above them. And the city is usually seen as an intense theatre of this capitalist process at work; movement in it is more rapid, more ambitious, more unchecked, more inventive than in the tranquil hinterland of country and small town. This folkloric view of the city has little basis in contemporary social fact.

For since the second wave of the industrial revolution in the latter part of the nineteenth century (a wave more of techniques of communication than of processes of manufacture), cities have become less and less directly productive. They have been the nerve- and distributive-centres of industry, but the factories and raw materials, both the hard muck and the hard money of the system, have either stayed or been moved elsewhere. The average city worker is not a producer : he helps to handle and transmit goods, he transports other workers, he liaises. Entrepreneurism happens at every income level, from the man who takes the tickets in the tube to the man whose signature commits a corporation to a contract. But, most significantly, entrepreneurism gives the pyramid a grossly swollen waistline; it fails to reflect the proportions of society as a whole by exaggerating a single level of education and communicative skill, and the relatively greater rewards accorded to people who handle rather than make goods. The clerk, the computer operator, the secretary, the systems analyst, the office-manager and whatever mysterious occupations lurk behind the much-advertised titles in the Appointments columns, 'supervisor', 'co-ordinator', 'promoter', and 'negotiator', are the staple people and jobs of the modern city. The typewriter and the telephone are the most common urban tools; paper the city's most necessary raw material.

This enlarged entrepreneurial middle – the salariat – makes the theory of upward movement and incentives much harder to apply. Theoretically, there ought to be a clear relationship between production, profit and mobility; you work harder, you produce more, and you are promoted into the slack which your effort has helped to create. But the urban entrepreneur is radically divorced from the process and the means of production; he is not in a position to create slack, and his own productivity is determined by forces beyond his control. The upward-and-downward perspective, essential to the functioning of the pyramid as model, becomes hopelessly blurred and elongated. 'Upward' means into the stratosphere of higher finance; 'downward' means, perhaps, a dimly remembered view out of a grimy train window of tips and slagheaps in some distant part of the country, with flat hats and flatter vowels. Economic movement in the city, for the salariat at least, is a matter of joggling about, keeping roughly in the same proportionate position, changing firms, waiting on increments, getting salary-rises which may improve a standard of living but hardly affect status at all. As a number of sociologists have observed, social position in this increasingly numerous class is determined not by what a member produces but by what he consumes. In today's great cities, the most visible and vociferous inhabitants tend to be useless (by any standards which rate bread as being of greater utility than circuses), disproportionately well-paid for their uselessness, equipped with the money, the time and inclination to spend a large portion of their lives out shopping. It is these people, that statistical minority from whose ranks come the heroes of a great deal of newspaper and television advertising, and whose values are more widely promoted than actually lived out, with whom I am concerned here. For however much moralists may justly berate their superficiality (and, indeed, question whether such people exist at all outside the studios of advertising agencies), they have coloured contemporary metropolitan life as boldly and distinctively as 'the mob', that older mass-produced image, coloured the Victorian city and had so profound an influence upon nineteenth century architecture and demography.

Just as Mayhew found it convenient to classify his street folk by the objects they sold, we may need to label ours by what they buy. For the modern city, at least in its middle class quarters, is a temple of useless consumption. If a class of non-producers distort and swell its social structure, its commercial life is correspondingly inflated by the trade in objects whose sole function is to enhance the identities of their purchasers. A list of shops on the nearest block in the inner London suburb where I live illustrates this quite dramatically. The block is more raggy than grand; the shopping area for a honeycomb of flats whose owners and tenants look fairly tatterdemalion – not poor, but not within sniffing distance of surtax and trustees either. There are 32 establishments on the 80-yard-long block, which also has a number of rococo fronted service flats with brass nameplates and buzzing doorphones. Of these, two are pubs and one a wine bar. Six are foreign restaurants, ranging from a smart Italian pastiche of a Venetian trattoria to a low curry cavern which serves business lunches; there is a fish-chicken-and-chips take-away, and a coffee bar with a downstairs folk cellar; shops selling leather goods and craft objects; a stripped-pine and Japanese lampshade furniture showroom; a cupboard-sized antique boutique; a continental supermarket, a delicatessen, a chain grocery, and a fancy greengrocer's (with avocadoes more in evidence than carrots); a tobacco kiosk, a store which sells camping equipment for hikers; two travel agents; three fashion boutiques; a radio, TV & electrical shop; an off-licence; a dry cleaner's and a launderette. An ordinary chemist's at one end has just been turned into a bistro full of rubber plants and dessert trolleys; while the newest venture is a shop that sells only white-painted Moroccan birdcages.

No urban planner, puzzling out the rational requirements of a new city development, would ever have arrived at the Moroccan birdcage shop. Yet of all the businesses on the block this is the one which is most typical of the peculiar big-city flavour of the quarter. It is an example of pure, bedsitter-entrepreneurism; you import a functional object from a distant place or period, make it both useless and decorative with a lick of paint, then sell it at a fancy price as a status-enhancer. If the bottom falls out of the birdcage market, no doubt the shop can quickly adapt to selling cracked 78 rpm rock-and-roll records, 1940s Aztec-fretwork radio sets, or glass liquid-gas jars for growing miniature gardens in. The market in fashion is omnivorous in this improvisatory, make-do-and-mend way; it transforms junk into antiques, rubbish into something rich, strange, expensive and amusing. It is solely concerned with effecting arbitrary changes of value; its raw material is the continuous stream of waste products which we leave behind us in our crazes. It is cyclical and self-sufficient, replenishing itself as demand dictates, from the reservoir of refuse from which we have temporarily averted our eyes. One blink, and we are making out a cheque to pay for some *objet d'art* which we tossed into the garbage can only last month. The Moroccan birdcage syndrome is a useful model for a certain kind of urban industrial process – a process which both supplies a demand for commodities whose sole feature is their expressiveness of taste, and becomes, by virtue of its laws of economic transformation, the ultimate arbiter of that taste. The stylistic entrepreneurs who make their living out of this curious trade go, along with gangsters and dandies, into the bracket of people possessed of a special kind of city knowledge.

What they have grasped is a fundamental change in middle-class attitudes towards possessions. Traditionally, the working class are supposed to be the major consumers of society; the middle class, adept at looking after their own, are investors – the commodities they purchase, like houses, antiques, pictures, are, according to the theory, durable, capable of being passed on to the next generation, likely to accrue in value. It is left to the East End hoods and barons to swill down astronomically priced cocktails, smoke fat cigars, and buy American-styled chromium cars which rust away as soon as purchased. In the myth of middle-class thriftiness, neither moth eats nor rust corrupts; and everything in the drawing-room gains steadily in value. But for our contemporary entrepreneurial class, for whom the pyramid is no longer sufficiently real and enticing as a social model, and whose position is determined more by skill than by property, no such comfortable conviction of continuity, of the reality of the future, is possible. Their gains are temporary, increasingly *for now* – the gains of chronic jogglers . . . in short, gains of taste, and the value of taste rather than the value of property.

Thorstein Veblen was the first chronicler of this new, lavish, non-investing class, and from the 1920s onwards, its heroes appear regularly in American fiction (in England, Evelyn Waugh's Margot Metroland valiantly spends for her country, but she has few rivals): in Nathanael West's novel of Hollywood, *The Day of the Locust,* for instance, the most telling symbol of a film producer's mighty wealth is the repulsive dead horse, made of inflatable rubber, which he keeps in his swimming pool. And in Scott Fitzgerald's *Tender Is The Night,* Nicole Diver became the exquisite, deranged heroine of consumption carried to the point of moral principle. Already in *The Great Gatsby* Fitzgerald had drawn the portrait of a bewitched immigrant to the city who lived out a tragic fantasy of possession: Gatsby's 'yellow bug' of a motor car, his wardrobe of shirts so beautiful that Daisy weeps over them, his patent gadget for gutting oranges – these are the perishable constituents of a dream which is bound to crack up, carrying the dreamer in the wake of its disintegration. With Nicole, Fitzgerald pursues the theme a stage further. Harder, more alive to her own desperation than Gatsby, she commits herself to her shopping with the serious frenzy of a determined suicide:

Nicole bought from a great list that ran two pages, and

bought the things in windows besides. Everything she liked
that she couldn't possibly use herself, she bought as a present
for a friend. She bought coloured beads, folding beach
cushions, artificial flowers, honey, a guest bed, bags, scarfs,
love birds, miniatures for a doll's house, and three yards
of some new cloth the colour of prawns. She bought a
dozen bathing suits, a rubber alligator, a travelling chess
set of gold and ivory, big linen handkerchiefs for Abe, two
chamois leather jackets of kingfisher blue and burning bush
from Hermes — *bought all these things not a bit like a high-
class courtesan buying underwear and jewels, which were
after all professional equipment and insurance, but with an
entirely different point of view.* Nicole was the product of
much ingenuity and toil. For her sake trains began their
run at Chicago and traversed the round belly of the continent to California; chicle factories fumed and link belts
grew link by link in factories; men mixed toothpaste in
vats and drew mouthwash out of copper hogsheads; girls
canned tomatoes quickly in August or worked rudely at the
Five-and-Tens on Christmas Eve; half-breed Indians toiled
on Brazilian coffee plantations and dreamers were muscled
out of patent rights in new tractors — these were some of
the people who gave a tithe to Nicole and, as the whole
system swayed and thundered onward, it lent a feverish
bloom to such processes of hers as wholesale buying, like
the flush of a fireman's face holding his post before a spreading blaze. She illustrated very simple principles, containing
in herself her own doom, but illustrated them so accurately
that there was grace in the procedure . . . (my italics)

That 'different point of view' is one from which the world
offers no continuity, no future to invest in. It belongs very
specially to the city, whose particular social discontinuities
have exacerbated — or confirmed — the conviction of our age
that temporariness is a fate we have been condemned to by
history. The consumer is the hero of a life considered as a
series of fleeting occasions. He lives as if both past and
future had been foreshortened to residual stumps: both the

beginning and the end of things are in stifling proximity to each other. Ecstasy, terror and insouciance combine in him into a permanent style. The doom which Nicole carries with her is her familiar; it inflects every action, makes survival miraculous. Like Nicole (and like both of those urban, supremely temporarist artistic communities, the *Yellow Book* group of the 1890s and the Dadaists of the 1920s.) the consumer's habitual form, in both art and life, is the epigram – that compressed, disconnected, transistorised circuit of language which transcends history and continuity by the exactitude with which it illuminates the instant. Buying a rubber alligator is an epigram : a rapid, oblique, witty gesture that transforms an object into an idea by the mere act of acquisition.

There are examples of this impulse all around us. Most of the goods we consume come in two kinds : as objects of nutrition and investment, or, in a slightly modified form, as epigrammatic ideas, liberated from their strict function. In the domain of food, for instance, whimsical and exotic eatables – foods whose consumption conveys an idea about the consumer as much as it nourishes him – are usually very close relatives of cheap commonplace foods. Thus the melon shares its texture, its flavourlessness and its botanical genre with the vegetable marrow. Melons, however (like the elusive sturgeon, whose roe when potted turns into caviare), come from faraway places and are luxuriously expensive. Beef is the staple family meat; in its immature, synthetically anaemic and notably less nutritious form as veal, it belongs to a style of cuisine. Marrows, cods' roes and sirloin steaks are investments, bought for their nutritive value; melons, caviare and veal escalopes are, like Moroccan birdcages and rubber alligators, objects whose consumption is its own point. Their most important function is to tell us something about the people who buy them; they belong to the hazardous but necessary urban art of self-projection.

I am beginning to trespass here on the ground of Roland Barthes's *Mythologies* (1972), but I should like to explore this general idea a little further, and broaden it to include two centrally important classes of objects, cars and houses.

Cars clearly provide a highly developed communicative code, ranging from superfluously durable investment objects to the most flimsily transient of stylistic affectations (the vintage Rolls to the Bond 'Fun Bug'). But the melon-marrow pattern of generic similarity, combined with a sharp distinction between investment and consumption still holds true. When British Fords introduced their new Capri model at the 1968 Motor Show, it had broadly the same mechanical layout and basic capacity as their long-running Cortina. But the Cortina, a sensible-looking boxlike car, is thoroughly functional; it might most readily be associated with commercial travellers and fathers of families – it is efficient, upright, thrifty without being cheeseparing, a middle-class utility object endowed with about as much glamour as a washing machine. The Capri, happily echoing the name of the holiday resort and 'caprice', was really no more than a body-shell, impressionistically reminiscent of the high-haunched shape and 'spring' of the American Ford Mustang. This pretty carapace was locked over the guts of the prim Cortina. Its most original feature was the way in which the company advertised and sold it. The minimum price purchased a standard model; then, for increasing sums, all sorts of extras, accessories and boosts of engine capacity could be clipped on. These were registered in prominent chrome insignia on the car's rear end. The purchaser of a Capri is thus able to advertise a sequence of personal choices; in a neat antithesis, the Ford Motor Company are able to market both a mass-produced vehicle built to a single design and a symbol of discriminatory consumption – the actual symbols of this discrimination are such things as dummy air scoops and strips of chromium plate which are pinned up along the side of the car.

There is a similar degree of deliberate uselessness or inefficiency built in to some of the most solid 'investment' cars; an inefficiency which effectively advertises their owners' wealth while at the same time playing its small part in the diminishment of that wealth. The motoring correspondent of the *Guardian* recently pointed out that the slab-fronted shapes of the Rolls and the Daimler make them 'aerodynamicists' nightmares'. Like the bleeding-out process applied to expensive cuts of veal, these imposingly solid porticos of bumpers, radiator grills and windscreens (not unlike the fronts of the Victorian town houses of wealthy merchants announcing their encastellated position above the mob) impair the vehicles' nutritional value. Presumably anyone who buys a Rolls or a Daimler can afford to ignore the loss of maximum speed and increased amount of petrol required to haul its fortifications through the resisting air. His indifference is a part of what he has paid for, a symbol of his freedom to choose independently of the constraints of utility and economy.

Cars have had to carry an excessive burden of symbolism; they have been decked out with every sort of frippery, used as promiscuously as tailors' dummies to promote a style. The car is a special simulacrum of the self; it goes where its owner goes; it forms his outer suit, his most visible and ubiquitous expression of choice and taste; it is most often seen briefly, on the move – like the citizen himself, it has to make its message plain in an instant. The epigrammatic possibilities of automobile design have been realised in a handful of models, the best known are, perhaps, the Mustang, the Volkswagen, the Morris Minor, the Rolls, the Jaguar, the Citroen 2CV, the Cadillac – and all these cars have been used as cult-objects, to make a condensed statement about the people who drive them, as legible as the symbols on a medieval shield seen in the thick of a battle. Earlier this century, before over-population and suffocating traffic jams alerted us to the fact that the motor car is one of the city's greatest menaces, the city was seen as the special province of the automobile. An imaginary city, Le Corbusier's Ville Radieuse, and a real one, Los Angeles, were built as shrines to the vision of the citizen as motorist. His changed scale of speed and distance gave rise to a city plan in which individuals were perceived as voyagers: the neighbourhood and the street were replaced by the super-highway, and the old supportive systems in which one knew who one was by the reflections given back by familiar faces from next door or the corner shop gave way to the bold, curt announcement of identity made by the motor.car. On an eight-lane carriageway, travelling in to the city at 60 mph, a Cadillac running side by side with a Volkswagen is as eloquently wordless a dialogue as the modern city often affords. The peculiar fakery of the car-customising business – the air vents which take in no air, the superfluous body-bulge over a drive shaft which has no need of that extra space, the extended bonnet projected over a short engine – deftly transforms a sense of self into a series of easily-read slogans. This one is powerful and ambitious, this one rich and secure, this one sensible and down-to-earth, this one sensitive to line and colour. Small adjustments, ironies and qualifications can be clipped on, until the car is a working model of how you see your self, a stand-in, able to communicate at speed without any further effort on your part.

With houses, in the city at least, their epigrammatic possibilities reside primarily in the postal district in which they are located. Certain areas, at both ends of the property market, clearly belong to the 'investment' category: Belgravia, whose denizens talk of it as 'just round the back of Harrods', or, several tens of thousands of pounds lower down, Hounslow or Catford. Some London suburbs are traditional class ghettoes; ownership of a house in, say, Golders Green or Cockfosters, merely reflects the income bracket and status within the middle class of the purchaser. But there is a great deal of soft territory where people buy houses to announce something distinctive about themselves, and not just that they have a certain quantity of money. I have already mentioned Islington and Camden Town as places of this kind; as I write, it is becoming a very clear signal of personal identity to buy a house in Kentish Town, a recently resurrected dark quarter of the city, to which those who are discriminatory, left of centre, but scornful of the swarm of Islington camp-followers, are currently flocking. The NW5 postal district is moving into the pantheon of style, where it joins N1, NW1, NW3, SW6, W8 and others. A year or two ago it had all the characteristics of an area awaiting rediscovery: heavy dilapidation, absentee landlords, houses let off in single rooms, a high proportion of immigrants and students, and relatively low property prices. As these things go, it was a junk quarter, a natural piece of raw material for the stylistic entrepreneurs. Its very unlikeliness was part of its charm. Kentish Town is a mess of hilly streets around a tube station, sliced into segments by noisy through-roads. Most of the houses are survivals of the most notorious period of Victorian speculative jerry-building. They were erected in short terraces of what were accurately described by their builders as 'fourth-rate residences', at a cost of about £200 for a single house. Their doors and windows are cheaply gabled and scalloped, and in line on the terrace they look like brick railway carriages, their decorations skimped, their narrow front strips of garden a long balding patch of tarry grass with motor scooters parked under flapping tarpaulins with holes in them. In 1885, the magazine *The Builder* said of the contemporary jerry-builder that 'he found a solitude and leaves a slum'. Kentish Town is one such slum; but time, and the pressure on metropolitan living space, have rendered its cramped terraces quaint . . . it now has 'possibilities'. Like the Moroccan birdcage, it is ripe for transformation. Jeremy and Nicola, out on Sunday for a trip around the house-agents' boards, find its ugliness lovable; for the first time in its history, Kentish Town is being chosen, adopted, an object to advertise not to conceal.

It has become an idea, the most precious of all commodities in this curious system. Three years ago I lived just above Kentish Town, and it was merely a place to be crossed in order to arrive at somewhere more interesting. Now it has an exact identity; it communicates thrift, intelligence, foresight, a refusal to be taken in by the showy charms of more obvious quarters. Thus transformed, it can now be used as badge of affiliation to a caste, a symbol not of status but of taste and identity.

Just as things can be converted into ideas, so ideas may be used as commodities. In his 1972 Thomas Jefferson Lecture, the American critic Lionel Trilling remarked:

It can be said of ideas that they are, like money, a mobile and mobilizing form of property. They are, to be sure, accessible to all and held in common, but as they come to have power in the world, it is plain that a peculiar power or, at least, status accrues to the individuals who first conceive them, or recognise them, or make them public. Men of ideas, perhaps even more rapidly than men of money, move towards equality with men of birth. Voltaire, Rousseau and Diderot appear on the eighteenth-century scene as sovereign princes of intellect.

But it was not until late in the nineteenth century that ideas, like so many other things, became cheap and mass-produced, and entered the urban industrial market. With the creation of the penny paper with its enormous circulation and trade in bizarre disconnected facts, the notion of the 'man of ideas' became available in an inexpensive popular form. The press barons, Harmsworth and Northcliffe, virtually invented a new kind of proletarian reading matter, aimed at the undifferentiated mass of city workers. (One indication of the overwhelmingly urban circulation of these papers is the fact that they consistently treat the country either as a weekend play-park or as the habitat of hay-chewing bumpkins who arrive in London asking policemen where the church is. The editorial slant, the jokes, the gossip columns of *Tit-Bits* and the *Daily Mail* were exclusively directed at readers who were self-conscious city-dwellers.) Unlike the sensational stories of the *Police Gazette* and other early precursors of the popular newspaper, *Tit-Bits,* and the vastly successful Harmsworth encyclopedias, built their circulations on the growing craze for popular knowledge, conveniently chopped up for instant consumption in two-sentence, short-worded paragraphlets. Strings of 'astounding facts' – the highest mountain in Asia, the heaviest man in history, the latest figures for Brazilian coffee production, the eating habits of the peregrine falcon – trailed down column after column of cheap, rather hairy and smelly newsprint. By memorising these useless scraps of information, one might become an 'educated man',

possessed of those commodities which, in this age of expertise
and skills, promised wealth and success. Insofar as these newspapers seriously pretended to be a force of mass education,
they cynically exploited a gullible public; they flung a pigswill
of silly statistics at their readers – perhaps it was the cheapest
and laziest way of finding something to print. It required no
reporters, only a rack of encyclopedias and HMSO reports.
For the man on the train or the tram, anything would do –
all he was presumed to want was a page full of words to hide
behind.

But it was an astute strategy. *Tit-Bits* seemed to offer
every man the chance to make himself an expert in something. He could find his own private corner of the learned
world. Rather than devouring the columns wholesale, he
could pick from them certain obscure fields and cultivate them
intensely – *everything* about falcons, or mountains, or Brazil.
Expertise, in this form, was the most accessible kind of
individuality. From the outside, one might look no different
from one's fellows, but inside, in the head, there one might
be – if not a prince of the intellect – at least a junior executive,
a figure of some real, if secret, authority. It was an illusion
pathetically and hypocritically fostered by the tycoons: the
strongest recommendation for *Tit-Bits* was that it was innocuous. At a time when the masses were widely feared to be
capable of some unspeakable revolution, the paper offered them
a soft, anaesthetic pap which actively prevented the possibility
of thought and the intelligent exercise of reason. The longer
the working class were kept interested in the trivial, the
exotic and the worthless, the better the middle classes slept
at nights. Few readers of these papers had any other standards
to judge them by, and habit and repetition were the surest
guarantees that the working class would grow to love what it
was given (a stage-managed coincidence which has, unhappily,
survived into our own time and into other media as the
classic and incontrovertible argument for every new tub of
dirty bathwater.)

Yet these papers did help to assuage a genuine deep hurt:
the tragic conviction that in a city mass, alone, unnoticed,

one has lost one's personal identity, become just another
blank face in the crowd. The encyclopedia offered a balm
to this profoundly private anxiety. Like the city itself, it was
available to everyone, an impersonal mass product; but what
lay inside, your individual reading of its pages, could be
yours alone, endowing you with the dignity of a solitary
empire. George Gissing opened a short story – called, with
heavy irony, 'The Salt of the Earth' – on a description of the
'morning tide of humanity' passing over Blackfriars Bridge.
Then, zooming in on a single clerk, arbitrarily picked out
from this wave of identical faces, Gissing says: 'No eye
surveying this procession would have paused for a moment on
Thomas Bird.' But Gissing, as attentive as God to the humblest
of creatures in his world, does pause, and he describes the
contents of Mr Bird's head:

> He delighted in stories of adventure, of bravery by flood
> or field, and might have posed – had he ever posed at all
> – as something of an authority on North Pole expeditions
> and the geography of Polynesia.

This is *Tit-Bits* stuff; a parcel of trifling odds and ends of
information, yet desperately precious to its possessor for it
is the only thing which gives him a place in the world, a
sense of who he is, an individual status in the crowd. The
Thames, for Gissing as for Dickens, is the supreme symbol
of London the city – a place where it is easy to drown in
the stream, and in which survival depends on finding some
raft, however thin or precarious, to keep one's head above
water. Such snippets of knowledge and dim intimations of
personal uniqueness do provide a raft, and the conditions of
the city make us cling to them with a hope and a vanity which
can, from the outside, seem pathetic or absurd.

Ideas are both the cheapest and the most intensely private
objects with which a man may furnish an identity. They are
also uniquely clubbable: groups of devotees huddle cosily
behind them, 'like-minded people', coteries, cliques, cells.
In the city, there are clubs for people to have weekly dis-

cussions of the work of Pushkin, or Theosophy, or Buddhism, or Humanism. The back page of the *New Statesman* is the London noticeboard for groups like this; here the Muswell Hill Humanists and the South Place Ethical Society advise that this Friday they will be considering the future of internationalism, the role of the free school, the origins of anti-semitism. Eleanor Rigby, a keen Fabian, puts on her hat and the face which she keeps in a jar by the door, and takes a tube to a rented hall with browning photos of obscure dignitaries on its walls; at the break for coffee, kindly provided by mesdames Lovegrove and Massingham, Miss Rigby is ardent on the issue of workers' control. November is the happiest month for these covens : at the darkening of the afternoons and the first frosts, people come in out of the cold, glad for the chance to talk of the world; but by spring, these gatherings thin out, and halting friendships, made over dry petit beurre biscuits and argots as occult as Mayhew's thieves' slangs, die in the April sun. At the meetings I have been to, the groups of people have looked much the same; single women with worried faces and genteel accents, bearded balding men in duffel coats and threadbare university scarves, doomed to a perpetual studentdom, and grizzled men of impoverished distinction, like unemployed bishops. When I went, it was as much to look for a Friend as to meditate on the future of socialism, and I felt kin to others there; the same stutter, words spilling out for the first time in the day, the same nervous glance at the watch and wrench at going back out into the dark street. For us, ideas were an excuse to gather; they filled out the dead spaces, protected us from too much of ourselves, made us, for the space of the evening, people with a purpose, with cards of identity. In the Fabian Society – and perhaps in the Theosophical Society too – you become a citizen.

But certain families of ideas are particularly amenable to this treatment as escutcheons for a coterie; and the history of popular ideas – of intellectual fashions which have taken fire in society at large – is itself essentially a city history, and the basic outlines of its major movements curiously resemble each other. Some ideas are more clubbable than others, more easily turned into commodities and advertisements for oneself. The Victorian craze for spiritualism is a remarkable example. An oblique offshoot of major intellectual movements in the nineteenth century, American transcendentalism and European romanticism, it was thoroughly bourgeois in its clientele. It belonged to the dabblers, the hobbyists, the dinnertime intellectuals. In his monologue for a fraudulent spiritualist, 'Mr Sludge : "The Medium" ', Browning described the people who held post-prandial seances in their drawing-rooms :

> There's a . . . hateful form of foolery —
> The social sage's, Solomon of saloons
> And philosophic diner-out, the fribble
> Who wants a doctrine for a chopping-block
> To try the edge of his faculty upon.
> Prove how much common sense he'll hack and hew
> In the critical minute 'twixt the soup and fish!
> These were my patrons . . .

The spread of the craze coincided with the peak growth-period of the industrial cities, from the 1850s to the 1890s, and its centres were London, New York and Boston. Certainly it had a great social cachet. Mr Sludge was able to say :

> Who finds a picture, digs a medal up,
> Hits on a first edition, — he henceforth
> Gives it his name, grows notable : how much more
> Who ferrets out a medium?

Spiritualism had an impressive, quasi-scientific jargon, with its notions of 'the ether', 'the other side', 'materialisation', 'ectoplasm', 'medium', and so forth. At the same time at which the physical sciences were devoted to constructing empirical catalogues of the properties of this world, spiritualism was earnestly parodying the process for the next. Mr Sludge observes of the other side that in it 'all our conventions are reversed'; the spirit world is a reassuring mirror of our own, where the reversed ghosts of the dead may be seen acting out their own mimicry of the comfortably well-placed middle-class existence of the living. It offered, in other words, a happily tautologous set of explanations.

These ingredients made a perfect soothing mixture for many of the nagging uncertainties of the Victorian world. Science, already growing distressingly complicated, beyond the reach of the gentleman's study with its jars of crystals, lengths of rubber tubing and blown-glass retorts, was turned, in spiritualism, into cosy gobbledygook, within the understanding of the dimmest maiden lady. The physical universe, which had been rendered by science into a suddenly lonely and directionless crust, was shown to be so presumptive that it could accommodate the supernatural and eternal too. Science could seemingly be made to bring immortality closer, not to hustle it out of existence. Most important of all, in a period when communities were felt to be breaking up, when the loss of human contact seemed fearfully imminent, especially in the jungles of the cities, spiritualism brought people close. The seance hinged on holding hands; the coterie clung together as they joined not only each other but the dead as well – the famous, the fabulous, and the domestic, family dead – in a sensuous orgy of community life.

Glasses, communally fingered, still scrape over Ouija boards in bedsitters, and forceful women with throaty voices still summon Zarak the Egyptian to ethereal music on long-play stereo records in darkened halls full of stacking chairs. ('The lady in the third row in the blue hat. I feel someone close to you has recently departed to the other side . . .' The lady in the blue hat nods solemnly. 'Your husband, I feel he is called Harry . . . H . . . H . . .', 'Henry!' 'Henry says you are not to worry, he is very happy . . . I feel there is some little financial difficulty . . .') But the palliatives of spiritualism survive in more respectable and secular forms, in currently fashionable ideas which are both valued highly and serve as prestigious screens·for coteries to shelter behind.

What distinguishes those ideas which make the transition from the study and the learned periodical to the gossip of the dinner table? It is not, I think, simply their current standing in the intellectual community which makes them valuable social objects, but a set of properties quite contingent to their truth or mental force. In London in the last few years such ideas have been sounded more frequently than any others over soup at the Veneerings': the zoological model of human society as propounded by writers like Desmond Morris and Jane Goodall, the basic theory of Levi-Strauss's system of structural anthropology, and the more abstract and intellectually titivating aspects of ecology. They have a number of features in common. Each one lends itself to being stated in an epigrammatic form. Each reduces the world to a simple universal model. Each offers some sort of general explanation about the nature of human society. Each has its own occultly-scientific technical jargon. They are all elegant, commodities with a high surface finish – new, bright, conclusive. They are, as ideas go, unusually communicable: we absorb them by a process of cultural osmosis, from humour, gossip, and television programmes.

The ideas which have become negotiable as prestigious social commodities in recent years have all conformed to this stringent set of conditions. The fashionable philosophies of Herbert Marcuse, Marshall McLuhan and Noam Chomsky have proved themselves capable of being transmitted as slogans, often to the alarm of their originators. They have been turned into industrial objects – cheap, easily acquired things which have a brief popular currency and are then discarded. Their other life, in the university and the professional journals, may go on unimpeded; but at the middle class dinner table they are as transient and modish as the clothes and cars which in so many ways they resemble. Yet if one attends to the undertone beneath the hectically bright surface of this popular trade in debased academic ideas, one can hear a dark, anguished entirely serious note.

The world postulated by these ideas is a world on the brink of devastation and disintegration. Levi-Strauss's structural anthropology begins by revealing the baffling diversity of human cultures; to every tribe and nation an exclusive and highly developed network of patterns of ritual, custom and kinship. Yet in this global disunity, he discerns a single repeated thread, a universal impulse; the Parisian and the Hopi Indian have different languages and symbols, but the basic structure of their minds is one. Levi-Strauss is voraciously interested in the cultural details which divide men from each other, but he is finally concerned to resolve these details in a universal model of the Human Mind. He has borrowed the notion of the binary opposition from computer science, and has adapted the techniques of phonemic and morphemic analysis from linguistics. The surface of his writing frequently looks highly technical, but this appearance of hard science is deceptive: most of the terminology turns out to have been grafted on to a prose as direct, simple and moving as that of a good novelist. When, in the last chapter of *Tristes Tropiques,* Levi-Strauss speaks without his professional mask, appealing for an ultimate brotherhood of man, he reveals the vital component of structuralism which has made it into a popular cult. However elaborately dressed in scientific terms and fine academic distinctions, it promises a reunited world, renders inessential the violent divisions of politics and culture. If we sometimes seem to be suffocating in the details created by our own over-active ingenuity, Levi-Strauss shows us how to rearrange them so that they become a simple universal pattern, varying only in minor structural qualifications. He offers the oldest of all consolations of philosophy: he sees harmony in chaos, extracts fundamental principles from a bewildering sea of particulars.

The parallels between structuralism and ecology are precise and significant. Where Levi-Strauss enshrines the binary opposition (*nature/culture raw/cooked*) as the fundament of the human mind and its expression in culture, ecology presents the cycle, the self-sustaining eco-system, as a universal model of life. The world it seeks to regulate is seen as a wasteful, over-productive place; it generates commodities out of all proportion to its needs, and the task of the ecologist is to construct an inventory of essentials, to eliminate the excess from the system. Both ecology and structuralism recognise that the world we live in is too massively diverse, too superfluous in its details, for us to manage capably. Structuralism makes it accessible to the imagination; ecology to practical scientific action.

The wider social force of these ideas is both powerful and dubious. The people who have attached themselves to them, and espoused them as if they were religious beliefs, have frequently used them to conjure alternative, simpler worlds, imaginary Edens. The eco-system is an effective metaphor for just the kind of small, self-sufficient community from which people living in large cities believe they have become disastrously divorced. It lends itself too, to a philosophy of immediate self-help, of consumer action. An article on kitchen gadgets in the Women's Liberationist magazine *Spare Rib* :

> An ecologically orientated friend of mine chews up her baby's food for him rather than use the blender that she has been given. She believes that turning-on the blender contributes unnecessarily to the pollution produced by electric power plants.

It is a wonderfully cosy way of avoiding the abyss. When ecology entered the language as a popular epigram, it was easily converted into a series of simple injunctions : we were to go back to the country, live with bicycles and mangles, eat vegetarian food, and stoke log fires under the leaky thatch. Science had given its imprimatur to rural nostalgia.

People often complain of metropolitan life that it coarsens thought, that the intellect is held cheaply, that serious issues degenerate into trends of the moment and the coterie. From the judicious distance of a provincial university town, London and New York often look like circuses, their intelligentsias as sleek as performing seals. So much of talk is fashion and frippery; its buzz of new ideas is brazenly decorative, there to adorn the talker and to protect him from the incursions of the world. When an idea becomes a commodity, readily transmittable and exchangeable in the bazaar of society at large, it takes on the characteristics of other commodities. It may be unpalatable to think of ideas as if they could have the same function as housefronts, cats or handbags but it is surely true that they very often do so. People gather behind them, for private and highly partial reasons. The inexpensive synthesis, of the kind that can be extracted from ecology, or structuralism, or *The Gutenberg Galaxy*, or *One Dimensional Man*, comforts and assuages those who embrace it. It makes the world simpler, gives a thrust of direction and authority to the individual living in a prolix and confusing city. We are not so far here from Gissing's Thomas Bird, picking himself out from the crowd with his treasured private knowledge of the geography of Polynesia.

These narrow, passionate *cognoscenti* bolstered by received ideas, given to clubs and cliques and intense sectarian debates, are part of the essence of city life. For the member of an urban guerrilla cell, or an ecological watchdog organisation, or a neo-mystical commune, or one of the countless coffee-and-discussion groups that are always springing up in big cities, his ideology is a *route,* a consecrated path through the unintelligible scatter of city streets. A sense of community, and the perspective which we acquire as one of the privileges of belonging to a community, are hard to come by in the city. Neither the street nor the neighbourhood (except in some of the leafier suburbs and odd clusters of besieged roads of working-class terraces) confers a sufficient sense of membership on its residents. The turnover of owners and tenants is too rapid, and the sheer physical density with which metropolitan space is occupied makes for a warren of private cubicles in which people jealously and secretively protect their own patches. Ideas, unlike neighbours, are chosen; and a community of people who share an idea, a craze, a belief is perhaps the most precious of all the associations which a man may make in a city. There is a café around the corner from where I live which is a nest of coteries in the long dull middle of the afternoon. Italian *au pair* girls go there, so do folk music enthusiasts and loitering record collectors. But there is also a curious group of young men in fishermen's jerseys who have the activist's look of glinting, mildly fanatical anaemia. One day I learned

how to make a bomb; and the technical jargon of revolution
spills from their table in single overheard phrases. I am not
a party to their beliefs, nor do I know what they are
(Trotskyists . . . anarchists . . . People's Democracy . . .
midnight slogan painters . . . colourful fantasising about the
lives of other people is a chronic urban habit); and this very
quality of unknownness scares me. But there is a real resem-
blance between this tableful of revolutionaries, if that is in
fact what they are up to, and some of the less exotic coterie-
milieux which I know better. I sometimes go to a pub in
Soho with a corner full of book reviewers, and one catches
the same note there: the same pitch of voice, the technical
talk, the possessive hunch over the table of people making a
close, improvised, temporary community in the middle of a
city of strangers. Communities like this, which come to life
around an idea, are constantly dissolving; they are not fixed
in place or time, although membership of them is a permanently defining feature of one's identity.

A large city is a honeycomb of such groups. To the outsider, they are likely to seem silly or sinister, and certainly
evanescent. For every group which establishes itself with
capital and property in a quarter, there are many whose out-
ward and visible signs are known and valued only by their
members. Their most important possessions are their ideas,
and these are preserved for fellow-initiates, not exposed to
the hostile examination of the world outside. They communicate by rumour and the telephone; they meet in public
places – in halls, in parks, in pubs and cafés, and on streets
and squares. Like their members, they are in a state of
constant locomotion in the city. One or two established organisations – the Salvation Army is the prime example – have
borrowed the mobile structure of these groups; grasping,
as General Booth grasped, that the most effective institutions
in a big city must keep on the move with the people.

Sometimes such a group will suddenly move into visibility
and claim the attention of outsiders in the crowd with its
extreme and bizarre public symbols. In New York, Los
Angeles and London, there is a wandering tribe of street

folk; they live in Radha Krishna temples, their heads are shaved except for a scrubby tuft on their crowns, they process through the streets in sandals and saffron-dyed sheets, chanting the 'Hare Krishna' mantra and beating on tambourines. On Oxford Street, motorists caught in the continual traffic jam yell cheerful obscenities at these outlandish communards. They seem indifferent. Their vegetarian diet and life of indoor meditation have pulled the skins of their faces away from their lips and eyes so that they have a curiously protuberant, root-vegetable look. Yet they are not without dignity: their voices are gentle, hazed, their accents invariably English urban, and patches of Manchester and Stepney show through their stiff, devoted impersonation of the mystic east. They are keen to evangelise, and methodically explain themselves with the rehearsed precision of a telephone answering service. I sat in my socks in a basement, sharing their bowl of grated oranges and vegetables, as they talked at me earnestly, not expecting to be believed, knowing, I suspect, that many of their visitors only come to smirk and peer. They are solemn, courteous, and extremely ugly: their scraped turnip faces nod slowly under the naked 200-watt bulb, which itself looks rather like another communard. Each word and gesture is reverently drawn out; everything here is ritual theatre – self-consciousness is elevated to mystical consciousness of the self, and everyday life turns into a studied allegory.

The International Society for Krishna Consciousness promotes a rural peasant culture as a spiritual antidote to and romantic release from city life. It recruits the disaffiliated young from the streets, offering them spartan communes and a simple, hokum-scientific doctrine of mind power. Like nineteenth-century spiritualism, of which it is a less sophicated replica, it preaches an ethic of impoverished literalism. The movement's *swami*, in a characteristic booklet called *Easy Journey to Other Planets*, invites you to join a bargain coach-trip to the spiritual world:

The material world is only a shadow representation of the anti-material world, and intelligent men who are clean in heart and habit will be able to learn, in a nutshell, all the details of the anti-material world from the text of the *Gita,* and these are in actuality more exhaustive than material details . . .

. . . The gross materialist may try to approach the anti-material worlds by endeavouring with spaceships, satellites, rockets, etc., which he throws into outer space, but by such means he cannot even approach the material planets in the higher regions of the material sky, and what to speak of those planets situated in the anti-material sky, which is far beyond the material universe . . . Master *yogis* who control the anti-material particle within the material body by practice of mystic powers can give up their material bodies at will at any given moment and can thus enter the anti-material worlds through a specific thoroughfare which connects the material and anti-material worlds.

This is a sad piece of writing; barely literate twaddle in which the jargon of popular science is treated with a superstitious reverence. Reading it, one suffocates in the appalling intellectual constriction of its vision of the world, and senses, too, in its ramshackle and reduced vocabulary and grammar, some of the sheer difficulty which its intended audience must experience when they try to think about the world at all. (A more unpleasant, because more grandly commercialised version of the same style, may be found in the work of Ron L. Hubbard and the Scientologists – another group of urban evangelists who operate in London from a shop in the Tottenham Court Road, and have had some success in converting people off the streets of the city.) The liberation of spirit which it purports to offer is a liberation into chains; it drops one into a mental abyss in which the simplest of ideas, the most elementary of rational processes, is impossibly large, foreign and unwieldy.

But when the *swami* writes of a 'thoroughfare', he indicates a route for believers which goes not so much to the stars as through the city streets. For the devotee, London becomes legible by being relegated to a plane of inferior consciousness. It turns into a chimera: the 'material' city is there to be transcended by home-made mysticism and holy gobbledygook. The chanting, the amazing dress, the razored skulls of these young men are there as a fierce announcement – they have seen through the illusory life of shops and automobiles; for them, the city we inhabit does not exist. In their city, the stars are under their feet, and the cosmos has blacked-out Bourne and Hollingsworth; they process through the chimerical void to the unearthly tinkling of their tambourines.

Krishna Consciousness presents its ideas as uniquely expensive commodities: but they are freely available to anyone who is prepared to pay for them with self-abasement, discipline, and by wearing the proud stigmata of robes and tonsure. One of the most significant features of the movement is the way in which it embraces the caste system; it promises the status of a *brahmana* to the believer. 'The caste system', writes the *swami*, 'is very scientific'; but the castes of which he writes are fundamentally different from real castes in that anybody may elect himself to the caste which he considers himself fit to belong to. We are instructed to search our hearts for signs of 'spiritual advancement', and if we find ourselves qualified, then, automatically, we become Brahmins. Status is a matter not of external circumstances but of the deliberate exercise of will over consciousness. It is inside our heads that we are aristocrats; the impersonal world, represented by the judgments and deferences of society at large, is, in the rhetoric of Krishna Consciousness, an irrelevant delusion.

It might be consoling to see the beliefs of the Krishna people as merely grotesque or dotty – the extreme responses of faddish, under-educated, under-employed young people to the unassimilable scatter of the city. But there is something more to them than that. Every western metropolis is at present swarming with bands of devotees, some flying political colours, some resurrecting or inventing exotic religions, some committed to eccentric hobbies and crazes. Some are as harmless as the radio-controlled model glider enthusiasts who foregather every Saturday on a corner of Richmond Park, cocooned from public inquisitiveness by their impressive technicalities, their talk of thermals and wavelengths and launching-ropes, mightily oblivious of the dogs and children who scamper among their balsa wood aeroplanes. They have a weekend world of their own, a private city which is invisible to the uninitiated. But at the other extreme, there are the revolutionary cells, and gangs like the Envies; people who have – like the members of the Hare Krishna Temple – concocted elaborate philosophies to prove that the city is a bead-curtain of illusion. The convicted conspirators of the English 'Angry Brigade', who had been accused of planting bombs in a number of public institutions and in the London house of a cabinet minister, subscribed to the theories of the Paris Situationists – who speak of the 'spectacle' or 'facade' of capitalism, and of revolution as imagination liberated from hierarchical modes of thought and behaviour. There can surely be no doubt that the unreality of the city, its prolixity and illegibility, its capacity to exceed all the imaginative shapes we try to impose upon it, enables its citizens to treat it with a terrifying arbitrariness. Georg Simmel, the nineteenth-century German sociologist, identified the characteristic urban habit of mind as *blasé*; Engels saw the city's major evil in the lack of curiosity shown by members of the crowd for each other. When the city becomes a mere facade, when Oxford Street ceases to exist, when violence can be casually inflicted by one metropolitan group upon another, then realism – a respect for detail, objects, independent and various lives – becomes the most pressing of all necessities.

At the Radha Krishna temple near the British Museum in Bloomsbury, a pale communard with a Glaswegian accent pointed to a man with a droopy moustache who was sitting next to me. 'Telex operator, right?' said the communard. The man stopped turning the pages of *Krisna Consciousness: the Topmost Yoga System,* and nodded slowly, reverently. 'To me', said the communard, 'he is pure consciousness. We do not see a person's job, or his clothes, or his house and family. We see his soul.' The man with the soul looked grateful; few other telex operators can visit distant planets or

turn, like magic pumpkins, into Brahmins, the ultimate aristocrats of the world-soul. He was leaving the street outside far
behind; its dense puzzles, its intricate social networks, its
inequalities, its confusion of noises and smells, were, he had
learned, just dull impediments from which he could liberate
himself at a blink.

Such subjective inspirational clairvoyance is a hallmark
of these isolated groups within the city. It is shared by
Weathermen, Diggers, Sufists, Envies, by moralistic thugs
and by placid vegetarian contemplatives. Each holds an idea,
an idiom and a uniform in common; and each believes
that the city is a 'facade', easily transcended by an act of
will, a trick of the mind, or the lit fuse of a bomb. The word
'consciousness', whether employed by the revolutionary or
the religiomane, is a shorthand-notation: it conveys the
notion that the intuitive self might actually come to replace
the edifice of society – that the world on the ground might be
moulded into the shape of a totalitarian world inside the
head.

It is a dangerous kind of dreaming, this solemn, simple
mentalism. It releases the dreamer into a domain of total
possibility in which his reality is as inventive, psychotic or
banal as his own imagination. He imagines himself a
Brahmin . . . he is a Brahmin. If a toolmaker's apprentice
from West Ham wants to turn into an Asian mystic, he may
do so simply by rigging himself out in the appropriate uniform and chanting the prescribed abracadabra. If one shifts
from group to group, one watches London dissolving; from a
paddy field of disembodied souls, to a systematic capitalist
conspiracy of banks, police stations, court-houses and monuments, to a range of Cuban hills where fellow guerrillas
squat in waiting wearing patched jeans and ex-WD wind-
cheaters, to the gothic, magical city of signs prophesied in
the writings of Nostradamus.

In a television interview transmitted the day after her
conviction in the 'Angry Brigade' trial in 1972, Anna Mendel-
son talked in what is increasingly becoming a characteristic
idiom of our time; a style in which familiar words are pro-

nounced as if they were components of an arcane code. She
spoke distractedly in a dream-monotone: phrases like 'working class', 'conspiracy', 'change of consciousness' came out
rounded as pebbles, but what they meant to me was clearly
not what they meant to her. When she was asked whether
the bombings had had any tangible effect on the progress of
the revolution in England, she stared mildly, apparently in-
comprehendingly at her interviewer and said 'I suppose they
must have . . . yes . . . they must have, mustn't they . . .' so
vaguely that one felt that one had trespassed illicitly over the
far side of her dream.

These intense, private groups, compacted around a core
of symbolic objects and ideas are very serious symptoms of
a metropolitan condition. They may or may not be politically
important in themselves; and when they take a religious
turn they may indicate nothing about the spiritual awakening which fond members of the clerisy enjoy forecasting.
But the club, the clique, the cell, the commune, the code are
proliferating forms in the city. Huddled, defensive, profoundly
complacent in their indifference or hostility to the rest of
the city, they are the foxholes for all those whom the city
has isolated, for whom no larger reality is habitable. Mayhew
saw the illegible mass of the nineteenth-century city as a
network of tight castes, each one operating independently of
the others and of society at large. Money, education and social
welfare provisions have largely released the castes of the
modern city from thraldom to their occupations. Just as the
poor can render themselves invisible in cheap fashion-styled
clothes so they can acquire ideas and identities of a much
wilder and grander kind than could Mayhew's costermongers
and mudlarks. In our city, it is easy to drift into a privacy
of symbols, a domain of subjective illusions made concrete
by the fact that two or three people have gathered together to
conspire in them.

It is impossible to miss the crackle of tribal hostilities in
London and New York today. What is most worrying is the
subtlety, narrowness and parochialism with which the lines
are drawn. The fierce antagonism between blacks and whites,

between haves and have-nots, is tragically comprehensible. What is not so easy to understand is the continual barrage of explosions from wars so small that only the participants can explain which sides are fighting them. *Gay News* reports vicious factional quarrels between opposed groups of London homosexuals, with smashed typewriters and bloody noses. A party for the opening of the Women's Lib magazine *Spare Rib* ended in an internecine brawl. Like the cross-hatching of bitchery which keeps literary coteries (themselves highly-developed examples of self-conscious caste groups) alive, the malevolent buzz of city life is a way of marking boundaries of taste, staking out the ever-more-questionable frontier between us and them. People in one postal district despise those in the next; the owner of the baby Renault reproves the driver of the expensive Jensen; the revolutionary dismisses the Buddhist, the Buddhist the revolutionary. It is a war of ideas and epigrams, in which objects are called on to play the parts of ideas, to express the ideologies of their owners; and its local battles are passionately territorial in nature. Each party has its own city, its own version of the self, its own route through that other, endlessly malleable city of fact.

A two-year-old conversation, if that is the word, with the manager of a pop group . . . He and I were about the same age; he smoked a joint of marijuana while he talked. He spoke, since our only purpose was ritual disagreement, with unctuous priestliness; no doubt he would describe my manner as equally odious. But this is my story. His eyes, slow-lidded, were fixed on a spot ahead of him on the ceiling.

'If you don't know what I mean, man, it'd be, like, redundant to explain it.'

'You might condescend to try.'

'It's where you're at. The level of consciousness. What you know, not something to explain. That's the whole rational hang up . . . like . . . justifications. I can't tell you what you can't know.'

'I thought that was what language was for.'

'Oh, Jesus, I am light-years ahead of you, you know? Like in experience. Words are shit. You'd only know it if that was where you were at, right?'

His accent was brisk public school, slackened at the edges with Notting Hill Gate-stoned, and his face was cold, fair and beatific. He was merely hardening the boundaries between his caste and mine on the principle that good fences make good neighbours. The exchange was a piece of formal theatre which one might find duplicated – with slightly changed vocabularies – again and again in the modern city. *The* sound of New York in 1967, so an excited expatriate told me, was Bob Dylan singing with what I thought was quite excessive relish, 'Something is happening here, and you don't know what it is, do you, Mr Jones?'

'Mr Jones' is a ubiquitous punch bag. Every group in the city seeking self-definition invents him; he is the indifferent, unknowing other, the man in the crowd who never managed to pick himself out, the loser dogging one's footsteps as a continual reminder of what the city threatens – its anonymity, its conformist anomie, its tacit hostility to all its citizens. To become someone in the city, it is first necessary to affront Mr Jones. He is the recipient of everybody's messages : the man who envies your car, is suspicious of the revolutionary content of your magazine, throws sidelong glances at your hair and clothes, disbelieves your ideas, stands alone in the street gazing at your housefront. Every coterie assures itself of its own tightness and rightness by excluding him. His incomprehension validates, his dullness is a measure of our own brilliance. Even Thomas Bird despises Mr Jones.

A city life is, in very large part, a life lived through symbols. Possessions – both the hardware of purchasable objects and the software of beliefs and ideas – become precious in exact ratio to their expressiveness, their capacity to define the relationship of the self to the city, and, more especially, of the fellow devotee to the depersonalised outsider or enemy. Perhaps the city forces these strategies upon us, or perhaps we have resorted to them thoughtlessly and unnecessarily. At any rate we have found ourselves living in an elaborate and barely understood system of castes. The intense cliquishness of metropolitan social life, that patchwork quilt of

cells, communes and coteries, everywhere provides evidence
of a society which has drifted out beyond our conventional
means of thinking, talking and feeling about it. The groups I
have described, exist side by side in a state of ignorance,
hostility or indifference to each other. They all command
a route through the city, but no common economic necessity
nor any system of direct industrial dependence binds them
together. There is no special reason for them to unite as a
class (and the recent attempts to forge links with the union-
ised working class, made by cells of young revolutionaries,
have been hopelessly unsuccessful). Their possessions, their
cult ideas, their arcane codes and jargons, form stockades
around each group. The social diversity of the city, which so
delighted the eighteenth-century citizen, has, during the course
of the twentieth century, multiplied to such an extent, accelerated by the industrial processes which have manufactured its
essential symbols, that no overview is possible. London now is
not so much an encyclopedia as a maniac's scrapbook, filled
with colourful entries which have no relation to each other,
no determining rational or economic scheme, merely a common drive to find an identity, a route, in an environment which
is perceived as invincibly impersonal and alien.

The small worlds of the devotees are concrete and self-
contained. They have managed to make their dreams real
with ornaments, toys and philosophies. They have little to
say to those outside their caste, and the boundaries become
continuously hardened and more finely drawn. The street-
Buddhist, the book-reviewer, and the bandannaed guerrilla
are not unrepresentative city men (though their styles of self-
advertisement may be more garish than most); but the cities
in which they live might as well be separate planets, so little
do their individual routes cross one another. Perhaps this
freedom to live out a dream of an exclusive community, cosseted by consumables, is the most important freedom that
the city offers; it invites a dramatically extended conception
of the self, it provides a stage for grand and uninhibited
performances. It is also heavily shadowed with loneliness,
indifference and the possibility of a pervasive unreality.

SIX

No Fixed Address

The very turmoil of the streets has something repulsive, something against which human nature rebels. The hundreds of thousands of all classes and ranks crowding past each other, are they not all human beings with the same qualities and powers, and with the same interest in being happy? . . . And still they crowd by one another, and their only agreement is the tacit one, that each keep to his own side of the pavement, so as not to delay the opposing streams of the crowd, while it occurs to no man to honour another with so much as a glance.
> Friedrich Engels, *The Condition of the Working Class in England in 1844*

It is as easy to lose other people in a city as it is to mislay one's umbrella. They are always being carried away with the crowd. When the Victorians looked at London, they saw with some shock that one of its chief evils was the ease with which the individual disappeared on the streets. The work of both local government and social and charitable agencies was made harder by the labyrinthine nature of the metropolis. Here was a place where the thief and the footpad could fade into thin air, where those people most in need of help – the poor, the witless, and the diseased – could render themselves invisible in their trek through successions of furnished rooms, where no-one could keep track of the citizens who strayed from the narrow path of a permanent home and a permanent job. The image of the nomad, employed independently by Mayhew and by Charles and General William Booth, haunts nineteenth-century writing about the city; and nomadism – the vision of a city of aimless and irresponsible wanderers—was seen as just as great a threat to the health of society at large as revolution, destitution and physical disease.

The street-folk whom Mayhew talked to revealed a great deal about the haphazardness of the honeycomb of mid-nineteenth-century London; a structure into which a person might drop, only to fall and fall, going ever further out of touch with his family and friends. There is no trace now of Mayhew's original questionnaire, but it is clear from the portraits in *London Labour and the London Poor* that he started each conversation by asking how many relatives each of his informants knew, and how frequently they saw them. The answers added up to a general picture of families that were shrinking drastically in size as the husbands or the children went deeper into the city. The closest relatives of many of Mayhew's interviewees had already faded into the distance; and the city immigrant—probably illiterate, certainly inadequately equipped with the basic skills needed to trace and communicate with his family across that widened space which the metropolis brought with it—became a nomad, a loner, scratching acquaintances off the street or in the gin-shop. An Irish girl of 22 who sold apples, told Mayhew: 'I'm an orphan, Sir, and there's nobody to care for me but God, glory be to his name! I come to London to join my brother, that had come over and did well, and he sent for me, but when I got here I couldn't find him in it anyhow.'

General Booth, whose *In Darkest England and The Way Out* is a remarkably sensitive and humane study of the nineteenth-century city, suggested that the Salvation Army should set up an 'Enquiry Office for Lost People':

Perhaps nothing more vividly suggests the varied forms of broken-hearted misery in the great city than the statement that 18,000 people are lost in it every year, of whom 9,000 are never heard of any more, anyway in this world. . . . Husbands, sons, daughters and mothers are continually disappearing, and leaving no trace behind.

Some of these people were no doubt embracing the darkness
of the city, using its streets as an escape, and holing up in
some obscure quarter with an assumed name and a new life.
Others must just have fallen through, finding themselves
fronted with a terrible dead blankness – because they had
lost the bit of paper with a crudely inked address, or it had
run in the rain, or they had misheard, or the house had been
pulled down . . . no name on the doorbell, no address for
forwarding, the mistrustful stare of landlady, or new tenant
in braces and shirt open at the neck. Suddenly the city must
have changed from a labyrinth with a route to its centre
into a hopeless scatter of streets, too many to count or
imagine, unsignposted and menacing.

For the Victorian writer, the industrial fog which hung
over London for so much of the year was very much more
than a chemical inconvenience, or even a romantic visual
effect; it was the supreme symbol of the city's capacity to
make people disappear inside it. At the end of the century
Oscar Wilde was complaining that the London peasouper
was an invention of the novelists, and that the city would be
a notably healthier place if the convention were dropped
from literature. 'The whole metropolis', says Dickens of a
grim morning in *Our Mutual Friend,* 'was a heap of vapour
charged with the muffled sound of wheels, and enfolding a
gigantic catarrh.' It is an image which holds true for
Dickens's vision of London at large – an ectoplasmic soup
from which characters can be fished out then dropped back at
will. Narrating the novel, he moves about London as if he
were its travelling soul, illuminating particular groups of
characters then losing them in obscurity. When people
separate in Dickens, it is often in fog or mist : lovers literally
fade from each other's sight, just as grotesques emerge in
dim silhouette, mistaken at first for tricks of the fancy. The
city is always swallowing its citizens, receiving them into a
dark opacity which is too thick for even the novelist to
penetrate; and it is in this moral fog that the most shabby
and evil acts are perpetrated. So Fascination Fledgeby, a
scheming cuckoo who has come into a paper fortune, dis-

appears, alas only temporarily:

> The murky fog closed about him and shut him up in its
> sooty embrace. If it had never let him out any more, the
> world would have had no irreplaceable loss, but could
> easily have replaced him from its stock in hand.

In the sprawling casts of Dickens's fiction, in which the prolific creation of characters is a by-product of the city itself,
it requires a great deal of conscious effort merely to keep the
people connected; the fog is omnivorous, and in every
novel Dickens is persistently losing his characters then finding them again. Meredith accused him of 'damnable itera-
tion'; but restatement and repetition are an inevitable part of
the fabric of the life of a city in which loss so perpetually
threatens.

Clean Air acts and smokeless zones have largely succeeded
in depriving us of the great nineteenth-century symbol for
losing people. Our modern means are cleaner, less aesthetic
and more brutal. People disappear now behind the smoked-
glass rear windows of taxis, or into the tartarously-tiled maws
of tube stations. They are taken away. The last we see of
them is a raised hand, smudgy over a bobbing crowd of
heads, or diminishing in size as the traffic lights turn to green.
A few months ago, I lost a friend I'd known for five years
when she went into the station at Earl's Court. It was, I think,
a typical city departure: a stiff kiss, a shifty sideways glance,
then blank – nothing at all but the polyglot faces of strangers
. . . Arabs, Italians, milk-fed Americans, Australians glumly
hulking duffel bags, and F. nowhere. In small places, people
have to go on living with their social failures; in London
there is an uneasy ease of separation. One is so likely to be
left only with a phone number in an old address book, and
that answered by a strange voice, curt and suspicious. We
continually drop each other back into the fog.

It is no wonder then that making connection should become such a central obsession in the life of big cities. To
meet and hold on to other people is to fly in the face of what

the city threatens to do to us; when isolation and loss are
so casual and likely, we have to work as hard as novelists to
keep our society going, to keep in touch. Much of the social
work done in cities is of this simple, connective kind. A
caseworker in Islington spends nearly all her time intro-
ducing members of the Cypriot community to each other.
Many of them are single women working as machinists and
seamstresses, living almost exactly as Jewish immigrants in
the garment district of the Lower East Side did seventy years
ago. They work at home, are paid low 'piecework' rates.
They speak little English, and apparently are often unaware
that other Cypriots are living on the same street. For women
especially, isolated by language, by the custom of staying
in the home, and by bare subsistence wages, it is alarmingly
easy to get lost, to drift into a cocoon of uninvited privacy.
It may take state agencies and charities to find even their
neighbours for them.

For although the city offers a multitude of contacts, each
of them tends to be so brief and dislocated that it involves
no more than an elliptical interchange of signals. For the
newcomer, this is baffling and infuriating. You want continuity and the possibility, at least, of permanence; what you
get is a checkover, so rapid that the encounter is over before
it has had time to begin. When I first came to London
(and I have felt it since, in two moves within the city),
I felt I was clutching at disappearing straws. Every conversation I had seemed as if it might turn into a friendship, or
so I hoped at the first flutter of words. I was slow and lumbering; other people all appeared quick, polished and hard —
their syntax seemed quite different from mine, a grammar
that sped from object to object like the squashed prose of a
telegram. It commanded assent and recognition more than
argument, and I was lost.

On tube stations, I still rake the faces in the crowd for one
I know. I expect coincidences, can never quite rid myself
of the conviction that London is an enormous village, that
one day one might wake up to find that one recognised everybody. And if the face is not familiar, then the clothes, the

magazine, the book may be. Seeing someone reading the *New Statesman* or the *New York Review* on a tube, I quicken absurdly, sensing a friend.

Such impulses drive one to those parts of the city which are both public and consecrated to a shared cultural taste. Loners foregather in bookshops, especially around the poetry shelves, picking over other people's reading. To see someone else liking the latest Auden is almost to have a friend already. And on Sunday afternoons, the art galleries fill up; glum isolates wander through the grotto of portrait miniatures at the Victoria and Albert, or around the day-glo adventure playground of the Tate. Just looking at and liking the same painting might be sufficient for intimacy; who has not fantasised a conversation spontaneously struck between two devotees, mutually enthralled by the brushwork of Nicholas Hilliard? It may never happen, but in the cathedral atmosphere of the gallery, set aside in parenthesis from the impersonal scatter of the rest of the city, it is an always-tantalising possibility. The blistering isolation of a weekend spent by oneself is softened and mulled in communal contemplation : the gallery, cinema, concert hall fill with the lonely merging selves that have grown as swollen and blubbery as porpoises through the long winter of Saturday night.

By Sunday, the fog can seem impenetrable. Not surprisingly, it is the favourite day for suicides; for this is the day when everybody is supposed to have a family to go to, a joint on the table, and a woozy afternoon in the rubble of talk, scattered papers and a bad 'fifties film on the TV. But if you are alone, things sharpen unbearably : hypochondriacs remember glands forgotten since last week, the TV set is a source only of malevolent philistine squawks (nothing is more enraging that Lucille Ball in a smug family comedy), and one is tempted to put a brick through its lined face. It is time for dialling people who have gone to the country for the weekend, and listening to the mocking repetitions of the ringing tone, counting to twelve before hanging up.

A Christmas evensong in a London church : St Luke's in Redcliffe Square. The congregation is divided into two groups :

the majority are elderly women, in cheap winter coats and shiny plastic basketwork hats. They have rouged mouths and narrow, contracted jaws. One or two are very old indeed, and their silver hair is balding, showing jagged patches of unnaturally pink skull. They do not look like grannies on Christmas cards. Then there are the young: scrubbed, anxious, in pairs rather than couples. Girls who might be secretaries or primary school teachers; a pimply young man whose eyes swim before thick spectacles, and who has the long donkey face of a premature Mr M'Choakumchild. There is hardly anyone between the ages of thirty and sixty. One man is black, and he looks cold, woebegone and a long way from home.

St Luke's was built for the prosperous Victorian tradesmen and their families and servants – who originally lived in the square. The fashionables now go to church in Kensington or Chelsea, and the congregation has shrunk away from the wide walls and side aisles into the centre. But each member keeps his distance; few pews have more than one occupant, and the hymn singing is quavery, a ghostly chorus, conducted by a jolly choirmaster whose instructions never quite reach us. He loses a verse from the end of one carol, and the voices wind raggedly down like an exhausted piece of clockwork.

It seems a dim consolation, dimmer than the Victoria and Albert. To me, a long-unaccustomed churchgoer, the words of hymns – especially carols – have an embarrassing forced intimacy. 'Love', 'bliss', 'tender', 'baby', 'sweet', are the same words one heard in crooners' songs in my adolescence. God is addressed as a baby doll, a sentimentalised Jesus with the big eyes of a lap dog or the infant Petula Clark. And the special Christmas language, of fellowship, wassailing and merry gentlemen sounds an acid joke in the grey wintry reaches of Earl's Court. The vicar talks in his address of 'the parish' in an anachronistic Oxford accent, and one wonders if the bounds are still beaten on the far side of the Fulham road, from the gasworks, up past the council flats to the deserted hospital. Yet this thin fiction – of loving and being loved, in a world nostalgically located in a thatched

village of, perhaps, a hundred and fifty years ago – is still
the most evident contribution which sentimental Christianity
has to make to society. Each Sunday it draws its thinning
congregations of the devout, the home-sick and the lonely.
People still go to church to make friends; in a strange city,
the church is sometimes their only link with a familiar community, and as Sunday squeezes, they gravitate to these under-
heated yellow-lit mausoleums, to sing scrappily together and
to pray in icy privacy. In the evening after the service, there
is always a knot of people under the illuminated globe over
the church door, reluctant to break up and go back to their
separate flats and rooms.

A snapshot from the life: a rocking tube, shuddering
through the most deeply subterranean of all London tunnels,
the Piccadilly Line. The faces of the passengers hang and
shake, each one closed and solemn. A neat girl with a patent
leather handbag on her knees has travelling eyes; they come
to a stop on an advertisement pasted up opposite from
where she is sitting. It says 'Are you sitting opposite the new
man in your life?' The stretched-out *Evening News* beneath it
stirs and lowers; an elderly West Indian in London Transport uniform stares back at the girl, whose eyes start moving
again, over the ads for secretarial agencies and insurance
companies. At Green Park, the girl gets off, and the West
Indian runs a horny forefinger down the list of runners
in a horse race at Newcastle.

During the last two or three years the computer-dating
industry has mushroomed spectacularly in London; a new
kind of private-enterprise social service · which boldly exploits the shame of loneliness, and answers to the peculiarly
big-city condition of sexual isolation. In 1890, General
Booth wrote:

Everything in (a village) community lends itself naturally to
the indispensable preliminaries of love-making and court-
ship, which, however much they may be laughed at, contribute more than most things to the happiness of life.
But in a great city all this is destroyed. In London at the

present moment how many hundreds, nay thousands, of young men and young women, who are living in lodgings, are practically without any opportunity of making the acquaintance of each other, or of any of the other sex! The street is no doubt the city substitute for the village green, and what a substitute it is!

Booth pointed to the importance of the marriage bureau, but he envisaged something too localised, too humanly personal to match the appalling size and scope of the city. Outside of certain close-knit community groups in the metropolis – the Jewish quarter of New York, for instance, where the marriage broker has always performed a respected service – such bureaux have catered to a tiny minority of the lonely. They have been small, eccentric institutions, and they have never really attempted to deal with the city on the city's terms, finding it easier, I suspect, to stick to country widows and ex-officers stranded in provincial towns. That, at least, is their image: discreet, genteel, prim.

But the computer-dating agency is brashly citified. It has, so it assures its potential clients, super-modern electronic techniques for reaching into the fog and slotting isolates together. The computer is a streamlined, 24-hour, infallible Dickensian imagination: *it* knows where everybody is, sees connections invisible to the mere citizen, can summon a plot in a few clicks for the dullest and most ordinary of characters. It is, significantly, largely a creation of its advertising, and it is in the plausible, nagging appeal of its slogans (most of them located on tube trains) that its primary business is done. The image of the city which these slogans promote is of a crowd too numerous and dense for the individuals within it ever to find one another. 'Only Connect!' shouts one, confusing E. M. Forster with a martinet station-controller. 'If the last person to phone you was your mother, isn't it time you . . .' insidiously wheedles another, poking like a dentist for the raw nerve. 'Meet your opposite number', says another blandly, for in computer city a partner exists for everyone, and right now they are waiting for the phone to ring, telling them their punched card has come up. 'Is there anyone quite like you?' has a fingerprint superimposed upon it, simultaneously celebrating personal uniqueness and the ability of the computer to transcend it.

These slogans imply a close association between the computer and the city. Both are mysterious and impersonal. (One brochure makes great play with 'flow diagrams' which explain nothing, but help to mystificate the process of selection with a generous dressing of quasi-technical language.) Both store vast quantities of individuals whose contact with each other is determined by forces beyond their control. Both cities and computers are symbols of what we tend to find most frightening in technology – their workings are equally incomprehensible, their decisions arbitrary and unarguable. But the dating agency offers us a benign computer, a computer which will take trouble with us as individuals, which will enter our personal lives, not to intimidate or separate us but to bring us together, to find us lovers and friends. It is surely this paradox which makes the slogans effective; the suggestion that the benign computer promises magically to revive the fading dream of a benign city.

But it works, of course, largely by hokum. The questionnaire of one vastly successful agency which claims to have sixty thousand people in its bank of suitors is a tissue of pretensions to scientific and psychological efficacy. In its 'Personality Profile' section, one is asked to mark one's position on continua between such poles as 'Introvert-Extrovert . . . Modern-Traditional . . . Generous-Thrifty . . .'; in a series of questions about 'Attitudes', one has to register one's response to questions like 'Is communism a vice which should be eradicated from the face of the earth?' and 'Do you consider money to be the root of all evil?' (There is a sinister, strategically placed question here, 'Do you strongly object to receiving advertising through the post?', on whose answer more, I suspect, than your prospective soulmate may depend.) There is a colour test in which eight colours have to be listed 'in order of preference', and you are asked to state how 'attractive' you are. The manager of the agency said to

me that the questionnaire 'has been designed by psycho-
logists to work in a psychological fashion'. Just so. None
but the very careless or the very innocent could fill in the
form honestly; it is so crude and vague that 'Personality
Profiles' based on its answers could only be those of monsters
or matchstick men. I imagine that the success of the business
is based largely on the fact that any lonely man and woman
– matched in age and height at least – will have more in
common in their loneliness than in their mutual detestation of
communism or love of money. One hopes so, anyway. But
the pretence of depth-probing and the whiff of the complexities
of punched cards and transistorised circuitry makes the
operation credible; it convinces the customer that he is up
against a system as intricate and baffling as the city which
has temporarily defeated him. 'We exist', said the manager,
'to supply the best possible types of dates,' and – smooth,
hygienic pandar – he conjured a hypermarket of gift-wrapped,
bed-ready people, ripe for action and instant consumption.

According to the agency, their clients are nearly all city-
dwellers and fall into two peak age groups: 23-25 and 38-42.
They live most typically in rented flats, are predominantly
middle class and unusually mobile, the upper crust of the
nomadic tribes, shifting from job to job and place to place,
leaving the continuities of families and friends behind.
While their university- and school-fellows acquire mort-
gages, spouses, and the latest in artbooks and kitchenware,
computer datables come to rest stacked in the memory bank,
waiting for an electronic coincidence to liberate them back
into normality.

For the very temporary, willing to go blindfold into the
fog, there is always the prostitute, an essential character of
the city whose existence excited nineteenth-century writers
about London to a pitch of rhetorical extremity which combined moralism and lasciviousness in equal parts. But emphasis on the 'viciousness' of the 'harlot' obscured the real
function which she performed in the city – a refuge, however brief and depersonalised, for the acutely lonely, a reminder of intimacy and warmth. Flaubert, who understood

human nature rather more than General Booth, wrote to his mistress Louise Colet, 'One learns so many things in a brothel, and feels such sadness, and dreams so longingly of love!'

Alone in the city, off the main roads where one might be spotted by acquaintances, one can find advertisements for call-girls in hundreds of newsagents' windows. Between the rooms to let and Electroluxes for sale, there are invitations to bed couched in whimsically thin double-entendres. 'Young French Canadian Lady Gives Expert Tuition In French . . . Elocution Lessons Given Daily . . . Blonde Model Seeks Interesting Position . . . Ladies Theatrical Wardrobe For Sale . . . Miss Penny Gives Lessons In Dancing . . . Massage by Miss-Tress.' If you ring the numbers on these inky cards, they are nearly always answered by the 'maid', a middle aged woman who keeps the flat and makes appointments for the girl or girls.

'I'll give you the details, dear,' she said, flat-voiced, tired and businesslike 'Height five foot-seven, dark hair, age twenty-three, waist twenty-four, bust forty. The price starts at £3.50.'

'What do you get for £3.50?'

'Full service.'

'And after that?'

'By arrangement.'

Then the address and the time. It is as formal as a Health and Social Security office. Indeed, in Earl's Court most of the call-girls I tried ringing all lived on one square which looks more like a barracks or a prison than a residential quarter. Here loneliness is treated with spartan efficiency. The maids shield the girls from the closer human demands of their clients; and the professional conduct of prostitution has as rigid codes as those of lawyers. It is necessary, perhaps. The stranded and the desperate, lurching through the fog in search of someone – anyone – need the protection of the code as much from themselves as for the girls whom they pump. The sadness of the punter, cruising from advertisement to advertisement, comparing lists of figures to find his special girl, goes deeper than the most expensive service can set right. But he himself is a more pressing, more significant city figure than the girls he hires.

For the really lonely individual in the city, life becomes a string of disconnected occasions; each present moment is exaggerated, and its theatrical glare seems designed to illuminate and isolate his aloneness. Eating by himself in a restaurant he feels conspicuous; he catches the eyes of other lone diners, imagines himself the subject of other people's conversations, sees a world divided into two groups – the majority, complacent couples, parties and families, and an envious parasitical minority of single people, all with the picky eyes of gunfighters. He prickles at the imagined snubs or cursory service of the waiter. He calls for his bill with his coffee, knowing he has no further excuse to stay on. In a phone booth, he makes a cliffhanger out of the ringing tone, and gulps with relief when it is answered. When his own phone stays silent for a day, he suspects a conspiracy to drop him, and pesters the operator to check his bell. At a party, he stays too long, since there is nothing to follow it. Walking on the street at night, he sees himself in the third person, hero of a scenario without a plot, only an unending series of empty locations. He ransacks crowds for faces he knows, drinks alone close to the bar where the action is in pubs, resists obvious palliatives like cinemas for he feels that there he would be shamefully advertising his loneliness. People detect in him something strained and overbright; his talk is hectic, his condemnations too strident to be convincing. His brief oases of evenings in other people's houses are hoarded and counted; each engagement that he makes marks a small sod of safe ground in the bog of the future. He criss-crosses the city, moving fast and purposelessly; little surprises him, but then neither is anything – outside, perhaps, of his job and his sleeping-quarters – predictable. It lacks both causes and results. He begins to see his time as a pin-board which every week must be filled with scraps . . . cuttings, bottle-tops, anything to take the edge off emptiness. He is wholehearted about nothing; he is a skimmer and a flitter. It is comfortably married and socialised men who take to drink with conviction: for him there will be a couple of whiskies before the next shift in location, and a new tube station, dull as the last, slides into place in the carriage window.

This sorry character has a central place in the literature of the city. For George Gissing, he was Edwin Reardon in *New Grub Street,* and he stood for the lonely self-immolation of the writer in an industrial society. For Sartre, he was Roquentin in *La Nausée,* the cipher-man of absolute gratuitousness, absolute contingency. For Saul Bellow, he was Jacob in *Dangling Man,* a condensed Chicago version of Roquentin, the shadow of a supremely lonely shade. Sartre prefaced *La Nausée* with an epigraph from Céline: 'He is a fellow without any collective significance, barely an individual.' It is a comment of great pertinence to the condition of all these heroes. Our existence in society is vested in the collective and connective significance of all our actions; but in the city, sheer loneliness and physical dislocation from other people can turn us into petty Roquentins, sharing his experience without having his philosophy to support it. City life easily fosters a bleakly contingent view of the self and the world, an impoverished, home-made existentialism, as morbidly gay as a Juliette Greco song.

But being alone in a city does not of itself constitute a philosophy – a fact which seems to have escaped too many novelists in their enthusiasm for an abstracted version of the urban hero. The superb sketches of life in London and Paris published by Jean Rhys in the 1930s are almost alone in their accuracy and honesty to the real texture of the loner's private world. Her heroines are utterly isolated and disconnected, but they are not yet solipsists. Miss Rhys attended patiently to their rhythms of living and feeling, and the contingency out of which her novels are made is something that happens to you, not a construct which you make to make sense of the world. Her syntax has the painful clarity of a hangover; sentence comes after sentence, event after event, with truthful, distressing illogicality. Acquaintances, lovers and friends pass in a moving frieze, often incomprehensible, always unstoppable. People are lost, found, and got rid of. The landscape of the city is hard-edged, like the smooth walls of a labyrinth. Loneliness is so essential that love and friendship invariably seem artificial and untrustworthy, matters more of rhetoric than of life. Encounters with other people are stiff with evasions and pretences. Here is one from *After Leaving Mr Mackenzie,* in which Julia, the central character, has been approached by a lonely South African on a tube train:

> The man said, 'Will you write or telephone me at this address? I shall be here for another couple of weeks.'
> He gave her a card, on which were his name and the address of a club. Without looking at it, Julia let it drop into her lap, and said, 'Yes,' smiling mechanically, and: 'Yes, of course, Yes.'
> When the train stopped at Notting Hill Gate Station she got up quickly, and the card fell from her lap onto the floor. The man stared after her, and reddened. Then he looked hastily about him. No one was watching. He picked the card up, brushed it, and put it back into his pocket, crossed his legs, and composed his countenance.

The slightly creaky formality of tone here is part of the style of isolation. In Jean Rhys's novels, communication of any kind is awkward and hard-won; often all language allows is an embarrassed escape into cliché. Her defensive, chronically ironic heroines handle their words like explosives; they know that language can get you into trouble. And they live in the city knowing it to be a dangerous place where to be hurt and alone is the most one can reasonably expect. The flash of a romantic affair, a candlelit dinner party or a drunken spree through the cafés are gifts of unreal and unrepresentative connection, and Miss Rhys's heroines have to learn to treat them with proper scepticism — even though these occasions are the only glimpses they are given of a collective life within society.

It is out of this conviction that one has become logically, chronologically, syntactically and sexually and socially disconnected that the deepest and most painful feelings of loneliness spring. It is dreadfully possible to be persuaded that one has, in effect, fallen out of the world, dropped through the wide and raggy mesh of the collective net. Then only the *I* is real, and solipsism, like suicide, taunts and tantalises. An ex-convict describes being let out of jail into the London streets after a long sentence. At 7.30 in the morning of the Thursday before Easter, he heads for the nearest tobacconist, then for an 'early house' – a pub in Covent Garden market. Later there will be the Labour Exchange and the trail round landladies letting cheap rooms. There are queues and forms to fill in, but every action seems hopelessly divorced from its consequences, the rest of the world alien and darkly conspiratorial:

I was given a letter to go to the Ministry of Social Security, the queue was so long I gave up in disgust and as I had paid my rent, I was not worried. I then had to pay for certain things people had been looking after for me but found quite a few things missing; I have written regarding these and hope that they will come to light.

Friday, Saturday and Monday were holidays so I was without assistance during this time. I did call on a relation but had the door closed on me; this I did not really expect though my father and certainly most of my relations want nothing to do with me. It would have been pleasant if I had had someone to talk to over the Easter period.

Objects, personal possessions, become disproportionate in their significance; and one feels here the looming, nightmare connections of paranoia. The collective world seems to have links that are all too strong; what is impossible is to relate oneself to that bitterly exclusive net of relationships. Like most writing about isolation, this passage is stiff with a kind of brutal innocence; everything down to the days of the week has to be listed and named – the simplest things have become strange and untrustworthy. The hardest thing to speak of is oneself. For the identity which routine, occasional, institutional encounters confer upon the individual is enragingly incomplete. You crave recognition; all you receive is treatment – as an applicant, a prospective tenant, a potential employee, a case, a customer. The lonely person in the city finds himself regarded as a disconnected string of such bare functions; he feels himself swelling incoherently over the top of them, bulging in places where no bulge should be. Odd intimacies spill out at inappropriate moments; to a stranger in a bar, he suddenly says that he chucked out his wife two years ago after finding her underclothes in a saucepan, or that his sister has invited him to her home for Christmas . . . then he shuts up, instantly ashamed of his candour. In cities, the personal is constantly being suppressed; and it is often the personal – the bottled intimacy, the pride in one's own name and own feelings – which bursts out in poems, petty crimes, letters to strangers, drunken communications in bars and the interior movies of which one makes oneself the hero as one walks the streets.

Coming out of the fog, making oneself visible and available, is prickly and difficult. The routes out are as formalised – as consecrated by custom – as other routes in the city. Certain public areas are set apart for loners to signal to each other: and it is significant that those groups which have become most accustomed to stigmatisation, to being isolated by society at large, have evolved the most ritualised forms of contact. In London, homosexuals have a number of clubs and pubs where it is very easy for strangers to make one another's acquaintance. Even compared to the bars in Chelsea where boys and girls pick each other up, there is an astonishing freedom of eye-contact in gay pubs. Within the ghetto (and in London there is an acre or so of streets in the Earl's Court district which is at night so densely populated with homosexuals that it assumes many of the characteristics of a real ghetto), direct invitations and interrogations are the convention. You may catch someone's eye across the length of a crowded bar or basement discotheque and make an instant assignation – at least to talk. People move freely about the floor areas of these places, switching from group to group and person to person. As an outsider, my first impression of these clubs and pubs was that everyone knew everybody else; but that was quite untrue. They are used primarily by people cruising on their own, rare privileged corners of the city where the stranger is approachable. They. are sad places, full of fervid hothouse intensity, because they are so specialised; most of their clientèle live outside the ghetto, and the over-bright friendliness of their atmosphere springs in large part from the fact that everywhere else the homo-sexual is condemned to a form of stigmatised solitude by society. I shall deal with them in greater detail in Chapter 8.

But stigma does carry a certain perverse privilege in itself, and the homosexual or the ghetto Jew is able to lead a col-lective life in the metropolis of a kind which many less readily identifiable isolates might envy. One can, if one is sufficiently bold or desperate, advertise one's loneliness in the newspaper. Print, the most public of media, goes into the most private rooms; and in its impersonality, and the anonymity of the box number, there are real consolations. In the Personal Column, you can reach into the fog by proxy, then see who comes to you through the mailbox: Here lone-liness has a solidarity, even a kind of respectability; fellow isolates are stacked neatly in columns of fine type, and the language they use is as formalised and restricted as the code of a caste. Its expressiveness lies in its rigid adherence to convention.

The papers which carry most such advertisements are in-variably caste organs – the parish magazines of political, literary, sexual, and sub-cultural groupings. The *New York Review of Books*, the *New Statesman, Time Out, Gay News, International Times* . . . these are all publications whose tone encourages their readers to see themselves as bands of like-minded souls. Subscribing to the *New Statesman* is perhaps the weakest of all ways of affiliating oneself to a caste, but in its personal column the phrase 'New Statesman reader' crops up again and again, as if it was a magical measure of personal identity. So, if you are acutely lonely, you may fantasise a community of people like yourself, invisibly linked by print; fellow radicals, fellow homosexuals, fellow hippies, secret sharers:

Lonely young man (28) of average looks, interested in the arts, travel, etc.; would like to meet an honest, sensitive and warm-hearted girl with similar interests for genuine friendship . . .

Quiet guy, 28, radical, enjoys classical music, films, seeks girl 18-39 to share life, country weekends, etc. . . .

Attractive, slim widow, young 40s, Jewish, seeks friendship, secure, nice male 50s . . .

Tall fit man, mid-60s, separated (misfortune not fault) needs companionship of sympathetic woman, 50-plus, sharing compulsive love of books and classical music. London, preferably NW . . .

Man, 36, div., no hang-ups, cultured, capital, sks attractive lady pref. in establ. business who needs partner in both senses of word. All answered . . .

Youthful, personable, humorous, competent man, 50+; ex-husband. 12 st., 5'9". All faculties working order. Executive; interested visual arts, town, country, food, wine; non-smoker. Seeks feminine attractive bus/prof. woman in attempt to achieve mutual happiness, London area . . .

Platonic friend needed. I am lonely, would like someone who likes going to pubs, clubs etc. Would be a help to have car. I am 26 and honest. Please help . . .

Are you 25-32 and passive? Are you tired of being alone,

tired of trolling? I'm a professional man of 33, gay, but
masculine in outlook. Have flat in West London and car.
If you are looking for a permanent relationship and security,
please write with photo to . . .

These people, squashing their lives into abbreviated sentences at so many pence a word, have developed a disturbingly vague grammar of identity. The adjectives which recur
most frequently in the columns are oddly impersonal : 'kind
. . . attractive . . . warm . . . sincere . . . personable
. . . intelligent . . . cultured . . . sympathetic . . . feminine
. . . The standard formula for describing hobbies and special
interests is 'interested in travel and the arts'. The relationship sought is 'genuine . . . secure . . . happy . . . serene
. . . peaceful . . .' Country weekends and listening to music
are essential ingredients in these idylls, which sound remarkably untainted by reality.

Yet the loneliness is real enough; and it must take a lot to
screw oneself up to place an advertisement of this kind.
Most of the people who do so are of an age to know that
secure, serene, genuine relationships between cultured, sympathetic and attractive partners do not belong in this world.
Many are divorced; more will have been 'trolling', in that
expressive camp word for fishing for pick-ups. One can
hardly doubt that their search is in earnest, that they are
bruised with experience. Yet when they come to put their
most intimate selves and needs on paper, the words they use
are as empty of meaning as transparent counters. Do 'attractive slim widow, young 40s, Jewish', or 'Man, 36, div., no
hang-ups, cultured, capital', really believe that they have
found just the right forms of words to describe themselves?
Do they feel the satisfaction of the happy autobiographer,
sure that he has got his likeness to a T? Or are these empty
shells themselves signs that, in the city, personal life has
become so obscure and unavailable that any attempt to communicate its nature is bound to flop?

There is another characteristic style in the personal column :
knowing, jokey, defensively ironic : *Of course I should not*

be here and neither should you, it says, over-loudly:

> Female, 27, blonde, buxom, brainy/Virginia Woolf, seeks
> independent amusing, vastly intelligent male/or Leonard
> Woolf character . . .

> Bald, bearded male, full of Prufrockian hesitation, seeks
> shy, gentle, literate woman 30-40.

The aggressively partying manner of these advertisements
make them communicate even less than the hollow descrip-
tions of professional men in search of idylls; they are
joshing, shyly vain, too hard-worked in their humour. This
is the language of bruisedness, of feeling too exposed and
brittle to venture more than a nervous thrust-and-retraction
of oneself, like a snail trying the air with a tentative horn.
In the cold definition of print they sound thin and shrill, and
the people behind them seem to shrink lamely from the bold-
ness of their own sallies.

One of the darker freedoms of the city is the way in which
it puts the individual at liberty to barely exist, and the
personal columns bear witness to the stunted conception of
character which the city permits at its worst. 'Man 50,
div. *New Statesman*-reader' and 'Attractive f., youthful 40s'
are the other side of the coin to the gangsters and dandies;
people who have dwindled, even in their own eyes to rudimentary stumps of identity, like peripheral characters in a
novel. For them, their isolation has become their most distinctive feature, and they are possessed by it as wholly as
junkies. The latent discontinuity, emptiness and helpless
solipsism which the city always threatens have consumed
them. They merge into the fog, self-immolated shadows in
search of the beam of light which will give them their
identity back again. It is significant that both the personal
column advertisements and the computer dating slogans
continually harp on the theme of love as twinship: the aim
is not so much to find someone who is your complementary
opposite, but on coming across your double. *Is there anyone*

quite like you? Only the genitals should differ: in every other respect, your imagined partner looks like your own reflection in the mirror. Love turns into a way of awakening and establishing the self, yet another mode of desperate self-projection.

For in the fog we all become solipsists, creatures of the mirror. Confirming our own existence preoccupies us; every action is bent to that end of self-revelation and exposure. In T. S. Eliot's *Sweeney Agonistes,* Sweeney, the prototypical corrupted city hero, knowing, bored and irredeemably alone says :

I knew a man once did a girl in —

Any man might do a girl in
Any man has to, needs to, wants to
Once in a lifetime, do a girl in.
Well he kept her there in a bath
With a gallon of Lysol in a bath

Nobody came. And nobody went
But he took in the milk and he paid the rent.

He didn't know if he was alive and the girl was dead
He didn't know if the girl was alive and he was dead
He didn't know if they both were alive or both were dead
If he was alive then the milkman wasn't and the rent-collector
    wasn't
And if they were alive then he was dead.

For this man, who may or may not be Sweeney himself, the most final and dramatic of all *actes gratuites* serves only to further ambiguate his own existence, sending him packing into the solipsist's limbo where the *I* is both the only reality and the source of the growing conviction that there isn't any reality at all. Sweeney is led by these delicate and depressing convolutions into a state of sluggardliness, lapsing, like the murderer Barnadine in *Measure for Measure,* into a gross boredom with and contempt for the world.

> But if you understand or if you don't
> That's nothing to me and nothing to you
> We all gotta do what we gotta do
> We're gona sit here and drink this booze . . .

Stirrings of the self – advertising for your double, doing a girl in, writing a poem or going on a pub crawl – tend, too frequently for comfort, to expire in a Sweenylike brutish lassitude; the world contracts to the shape of the immediate local situation. Time is splintered and foreshortened, space becomes the sleazy here-and-now; the urban anti-hero, ugly, knowing and indifferent, emerges. He inhabits the city as if it were hell and he a fallen angel, too immoralised even to notice that it is a bad place. This, at least is the customary, official version of the consequences of isolation in the city. The urban honeycomb by its very nature clearly threatens to subvert the structure of society at large. If society needs continuity, cohesion, interdependence, the collective life, to go on functioning as a working body, the city encourages discontinuity, fragmentation, privacy and an egocentric personal life – and the loner, whether isolated by fate or by choice, is a constant symbol and reminder of the city as an intrinsically antisocial mechanism. Concern with isolation need not spring from philanthropic motives; a place seething with lonely people is the most dangerously atavistic territory in the world. Nor need isolation be confined to individuals; the most frightening of all urban images, from the point of view of the social administrator, is of whole groups of people behaving with the self-immersion and foreshortened perspectives of the loner or outcast.

In the nineteenth century, the growth of the sprawling tenements in Bethnal Green, Mile End, Hackney, Bow, to the east of the financial centre of the City of London, caused enormous apprehension amongst the middle class. For their own health and safety, the affluent moved as fast as possible to the northern and western suburbs during the 1880s, drawing a broad *cordon sanitaire* around the proles in the marshy east. Yet, thus isolated, the working class seemed even more alarming. Mayhew saw them as an exotic tribe with differently shaped skulls from those of respectable people. Charles Booth, whose survey of London was otherwise remarkably sympathetic to the poor, was able to say of the poorest of the East Enders:

> They render no useful service, they create no wealth; more often they destroy it . . . They degrade whatever they touch and as individuals are perhaps incapable of improvement; they may be to some extent a necessary evil in every large city . . .

And Charles Kingsley, lecturing to an audience of Bristolean ladies in 1857, conjured that evil chimera of the mob which was to haunt late Victorian England:

> We have . . . to face the existence of a dangerous class . . . into which the weaker as well as the worst members of society have a continual tendency to sink. A class which, not respecting itself, does not respect others; which has nothing to lose and all to gain by anarchy; in which the lowest passions, seldom gratified, are ready to burst out and avenge themselves by frightful methods.

It is the generalism of this rhetoric which gives it away; the most basic power possessed by the working class — the power to menace — grew in direct proportion to its isolation from the rest of city society. Decent people simply did not know the tenement dwellers of Stepney, and what they did not know they feared, and turned into figures, phantoms, of nightmare or worse. People who live in city ghettoes are liable to have hostile and paranoid myths built up around them; some make their own ghettoes, some find themselves ghetto-dwellers perforce. Once the blacks, the Jews, the poor have been isolated, they turn into the bogeymen of society's most disturbed dreams. In England, the dream took on a seemingly traumatic reality on May 17th 1900, when the working class took to the streets in extravagant celebration of the relief of Mafeking. Drunken louts stormed into august clubs and offices, and the mob looked as the mob was expected to look – alien, conspiratorial, uncontrollable,. capable of destroying civilisation in an orgy of thuggery. The word *Maffiking* passed into the language as an active participle expressing the hyperactivity of holidaying ghouls.

Since then, it has been an axiomatic principle of public housing that a policy of dispersal and infiltration should be pursued. The isolation of the blacks or the lower working class in large urban ghettoes has been widely felt to be tantamount to inviting a revolution. The idea of 'mixed housing' has been heavily propagandised, and suburban high-rise developments scatter their inhabitants in innocuous units of a few thousand here, a few thousand there. A great deal of English social legislation has been motivated by fear of the terrors of the mob; and in the United States, 'urban renewal' has consistently proved to be simply a process of concreting-out the undesirable elements who have begun to take over the centres of large cities.

People who are isolated from the mainstream of social dependencies and ambitions are always potential subversives, and it is in society's best interests to keep them as closely in touch as possible. 'Marriages', said Charles Booth, observing the destructive patterns of behaviour which obtained among single people of both sexes in London, 'are to be encouraged'; and he went on to quote a Congregationalist minister of his acquaintance who described marriages among the poor as 'permanent moralities'. We have come a long way since then. Isolation is promoted as a deeply shameful condition, and the twentieth-century family – a uniquely constricted institution of unprecedentedly small numbers and avid powers of rapid and expensive consumption – is canvassed as the optimum standard of human life. In America, the process has gone so far that it is hard for an unmarried person over the age of 25 to watch television without feeling he is a freak.

One is barraged with advertisements which announce that you should have a baby, a small boy to take to the ball park on Saturdays, a dog to guzzle something called *Alpo,* and a wife with an unremitting interest in the workings, needs, whims, and occasional breakdowns of the digestive tracts of all members of the family, not excluding the dog. After a few hours of this, torn between panic and nausea, you start looking around the room for the bassinet. In the world of TV ads, loneliness is worn like a Scarlet A; it is the prerogative of the man whose breath smells bad, whose nervous system has pooped, and who, through his own fecklessness, stays feebly on the bottom rung, scorned by the boss and the toothpaste-sparkling stenographers alike. To be alone is to fail yourself and society; away from the family or the boys at the office, you are not likely to consume enough, you may think too much, and you should certainly be made to feel guilty and perverse if you take any pleasure at all in your predicament.

Yet despite this insistent plugging of the oppressively collective life, people clearly do enjoy the privacy and anonymity of the city. Not knowing one's neighbours may be a privilege, not a dreadful fate; to be without a family is, for some, a luxurious escape, and an honourable one, from a state of repressive social bondage. The rules and condition of isolation, like those of other arts, may be liberating and invigorating to those who properly understand them and a straitjacket only to those who don't. Taught to fear the isolation both of ourselves and of others, commanded and cajoled to seek the cosiness of the herd, aloneness is an increasingly difficult craft to practise.

The isolate in the city may either find his loneliness so intolerable that it erodes his identity into a vestigial cipher, or he may discover that it offers him the most complete personal freedom that can be had in modern society. The instruments of communications technology, which to the unhappy loner can seem as wounding as racks and thumbscrews, can be pleasant tools for keeping one's distance, managing one's appearances and disappearances, making deliberate and controlled social choices. The telephone, the post, the subway or underground system, the newspaper and coterie magazine ought to be the arteries of urban life, not symbols of its capacity to starve and alienate the individual.

It is only a seeming paradox that the city, with its enormously high density of habitation, should give rise to feelings of such intense solitude. Lonely people often feel sick with guilt that they are suffering in the middle of such apparent abundance; what is wrong with *them* that they should be singled out to watch TV while millions are on the street below their window? At night, when the roisterers come out of the pubs, the loner hears their laughter as a cacophony of maniacal shrieks. He hates their jokes, their girls, their disturbances of the peace as they call good night to each other across streets. The slam of their car doors enlarges in his head to a wave of thunderclaps, and they are doors which are always closing on him.

Yet his solitude, which he has been taught to think of as an illness which he has brought upon himself, is the prize as well as the penalty of city life. And some of the people of the metropolis have learned, in spite of the weight of propaganda and ideology which has been stacked against it, to value solitude and manipulate it creatively. It will take a new chapter to continue the discussion into the territory of inner space, and the mental cosmologies of people who have adjusted to the isolation, the essential privacy of the city.

SEVEN

The Magical City

It has been a traditional axiom of classical writing about the city that urban structures are the domain of reason; that they are emancipated from the primitive, magical life of rural society. Lewis Mumford, following his mentor Patrick Geddes, saw the city as the natural habitat of civilised man; an environment of artifice, it was the highest expression of communal rationalism, and the problems it spawned could be solved by the exercise of reason. It was a question of finding the right transportation system, the logical pattern of urban housing, the right balance between work and play areas, the correct proportion of green space, and so forth. To all of these, Mumford applied himself with assiduity and vision, and he has infected several generations of architects and planners with his logical, level-headed optimism. Understand technics, he argues, and you will understand the underlying rational forces of the city as a human community. It is simply an exercise in controlling these forces rather than letting them control us. Mumford's essential tone is now part of the bloodstream of town planning, and his voice is audible whenever new schemes for improving the city are introduced. In January 1973, an editorial in *The Times* summarised the Greater London Council's programme for the 'renewal' of Covent Garden:

The plan drawn up was for the area as a whole. The number of places to live within the area was to be doubled; the uses of leisure and pleasure were to be cultivated; a differently aligned road system was to be supplied; vehicles and pedestrians were to be vertically segregated; a 'line of character', in which old buildings and spaces were preserved, was to stretch in a middle band from east to west, otherwise, it was to be largely a matter of demolition and rebuilding.

This is a fair measure of planners' rationalism, a diluted compound of Geddes, Mumford and Corbusier. What is important about it is the fundamental assumption which it makes about the nature of city man — that convenient, hypothetical creature whose needs are being so logically and economically satisfied in the Covent Garden programme.

The founders of the most influential group of urban sociologists, the Chicago School, were confident of the unassailable truth of the axiomatic rationality of city man — a notion which they had inherited, as they inherited much else, from the theoretical writing of Max Weber. In the bibliography of the Chicago School compilation, *The City* (1925), Louis Wirth flatly asserted that:

There is a city mentality which is clearly differentiated from the rural mind. The city man thinks in mechanistic terms, in rational terms, while the rustic thinks in naturalistic, magical terms.

Robert E. Park, the co-founder of the school, contributed two articles to the symposium which are of special interest here; one on magic and one on the mind of the hobo. He saw both as vestigial relics of a rural past; the hobo mentality and the superstitious magical cosmology were impediments to urban assimilation, and new American citizens must be weaned from them, or reasoned out of them, if they were to succeed in the city. Cities, in other words, were not places for negroes to practise *obeah* with other people's nail-parings, nor for pensioned-off frontiersmen to ride imaginary ranges. More recently, a latterday Boston Augustinian, the Christian sociologist Harvey Cox, has argued (in *The Secular City*) that the mobility, 'desacralisation', and 'disenchantment' of city life have effectively liberated us into reason, and have exorcised the mystificatory spirit of tribalism.

This overweening emphasis on the intrinsic rationality of the city offers a tantalising clue as to why urban isolation is regarded as such a dirty secret. In a rational community, the disconnected loner is a sport, a mutant; he exists in the minority statistics of the outcast and the maladjusted, as someone who has failed to recognise the consensus on which civic life is founded. Since Plato, definitions of the city have been essentially political : a place became a city by virtue of its legislative autonomy, and its economic power and complexity. Like a house of cards, the city was seen to depend on a featherweight balancing of interests and agreements. The myth of the fallen city, of Babylon and Byzantium, still haunts us : cities grow on reason and interdependence, they fall when private and sectarian interests swell without regard for the community as a whole, when people give themselves over to the egotistical pleasure of buggery and paganism. Mr Boffin took Gibbon's *Decline and Fall of the Roman Empire* as the starting point for his education; and there was good reason for the Victorian obsession with classical decadence. As London grew at a spectacularly faster rate than any other city in history, so, perhaps, it fostered the seeds of an even more dramatic collapse than those of Babylon, Byzantium or Rome. The city was to be saved by reason and Blue Books, and government bodies and private philanthropists invested vast amounts of time and money in social surveys, plans, projects, hypotheses. Victorian literature on London, Manchester and Birmingham is voluminous and dull, an ocean of statistics. Its sheer bulk reflects both the depths of our great-grandfathers' fears of the inherent susceptibility of the city to corruption; and the strength of their conviction that it could be rescued from that fate by knowledge, by taking thought. Speeding towards the millennium, what one needed most to decelerate one's progress was more research. Isolation, superstition and tribalism – the mortal enemies of citizenship – could, so it was thought, be eliminated by education and rational planning.

The idea that the city is in essence a rational structure, and that evidence of irrationality is a sign of decadent deviation

from its intrinsic cityness is entirely comprehensible; it is
even perhaps administratively and psychologically necessary.
But it seems intuitively wrong. It also accounts for the
curious sense of unreality that pervades so much of the literature of town planning and sociology. Reading Mumford,
Howard, Geddes, Corbusier, Park, Weber, I can never
manage to believe in their cities or their citizens. It is not
that people and social lives in these books are too schematised
and sketchy, but that they seem to belong to an entirely
different culture from mine; they are Houyhnhnms burdened with a few problematic Yahoos; and the import of a
great deal of conventional writing about the city is the
complex necessity of persuading apes to turn into horses.
The city I live in is one where hobos and loners are
thoroughly representative of the place, where superstition
thrives, and where people often have to live by reading the
signs and surfaces of their environment and interpreting
them in terms of private, near-magical codes. Moreover,
these people seem to me to be not sports or freaks, but to
have responded with instinctive accuracy to the conditions
of the city. It seems worthwhile – at least as a corrective
measure – to stress and explore some of the magical properties
of city life at the expense of the customary rational ones,
and to treat the evidence on this issue not as a vestige of
some inferior, pre-city stage of human development, but
as a possibly organic constituent of urban experience.

Park's essay, 'Magic, Mentality, and City Life', offers an
ideal springboard for a discussion of magic in the city, because it is persuasive in everything except its conclusions,
which seem so forced as to be capriciously untruthful. Park
borrows his terminology and definitions from Lévy-Bruhl,
calling magic a 'pre-logical' habit of mind and describing it
as 'a method of interpreting as wilful acts the incidents,
accidents and unsuspected changes of the world'. The primitive man, he argues, interprets everything according to his
own impulses and purposes; by dramatising the universe
in a way that is personal to the point of being solipsistic,

he evolves a mental style of 'participation', of continuous imaginative gate-crashing on external processes. He has 'no mental patterns except those offered by the mutations of his own inner life' and sees the universe as a 'society of wilful personalities, not an irrefragible chain of cause and effect.' Park observes, 'We are all disposed to think in magical terms in those regions of our experience that have not been rationalised, and where our control is uncertain and incomplete'; and it is this statement which effectively prevents him, as a prisoner of his own axioms, from relating the mental style he has been describing to the urban condition he is trying to analyse. Indeed, he drives a blunt hatchet between the two:

> The reason the modern man is a more rational animal than his more primitive ancestor is possibly because he lives in a city, where most of the interests and values of life have been rationalised, reduced to measurable units, and even made objects of barter and sale. In the city – and particularly in great cities – the external conditions of existence are so evidently contrived to meet man's most clearly recognised needs that the least intellectual of people are inevitably led to think in deterministic and mechanistic terms.

Of course Park was writing (in 1924) at a time when anthropologists were interested in the savagery rather than the modernity of the savage mind, before Levi-Strauss and the structuralists taught us all to hear the primitive dialogues rehearsed by civilised life. But Park is tethered here by more than an anthropological tradition: he cannot rid himself of the belief that Chicago is simply a megapolitan form of Plato's city-state, an arrangement not a fate, a rational structure arrived at by rational men. Cities, he assumes (and his assumption is shared by most of his contemporary successors) belong to culture not nature.

Yet to live in a real city is to live in just as indomitable an environment as any valley full of rocks and stones and trees. Streets, shops, cafés, houses, underground railways, office

blocks are not, for most of us, matters of choice and reason
merely because someone built them out of bricks and mortar
and decided that they would be useful there. The city dweller is constantly coming up against the absolute mysterious-
ness of other people's reasons. To get from my flat to the
nearest tube station, I have to walk round two sides of a
grassy square full of pigeons, then cross a tumultuous main
road on which heavy trucks persistently thunder. Park seems
to suggest that because these trucks fulfil someone else's
'recognised needs' I ought to say to myself: 'I don't mind
being kept hopping in fear of my life for ten minutes at
the side of the road, because quite clearly Mr X needs to
transport his tractor parts to the Continent in container lorries,
and I recognise his rights as a fellow-citizen to temporarily
inconvenience me.' In fact I feel about the road much as a
primitive tribesman might feel about a dangerous ravine with
a killer river given to unpredictable floods. I personify
and apostrophise it, I attribute mysterious and malign volitions
to its traffic, and it frequently disturbs my dreams. The
example is perhaps frivolous: the general point is not. When
the needs and reasons for things of 'culture' become sufficiently divorced from our own personal needs and wishes,
they turn as intractably alien as anything in nature. A road full
of container trucks blocking my path seems to me, at the
time of barely-avoided impact, almost uniquely irrational;
a park full of grass, trees and pigeons strikes me as a
thoroughly sensible arrangement.

And cities, by their nature, *as* nature, grow out of just
such processes of separation of ends from means. The industrial megapolis is a direct product of the division of
labour; its politics and economics dictate that each of us
must find the purposes and directions of most of our fellow
citizens increasingly incomprehensible, and often apparently
hostile. Mutual self-interest in a modern city means nothing
more elevated than that we have to put up with the goings-
on of the neighbours in a spirit of reluctant, because finally
impotent, toleration. If there was the faintest chance of you
personally recognising the driver behind the truck window, or

of him recognising you, things might be very different. As it is, we live in a world which is patently not of our own devising, in which we are perpetually baffled and inconvenienced by people we don't know and whom we suspect we wouldn't like. By contrast, the supposedly irrational life of the village seems logical and simple, its causes and effects clear and direct, its patterns of friendship, deference and hostility reassuringly predictable. (Surely a major reason for the passion of the urban middle class to possess country cottages is that, from the perspective of the city, life in the country has a refreshingly basic reasonableness – its rhythms, far from being primitive and magical, seem much saner and more straightforward than the perverse and complicated metres of city life.) For most of their inhabitants, cities like New York and London *are* nature, and are as unpredictable, threatening, intermittently beautiful and benign, as a tropical rain forest. That they are in point of fact *constructs* is a mighty and deluding irrelevance. Park's description of the savage mind groping with a universe of unrelated episodes and phenomenal accidents may apply as well in Earl's Court as in the Congo. That 'uncertain and incomplete' area of experience which is especially vulnerable to magical explanation may – at this notably uncertain and apprehensive period of history – turn out to be the very city whose ills are the major insoluble affliction of our century.

As we lose the immigrant's habit of mind, as we cease to see the city in perpetual contrast to the alternative life of the country (which diminishes in area even faster than cities grow), so more and more does the city come to usurp and so resemble nature. There is a dramatic illustration of this process in the series of paintings which Claude Monet made of London between 1871 and 1914. The earliest paintings represent the city as a castellated frieze on the horizon, seen from across the wooded meadows of Hyde Park; a jagged rectangular construct imposed on a lyrical nature of sweeping curves and intense greens. One painting of this period shows the Houses of Parliament and Westminster Bridge, half-shrouded in mist in the distance, their gothic pinnacles and curlicues softened, as if they might fade altogether into the sky; while in the foreground, the violent hard-edged out-lines of a half built jetty stand out against a river of pretty ripples. At this stage, the main content of each painting is the play of nature against culture, the arrogant rigidity of man-made shapes against the soft, diverse and promiscuous activity of things in nature. Later, in the brilliant studies of West-minster Bridge, painted between 1899 and 1904, Monet explored the visual osmosis which seemed to take place in the heavy industrial smog of the city; the bridge, an un-earthly blue, soft in shape but strident and surreal in colour, exchanges its characteristics with the river and the sky. Its colour spreads into nature, while it borrows from nature the rusty oranges and yellows which might come either from the sun or from the flame of some giant industrial retort. The freest shapes come from the smoke from chimneys; the most intricate colours from the traffic crossing the bridge. It is impossible to know where nature ends and culture begins. Later still, probably in 1918, Monet painted three night por-traits of Leicester Square in a style close to abstract ex-pressionism. From a distance, they look like pictures of a murky field full of flowers; close to, we see a human drift of colour, left behind like a sediment on a ground of the kind of oily grey-green to which all the colours on the palette might repair if they were left to themselves. Illumin-ated signs and people's faces provide the only points at which the paintings come defined and alive; the city is all movement, and the nature-culture opposition slides into unimportance compared to the tidal waves of social life which the paintings record.

Monet's progression rehearses a sequence of changes in the heart common, I think, to most people who come to live in a great city. As we adapt to it, it becomes our nature; we learn to feel about its docks, warehouses, neon signs, bridges, streets, squares, not that they are gross super-impositions (as we felt when we first arrived), but that they are as inevitable, as possessed of an intrinsic life of their own, as mountains and rivers. The currents of society which pass through them are, finally, as impersonal as the pressures, winds, and precipitations on a weather map.

As surely as any mountain face, the city throws us back on ourselves; it isolates us, both as individuals and as tribal groups. Just as it constrains the expression of individuality, threatens us with absorption into total anonymity, so it makes self-assertion and projection into overwhelming necessities. As Georg Simmel observes in 'The Metropolis and Mental Life': 'man is tempted to adopt the most tendentious peculiarities, that is, the specifically metropolitan extravagances of mannerism, caprice and preciousness'. Implicit in Simmel's statement is the suggestion of utter arbitrariness: the city is so large, so amorphous, its ends so remote from us as individual members of it, that any eccentricity or gewgaw might function as a token of our personal uniqueness. The nature of the city precludes, or at least makes unnecessary, a causal relationship between personal and corporate life. The extravagances of Wilde and Beerbohm, of Tristan Tzara, of Fitzgerald's doomed rich butterflies, were played against cities which had so lost their fixity of definition and purpose that they had reverted to inchoate jungles. And when reason is lost, magic is there to take its place; when people can no longer relate themselves to the overall scheme of things, to civic life as a programme and consensus, then they take to private attic-superstitions, charms, token, spells to win their personal fortune from the mysterious, florid abundance of the city.

Living in a city, one finds oneself unconsciously slipping into magical habits of mind. As I have tried to show in earlier chapters, surfaces are in any case of enormous importance to the city dweller: he has to learn to respond to a daily cascade of people and places in terms of briefly-exhibited signs and badges. His imagination is always being stretched. In a junky antique shop, I stop bargaining over what might be a late Georgian chair because the man selling it is wearing a navy-blue peaked Carnaby Street cap; his hair, dyed silver grey, curls coyly in ringlets round its rim. Just that hat and those curls make up a message, and

I do not trust it; it belongs to the area of the grammar used
by sharpies and plausible perfumed frauds. I know next to
nothing about Georgian chairs, but the cap and curls are part
of the everyday language of the city, and I understand—
believe I understand—them as well as if I had actually seen
the man spraying woodworm holes into the furniture with
a sawn-off shotgun. All the time, one is isolating such details
and acting upon them as if they were epigrams. Only rarely
is one able to put one's assumptions to the test, to discover
incongruities between people and the badges which they
wear; and one has to believe, however erroneously in fact,
that people behave 'in character', and to trust one's own
powers as an interpreter of symbols. For me, this gives city
life a curiously vertiginous feeling; I move on the streets
always a little apprehensive that the whole slender crust of
symbolic meaning might give way under my feet. At the
same time I collect more and more signs, a jackdaw's nest
of badges and trinkets, continually elaborating the code
which I use for deciphering my own world. When new cars
come out of motor shows, I watch who buys them: who
wears platform heels, buys *Time Out* or *Spare Rib*, ostenta-
tiously sports Harrods carrier bags? One becomes as avid for
permutations of details of passing fashions as any student
of the stars, a Gypsy Petulengro casting horoscopes and pre-
dictions out of the colourful trash of urban consumables.

More than that, we map the city by private benchmarks
which are meaningful only to us. The Greater London
Council is responsible for a sprawl shaped like a rugby ball
about twenty five miles long and twenty miles wide; my
city is a concise kidney-shaped patch within that space, in
which no point is more than about seven miles from any other.
On the South, it is bounded by the river, on the north by
the fat tongue of Hampstead Heath and Highgate Village,
on the west by Brompton cemetery and on the east by Liverpool Street station. I hardly ever trespass beyond those limits,
and when I do I feel I'm in foreign territory, a landscape
of hazard and rumour. Kilburn, on the far side of my northern
and western boundaries, I imagine to be inhabited by vicious

drunken Irishmen; Hackney and Dalston by crooked car
dealers with pencil moustaches and goldfilled teeth; London
south of the Thames still seems impossibly illogical and contingent, a territory of meaningless circles, incomprehensible
one-way systems, warehouses and cage-bird shops. Like any
tribesman hedging himself in behind a stockade of taboos,
I mark my boundaries with graveyards, terminal transportation points and wildernesses. Beyond them, nothing is to be
trusted and anything might happen.

The constrictedness of this private city-within-a-city has
the character of a self-fulfilling prophecy. Its boundaries,
originally arrived at by chance and usage, grow more not
less real the longer I live in London. I have friends who
live in Clapham, only three miles away, but to visit them is a
definite journey, for it involves crossing the river. I can,
though, drop in on friends in Islington, twice as far away as
Clapham, since it is within what I feel to be my own territory. When I first came to London, I moved about the city
much more freely than I do now; I took the liberties of a
tourist and measured distances in miles rather than by the
relationship of the known to the unknown. In Manhattan,
on my first afternoon in New York, I asked the man I'd
lunched with for directions to a part of down-town Brooklyn where I had to make a call. He puzzled over my question
and eventually needed to look at my map; he had lived in
New York for twenty-five years, and had last been to Brooklyn, just over the bridge from his office, twelve years ago.
It is the visitor who goes everywhere; to the resident, a
river or a railway track, even if it is bridged every few hundred yards, may be as absolute a boundary as a snakepit
or an ocean.

Inside one's private city, one builds a grid of reference
points, each enshrining a personal attribution of meaning.
A black-fronted bookshop in South Kensington, a line of
gothic balconies on the Cromwell Road, a devastated recreation ground between Holloway and Camden, a café full of
Polish exiles playing chess in Hampstead, a shop window
stuffed with Chinese kitsch, illuminated sampans and re-

volving perspex table lamps with tassels, in Gerrard Street —
these synecdochal symbols, each denoting a particular quarter,
become as important as tube stations. And the underground
railway itself turns into an object of superstition. People who
live on the Northern Line I take to be sensitive citizens; it is
a friendly communication route where one notices commuters
reading proper books and, when they talk, finishing their
sentences. But the Piccadilly Line is full of fly-by-nights and
stripe-shirted young men who run dubious agencies, and I go
to elaborate lengths to avoid travelling on it. It is an entirely
irrational way of imposing order on the city, but it does give
it a shape in the mind, takes whole chunks of experience out
of the realm of choice and deliberation, and places them in
the less strenuous context of habit and prejudice. My mental
city is a small Manichean place, divided between the angels
and the witches, and I tightrope-walk superstitiously between
them. I have found childhood spells coming back to me; I
avoid walking on cracks between the paving stones, I count
lamp posts in units of seven, at zebra crossings I am especially
wary of every third vehicle. From my study window, I see
people surreptitiously touching the spikes of the house-railings
in some occult combination of their own. In London, postal
districts, though often thinly related to the changes of
character in individual areas, have been endowed with curiously absolutist values. Prestigious ones, like SW1, SW3,
NW1, NW3, are like talismans, more important even than
the house or the street, magical guarantees of a certain kind of
identity.

These are small, perhaps trivial, rituals, but they do suggest that there is rather more than a merely vestigial magi-
cality in the way we deal with the cities we live in. It is
precisely because the city is too large and formless to be
held in the mind as an imaginative whole that we make
recourse to irrational short-cuts and simplifications. Magic
may be a major alternative to rejection of the city as a bad
unmanageable place; it offers a real way of surviving in an
environment whose rationale has, like a dead language,
become so obscure that only a handful of specialists (alas,

they are all too frequently sociologists, urban economists
and town planners) can remember or understand it. The
rest of us make do with an improvised day-to-day magic
which, like shamanism, works because we conspire that it
shall work.

Within the city at large there are multitudes of contracted,
superstitious cities, sequestered places with clear boundaries,
rituals and customs, whose outlines often correspond with
those of the tribal castes and styles. There is, indeed, a strong
case for interpreting the kinds of style I have described in
earlier chapters as manifestations of magical cosmologies.
But I am primarily interested here in magic as a technique
of urban life, in superstition and ritual as methods of interpreting the city as nature, and not as tools for welding
social organisations together. The distinction is flimsy – the
functions are complicatedly intertwined – but it is convenient
insofar as it reveals the individual alone with his city; and
I want to examine that private city as it emerges from his
personal symbols and taboos.

In Notting Hill Gate in London, or it might be Greenwich Village in New York, the unreasonable city has come
to the point where it cannot be ignored by even the civic
authorities. The streets around Ladbroke Grove, with their
architecture of white candy stucco, are warrens of eccentric
privateness; they are occupied by people who have taken no
part in the hypothetical consensus of urban life – the poor, the
blacks, the more feckless young living on National Assistance or casual jobs on building sites or bedsitter industries
like stringing beads or making candles. The district is notori-
ously difficult to police: it has a long, twenty-five-year-old
record of race-riots, drug arrests, vicious disputes between
slum landlords and their tenants, complaints about neighbours,
and petty litigation. Like many impoverished areas in big
cities, it is picturesque in the sun, and Americans walk the
length of the street market in the Portobello Road snapping
it with Kodaks; but on dull days one notices the litter, the
scabby paint, the stretches of torn wire netting, and the faint
smell of joss-sticks competing with the sickly sweet odour

of rising damp and rotting plaster. Where the area shows
signs of wealth, it is in the typically urban non-productive
entrepreneurism of antique shops and stalls. Various hard-up
community action groups have left their marks : a locked shack
with FREE SHOP spraygunned on it, and old shoes and sofas
piled in heaps around it; a makeshift playground under the
arches of the motorway with huge crayon faces drawn on the
concrete pillars; slogans in whitewash, from SMASH THE
PIGS to KEEP BRITAIN WHITE. The streets are crowded
with evident isolates : a pair of nuns in starched habits, a Sikh
in a grubby turban, a gang of West Indian youths, all teeth and
jawbones, a man in a fedora, greasy Jesus Christs in shiny
green suede coats with Red Indian fringes at their hems,
limp girls in flaky Moroccan fleeces, macrobiotic devotees
with transparent parchment faces, mongrel dogs, bejeaned
delivery men, young mothers in cardigans with second hand
prams. These are the urban spacemen, floating alone in
capsules of privacy, defying the gravity of the city.

Here magic flourishes, and everywhere one sees evidence
of a growing devout irrationalism. Little bookshops sell
the *I-Ching,* packs of tarot cards and fat studies of the obscure
mathematics of astrology. You can buy Sufi watergongs to
aid contemplation ('It helps you get into yourself, like know
who you are and who you're going to be . . .') and the
macrobiotic foodshop on Portobello Road, Ceres, even turns
the consumption of vegetables into a mystical religion.
Buddhist splinter groups have turned scrubby basement flats
into temples, painting the names of their *swamis* in erratic
red letters on white front doors. The politics of racial warfare are magical too: their cabalistic symbols and slogans,
as absolute and unlikely as mantras, seem to have largely replaced action with signs. The world of pigs versus people belongs to witchcraft; spells are cast with sprayguns, wax
images replaced by ritual terms of abuse. For people without
formal power who feel themselves to be on the ignored
periphery of the social system, magical display may be their
most effective course of action, at least therapeutic, at best
miraculous. (In the Golborne district of Notting Hill, a

neighbourhood policeman, Constable Jim Price, distributes chattily informative visiting cards to the mainly West Indian residents, and makes a point of helping everybody's children across roads and acting as a one-man citizens' advice bureau. As miracles go, Constable Price is rather a small one, but there is surely a direct relationship between the hopeless bloodthirstiness of the slogans on his beat and his studied friendliness and refusal to harass and arrest, in sharp contrast to generations of Notting Hill policemen.)

The fierce heterogeneity of the district makes it 'urban' in the sense of that word as it is used by the city's most powerful detractors. Here one feels the fragility of law, taut as a frayed guitar string; one can smell the foetid decomposition of the neighbourhood garbage, as if the human element, too, were being sucked into the cycle of decay; one can see and hear crackling hostilities between the people of the streets, always alert for enemies; and one shivers from the draught of loneliness, poverty and privation, where children have to play under the overhead thunder of the traffic, and elderly shiftless people sometimes go literally in rags with a glaze in their eyes as if they had already died. Yet here fashionable people buy little pastel-coloured terraced houses, and the bell-bottomed and caftaned crew of flat-dwellers talk about the place in affectionate diminutives. It is, simply, 'The Gate', as Ladbroke Grove is 'The Grove' – as if they were living in some model village in Wiltshire with retired brigadiers behind every elmed drive. Notting Hill Gate incorporates a central paradox of city life, in that its nature is as prolific and untameable as anywhere in London, yet for some at least of its inhabitants it has been accommodated to an order so benign as to be cosy.

The messy prolixity of the place makes it a perfect territory for the exercise of natural magic. Its unpredictability, its violent transitions from extreme wealth to extreme poverty, its atmosphere of being crowded out with disconnected loners, its physical characteristics as a maze of narrow streets and irregular crescents, combine to force the individual into a superstitious, speculative relationship with his environment.

He cannot, merely by studying the arrangements and amenities of the district, deduce from them who he is, for the answers he would get would be impossibly various. Society in Notting Hill Gate reveals no rationale, no comprehensible structure. The sets of values embodied in it are almost as diverse as the number of people on the streets. If untutored man were to be set down on a tropical island and told to construct a pattern of beliefs and morals from what he saw around him, he could hardly have more difficulty than a newcomer to Notting Hill Gate. It is a place where anything is possible, a nightmare – or paradise, perhaps, for some – of chance and choice.

It is no wonder that here the *I-Ching* has become a cultic accessory to life in the city. It is, says a girl in a poncho with fair hair to her waist and a knobbly zodiacal ring, 'quite . . . philosophical'. It preaches a doctrine of continuous change, of man's life as a series of chances, taken or rejected, against a background of universal flux. Shall I go to the shops or the cinema, does the day promise to be good or evil, will the milkman go for another week unpaid? One may toss slender yarrow stalks, or flip a combination of three coins, to find the hexagram of the moment. How should this paragraph go? The coins produce the figure *Chia Jen,* the sign of the family : 'what is most advantageous is that the wife be firm and correct.' The commentary goes on : 'The first line, undivided, shows its subject establishing restrictive regulations in his household. Occasion for repentance will disappear . . .' A book might, I suppose, be construed as a household, and the female element in writing is mythologically reputed to be style; but, even allowing for the most ingenious metaphors, this is not the most constructive criticism I have ever had. It does, however, indicate the way in which the *I-Ching* works; its oracular statements are wonderfully ambiguous, and, if you wish, you may see any specific question you choose reflected in them. It isolates events from the swirl, and the controlled chance of its operation satisfactorily excludes rational explanations and justifications. Its advice is personal, and pertains to the immediate moment; for someone who feels disconnected from society's intricate net of causes and relations, for whom time has atomised into a spray of haphazard occasions the *I-Ching* presents a system of choice which corresponds perfectly with the contingency and privacy of his view of the world. The sixty-four hexagrams and their variants make up a model of something very like a city; diverse, random, unpredictable, yet finally possessed of an order, even though it is an order which is beyond the grasp of the individual imagination. The play and ritual which accompany its use endow each consultation with a uniqueness of occasion. Universal forces, so mysterious, so apparently impersonal, miraculously bend themselves to accommodate the needs of a single person at a particular moment. If Notting Hill is a scramble of contradictory messages, the cosmos is benign and – if tapped with the right mumbo-jumbo – it will make itself simply and clearly audible to the honest inquirer. Raymond Van Over, the editor of the most widely available edition of the *I-Ching,* says in his introduction: '*form* is a mere illusory manifestation of underlying causes'. It is the same consoling message that the Situationists and the Hare Krishna people preach; believe it, and the city, with all its paradoxes, puzzles, and violent inequities, will float away before your eyes, a chimera to delude only the hopelessly, cynically earthbound. The computer dating agency and the horoscope render a similar service: science (especially mystical mathematics) and magic are closely allied – both promise to rip the veil from the troubling face of the world at one sweep.

Notting Hill Gate is a superstitious place because it seems to exceed rational prescriptions and explanations. On the Portobello Road, one feels oneself growing more insubstantial, less and less able to keep a sense of personal proportion in the crowd of people who all look so much poorer, or richer, or wilder, or more conventional than one is oneself. It is certainly hard to keep in touch with other people in the city; it may sometimes be almost as difficult to keep in touch with one's own self – that diminishing pink blob which rolls and slides like a lost coin in a gutter. The people who

float on the tide of metaphysical junk—freaks of all kinds
. . . into macrobiotics, yoga, astrology, illiterate mysticism,
acid, terrible poetry by Leonard Cohen and tiny novels by
Richard Brautigan—have managed, at a price. The new
folk magic of the streets promises to have some unhappy
political consequences but as a way of responding to the city
it does reflect a truth about the nature of the place which we
had better learn to confront.

The truth is one of an ultimate privacy, in which the self,
cosseted and intensified, internalises the world outside, and
sees the city as a shadow-show of its own impulses and
movements. Privacy and reality are profoundly equated, so that
what is most real is located in the deepest recesses of the
self. The external world turns into an epic movie, supplying
details on which to feed one's fantasies; like Disney's *Fantasia*
which, when shown in London three years ago, drew crowds
of hippies who dosed themselves with acid at selected points
in the film. Like Notting Hill Gate itself, it was perfect trip
material, and Disney's original intentions were as irrelevant
as those of the civic architects who first laid out those
streets and crescents.

In this search for the disappearing self, the physical body
becomes a central symbol; the stomach, intestines, and
organs of reproduction are solemnly attended to, as vessels
in which the precious self is contained. In Ceres, the macrobiotic shop on Portobello Road, I bought *Macrobiotics: An
Invitation to Health and Happiness* by George Ohsawa:

> The kitchen is the studio where life is created . . . Knowing
> that no absolute rules exist, or can be followed forever,
> we start with principles that are as adaptable to the constantly
> changing world we inhabit as possible. Only you are the
> artist who draws the painting of your life . . . Strictly speak-
> ing, no one eats the same food and the same amount even
> from the same cooking pot. Such recognition of individuality
> leads us to the fact that we are living by ourselves and we
> are creating our life by ourselves.

The girls who drift about the store, filling wire baskets with

soya beans, miso and wakame seaweed have the dim inward-
ness of gaze of Elizabeth Siddall in Rossetti's 'Jenny'. In
bedsitters in Ladbroke Grove, they create themselves over
gas rings, feeding their immaculate insides on harmoniously
balanced amounts of yin and yang foods. It is hard to tell
whether their beatific expressions come from their convictions
of inner virtue or from undernourishment. When they speak,
their voices are misty, as if their words had to travel a long
way from their inscrutable souls to the naughty outer world.
Serious, narcissistic, terrifyingly provident, like all fanatics
they brim with latent violence; when they exclude and con-
demn, they do so with a ringing stridency that smacks more
of mothers in Romford and Hornchurch than of Oriental sages
preaching doctrines of universal gentleness. 'Oh, man . . .'
withers its recipient as skilfully as any mean current of suburban disapproval. Their city is a pure and narrow one : they
are miniaturists in their talented cultivation of themselves.
In her scented room, Annette feeds herself on honey and
grape juice and brown rice; she reads haiku by Basho. 'I
thing that's really beautiful,' she said . . . a vague poem, with
a horseman and some bullrushes in it, a long way from the
things you see at the Gate. On her shelves, a meagre stretch
of paperbacks : *Trout Fishing in America, Steppenwolf, The
Macrobiotic Way, The I-Ching,* Louis MacNeice's coffee table
book on astrology (an awkward Christmas present from her
father), poems by Rod McKuen, Lewis Carroll, Barry
McSweeney, Blake and Leonard Cohen, *Slaughterhouse 5,
Alternative London, The Book of the Pony* (a relic). Annette
says Basho was really into himself, like . . . like Hesse, you
know? Her simplesse is acutely constraining; any sentence not
phrased in that mystical babytalk of ritual, contemplative
assent is met by the slow disdainful fall of eyelids which are
almost completely bare of lashes. Right, you say, picking up
the correctly slurred, drugged intonation, right . . . right.

Waste blows on the pavements of Ladbroke Grove like
tumbleweed in a western, but Annette is clean as a whistle,
inside and out. The scatter of coins by the door is a money
spell, she says; her vegetable knife is kept carefully wiped

to make sure no yang is infected with yin on its travels. At weekends she visits her parents at the far end of the Metropolitan Line, carrying her own food with her in a knitted Mexican bag . . . 'Daddy's heavily into meat and roast potatoes, he's very Leo.' She used to work as a primary school teacher, but she got all apart, and now lives on National Assistance. ('You meet some really freaky people down there, really strange. They all have a story to tell.') Her friends carry the same woollen satchels, and talk in the same half-American half-childish idiom. Some play penny whistles and chant mantras. Their parents are lower middle-class clerks and tradesmen, or skilled working-class labourers: 'straights' who, in their children's version of them, live in a state of amazingly ingenuous incomprehension.

The political world, the domain of reason and social organisation, is as vague and distant as a period of history in a schoolbook; Ulster, Vietnam, the British economy, belong to 'freaks' who are 'on' some bad foreign substance. The vogue for Kurt Vonnegut's novel *Slaughterhouse 5* is of relevance here, for it might seem curious that a book based on the experiences of an American prisoner of war during the days leading up to the Dresden bombing should make any impact at all on a group of readers so notably indifferent to history and to politics, for whom the previous literary craze had been Tolkien's pixie-gothic saga, *The Lord of the Rings*. But Vonnegut succeeded in making history available by putting it inside the head of his hero: the novel presents the war as an hallucinogenic trip, a reel of internalised sensations and fantasies, in which Billy Pilgrim moves, suspiciously easily, from the actual landscape of Germany to delusions of intergalactic travel and lonely extra-terrestrial wisdom. In the novel, the real is clouded and discredited; a POW camp, saturation bombing, exhaustion and suffering are, we are led to believe, no more or less than anyone might go through on a bad trip. We are told that Billy Pilgrim is haunted by what happened to him in the war, but it is a war which, the book implies, can be repeated for anyone, any time, for its bombs explode as much inside the head as on the ground. Vonnegut enforces

a pernicious democracy in which there is hardly any discrimination between fantasy and reality – a democracy in
which Annette gains and real survivors or real wars lose
(Dresden a bad scene, like a trip on inferior acid). Annette,
who in real life has grazed experience as lightly as a butterfly,
is as wise as the ages in her head : she knows wars, revolutions,
strikes, gross inflations of the mental economy, and beside them
Belfast is a dim shadow, too far out in the external world to
be real.

Where the world outside shrivels and fades, the private
world of the self grows correspondingly more solid and
detailed. If the social language of Annette and her friends is
detached and rudimentary, their vocabulary for describing the
contents of their heads is exact. 'Hang-up . . . spaced-out . . .
mind-fuck . . . together . . . freak-out . . . mind-blow . . .
buzz . . . high . . .' – the words, drawn from black slang,
psychoanalysis and communications-technology, domesticate
the mind; they turn it into a familiar usable instrument like
a wireless set. Just as the body is perceived as a vessel that
must be kept clean with yoga exercises and elaborate diets,
so the head is the ultimate casket of the self. The pursuit
of *satori,* of 'inmost happiness', is an epic journey into selfhood; and the illusion, at least, of this inward drift is made
dramatically real in the acid trip and the contemplative
smoking of marijuana.

Alcohol, the approved drug of 'straight' society, makes its
users voluble and communicative; in moderate quantities it
increases social participation, fortifies one's conviction that
one is part of a consensual community. But pot and acid
intensify the sense of privacy to the point where the outside
world becomes almost entirely blotted out. Smoking hash,
I have watched the people I was with growing smaller, heard
their conversation as a fading hum of nonsense syllables.
One's vision contracts, one becomes acutely conscious of one's
own body, feels the 'buzz' in one's limbs as if one was coated
with electric fur. Music, paintings, words turn into disembodied stimuli. They lose their contexts, and you can
appropriate them for your own mental furniture. An im-

provisation by Miles Davis turns into a long squeeze of toothpaste; you watch it thinning and thickening, coiling on itself as it falls. The image, like most images in psychedelic writing (R. D. Laing's *The Bird of Paradise*, for instance), does not at all illuminate the music; rather it deprives the trumpeter of his creation and makes it over for the smoker's fantasy. The automatic surrealism, which is an inevitable accompaniment to being high, tears experience out of the real world by the roots and uses it for play or decoration or as a mystical aid, like a watergong, for seeing not *it* but the perceiving self.

In such a state of mind, it is not hard to believe that the world is a dream, a three-dimensional moving panorama by Beardsley and Rossetti. What matters is that this egotistical and aesthetic view of life converts everything into food for the omnivorous *I*. Much of the hotch-potch of San Francisco Buddhism, dotty nutritional science, dope mysticism and star gazing is half-baked and second hand; its claims to being a culture or counter-culture are both pompous and impoverished. But these ingredients, however silly they may seem in themselves, add up to something more: they are the feathers, samples of blood and urine, and charred twigs of a magical ritual – and the magic in whose service they are employed is not to be so lightly dismissed.

The childish manner, the affected spontaneity, the baby clothes (shawls, loose dresses, and, for men, jean outfits that look like overgrown romper suits) of Annette and her kind have a special significance here. Lévy-Bruhl saw magic as a 'pre-logical' habit of mind: childhood is the pre-logical state of human development, and at the Gate it is used as a symbol of disaffection for the rational adult world. Annette still sleeps with a felt rabbit, plays with melting candlewax, gazes distractedly at comics (*Oz*, the English 'head comic', is a watered down version of a spectacularly savage American genre, whose most notable examples have been the deranged expressionist strips of Robert Crumb); but she is a bug-eyed innocent. Her play is whimsical and contrived; it is performed as much for the benefit of spectators as for herself.

Playing at being a Red Indian in a bandanna, or an Asian peasant in a tie-dyed sari, or a workman in a boiler suit, is a carefully stage-managed announcement. It trumpets a commonplace city freedom – the freedom to be who you want to be, without bonds of class, nationality, education, occupation, or even sex. It further expresses an allegiance to the irrational, mystical or magical values which the Red Indian, the peasant or the labourer are presumed to possess. The Mohawks and Cherokees of Notting Hill Gate belong among the lofty savages of Fenimore Cooper, not in the downtrodden reservations of the real USA. It is also a homage to 'dressing-up'. Grown-ups don't dress up and indulge in make-believe; children do, and the boutique is the industrial equivalent to the Edwardian dressing up box, that grotto of old wedding dresses, turbans, yashmaks collected by a grandfather on furlough, and clumpy shoes all buckles and straps. There is something of the same coy, schmaltzily 'fetching' little-girlishness in the way the young rig themselves out in their incongruous costumes on the Portobello Road – elderly children smirking complacently under broad-brimmed hats. But they take childhood seriously, more seriously than politics, at least. The tradition of childhood represents their only real foray into history; they see themselves as terrible Blakean infants, or as Wordsworth's boy evading the growing shades of the prison house, or as Alice, wise in her naivete. To be a child is to be in touch with dark, para-rational, para-urban forces, and to see the equivocations, arrangements and compromises of adulthood as a lunatic charade.

The mind of the child, as it imposes order on the abandoned scatter of the city, is superstitious, egocentric, full of taboos. In a moving autobiographical essay on the growth of sensibility in a city-bred child, Adrian Stokes described how he reconstructed Hyde Park out of a bundle of parental prejudices and overheard rumours, and from lurid scraps of theology borrowed from his nannies. The park sheep were 'wicked and guilty', the keeper an omnipresent 'magician'. The boy Stokes practised a continual, and characteristically urban, habit of synaesthesia; learning to arrange visual scenes in terms of their accompanying noises—'a street became *informed* for me by the sounds of a barrel organ . . . Thus the street was not only organised; it became an organism, it became alive'. The traffic on the misty rim of the park was absorbed into the gloomy metaphysics of low-church Anglicanism:

'Time like an ever-rolling stream, bears all her sons away.' We used to sing that hymn, the thin sounds torn by the wind. I had never seen a rolling stream. I thought of it as the low thunder of the London traffic. And Time was the gloomy sky over the Park, which, by turning into night, bore away the soiled fretfulness of all happenings there each day. The Park monuments, then, especially the would-be works of art, possessed in my eyes an almost masochist quality in their utter *poverty*; impotent under the lash of Time, borne away each night to build their grimy ugliness anew each dawn. Between Marble Arch and Albion Gate there is a kind of Gothic steeple whose function is to provide several vents of drinking water To this globuled monstrosity in particular I attributed a horrible masochism. There lingered no romance in its poverty nor in the poor frequenters; and as I was not allowed to drink such public water, I shunned it for being something blind and grey.

Here is a world laid out arbitrarily and passionately in terms of the self. The 'public water' which he is forbidden to drink, and the monstrous fountain from which it springs, are especially taboo: they belong to the Others—the impoverished tramps and wicked sheep, figures of all that the polite child is not. The water, traditional symbol of life, is 'blind', like the insensible sheeplike class of men whose thirst it slakes. It is a passage of considerable power and complexity, impregnated with an unconsciously ferocious snobbery, as well as with the charge of imaginative invention of the lonely child. I think it provides a very exact model of the way in which isolated, desocialised people respond to the

city, putting up a grand scaffolding of theology and superstition around quite small situations of social placement and
distance. Strangers turn into evil untouchables, there are
uncrossable boundaries and monumental symbols. A hymn
sung by a religiomanic nanny, or a few words found at
random in the *I-Ching,* might reveal the inner structure of
the whole city, with oneself at its centre.

The young tribalists of Notting Hill, approaching the city
with their mishmash of half-read Blake, oriental mysticism
and self-conscious babyishness, try for the same vision, even
though their efforts are much less intelligent and articulate
than Adrian Stokes's elaborate demonology. An anthology of
poems, *Children of Albion,* brings together a rag-bag of
verses from the 'underground', mostly written by people in
their twenties at the time of publication. A very large number
of these poems are simply about living in London, and,
more particularly, about living in Notting Hill. They are full
of borrowed apocalyptic images; they render their authors'
dazed emotional states in a turgid flow of substantives. The
Blakean '&' sign is used to join up the sounds, smells and
sights of an environment too fecund to articulate, and through
this swill of sensations there runs a steady thread of home-
made magic, a squinny-eyed view of London as a wizard's
coat of occult signs. A poem called 'vision of Portobello
Road' finishes up with a whimsical exclamation mark at
the impossibility of decoding it all:

> Screaming tricycles and melons
> lettuces and ripe negroes,
> stripe shirt,
> and others proud walking.
> It's gay and sad and rich enough!

Grammar has dropped out of this language altogether, and
we are left with a string of mechanically surrealist transferred epithets and lazy antitheses. This is not poetry so much

as a symptom of a condition; like much else in the anthology, it betrays the acutely taxed state of the writer's imagination — his fuses are blowing, and only abstraction and exclamation can save him from combustion. Beyond his last line lies, to take a phrase from another poem in the book, 'the sunpyre fire city' . . . the city of primitive magical apocalypse where reason and order are futile checks against the electric storm of sensations.

These people at the Gate have clearly embraced the idea of a magical city. Their clothes, their language, their religious beliefs, their folk art belong to a synthetically-reconstructed tribal culture ruled by superstition, totems and taboos. Most of what they have is borrowed, affected and contrived; it reflects a sturdy unoriginality. But perhaps its very tawdriness is a measure of the urgency of the need which has created it. We live in a society in which magic is supposed to have been outlawed or outgrown, in which secular rationalism is presumed to be the standard by which everyone lives. Yet at the same time we have created an environment in which it is exceedingly hard to be rational, in which people are turning to magic as a natural first resort. Television clergymen fondly interpret the evidence of Notting Hill Gate or the box-office returns of *Jesus Christ Superstar* as the first twitches of a spiritual reawakening. That seems, to put it mildly, doubtful. The kind of magic I have been examining is profoundly solipsistic, self-bound, inward. Its very ignorance of plan or creation is its most obvious strength. One would not deduce the existence of God from the Portobello Road; but one might register from it the force of the amoral, the relative, the anarchistic. One might also discover, with shock, one's own isolation, the space-suit of privacy and its attendant rituals, in which one travels in a state of continuous locomotion through the city. Leaning against the spiked railings of the Salvation Army Hall, next door to a Woolworths and a Wimpy bar, one could hardly be further away from Plato's city state and its supremely intelligible contractual relationships. The Gate opens not on to the gentle potsmoking whimsy of Gandalf's Garden, but

on a ruined Eden, tangled, exotic and overgrown, where
people see signs in scraps of junk and motley. It may look
like affectation, a boasting juvenile pretence, but perhaps it
is real—a state of natural magic to which the fragmented
industrial city unconsciously aspires.

EIGHT

Two Quarters

It is, perhaps, a symptom of our superstitious habitation of the city that we map it, quarter by quarter, postal district by postal district, into a patchwork quilt of differently coloured neighbourhoods and localities. For in fact urban man is less of a robin, less tied to rigid territorial boundaries, than his country cousin. The 'Italian', or 'Jewish', or 'Black' quarters are not exclusively inhabited by Italians, Jews and Blacks; they are more or less arbitrary patches of city space on which several communities are in a constant state of collision. A colourful and closely-knit minority can give an area its 'character', while its real life lies in the rub of subtle conflicts between all sorts of groups of different people, many of whom are visible only to the denizen. Conversely, a strong cultural community can exist quite outside the geographical definition of a quarter. I live in a community whose members are scattered piecemeal around London (some of them live outside the city altogether); the telephone is our primary connection, backed up by the tube line, the bus route, the private car and a number of restaurants, pubs and clubs. My 'quarter' is a network of communication lines with intermittent assembly points; and it cannot be located on a map.

Yet place is important; it bears down on us, we mythicise it – often it is our greatest comfort, the one reassuringly solid element in an otherwise soft city. As we move across the square to the block of shops on the street, with pigeons and sweetpapers underfoot and the weak sun lighting the tarmac, the city is eclipsed by the here-and-now; the sight and smell and sound of place go to make up the fixed foot of life in the metropolis. Place, like a mild habitual pain, reminds one that one is; its familiar details and faces – even the

parked cars which you recognise as having been there in
that spot for months—assure us of a life of repetitions,
of things that will endure and survive us, when the city at
large seems all change and flux. Loyalty to and hunger for
place are among the keenest of city feelings, reverenced and
prized precisely because they go against the grain of that
drift towards the formless and unstable which the city seems
to encourage in us. My two quarters are parts of London
where I have lived; a square in the north east of the city
on the border of Islington and Holloway, and a square in
Earl's Court, on the scruffy western fringe of Chelsea and
Kensington. They are not ghettoes, and to prise them apart
from the rest of the city entails a considerable amount of
surgery on the veins and arteries which, in real life, keep
them organically joined to the messier and much larger
entity of London. (This is not merely a problem of piety.
The outstanding weakness of much classical sociological
study of the city, from Louis Wirth's *The Ghetto* to Willmott
and Young's *Family and Kinship in East London,* is its insis-
tence on the neighbourhood as a culturally self-sufficient
community—as if it really was a village inside the city. My
quarters are both chronically dependent places, and when
they look most like villages or ghettoes it usually means that
some people are trying very hard to play at being villagers or
persecuted refugees, which is not at all the same thing.)

The northern square is not actually a square at all. It is
three sides, each with its own rather odd, cheapskate style
of Victorian architecture—one grand with balconies and rotting porticoes, one derelict-gothic, and one orotund fake-
Georgian terrace. It looks as if it had been put together by a
shady and squabbling trio of speculative builders, while
their fourth friend found a more profitable racket : the south
side of the square is a cutting, in which the goods trains of
the North London Line from Broad Street to Richmond
rattle through where the slaveys ought to have been steaming in a line of basement washrooms. In the centre of the
square, there is an ornamental garden, mostly grass and
flowering shrubs that never seem to be in flower, a children's

playground, the superstructure of a bomb shelter which has been turned into a pair of public lavatories, and a padlocked tennis court whose gravelled surface has cracked and subsided as if it had had its own earthquake. It is a square that architectural writers about the area leave conspicuously alone; it shows its own history, of unimaginative enterprises, both private and civic, all too well. Lots of people have had ideas for it at one time or another; none of them have been very bright ones. On the Georgian side, someone thought he would smarten his house up by slapping a coat of gravel-stucco on it three inches deep and painting it nightdress pink; and just by the railway line, on the central space, a truck owner built a large wooden-and-corrugated-iron hangar to unload his lorries in. Floodlit, on a winter evening, it looks as if he is putting on a passion play, a ghostly Islington Oberammergau.

Yet in the late nineteen-sixties, the council put a conservation order on the square – perhaps because it was, almost, a square and squares are in fashion; perhaps because no-one from the council had ever seen it (or maybe because they all lived in it); perhaps because Islington Council has a perversely sophisticated taste in architectural curiosities – and it was this, the most recent idea, which dominated the life of the square while I lived there, skunklike, in a newly-converted basement on the west side. For eighty years the square had been deserted by the middle classes for whom it had originally been built. They fled north, scared of their proximity to the East End and its suppurating brew of cholera and typhoid germs. By Edwardian times, their only relics were the kept women of gentlemen in the City, who sat out, so people remembered, on the sunny balconies of the north side, waiting for the clank of carriage wheels coming up Liverpool Road from the Angel. But the carriages stopped coming. The houses were broken up into flats. It was a cheap place for immigrants to get a peeling room; and it bulged with Irishmen who had come to London to burrow tunnels for the underground railways, with Greeks who were in the tailoring trade as machinists and hoped to open cafés, with Poles, and West Indians, and the more feckless members of the Cockney working class for whom the square was a vague stopover, a place they had landed up in on the way to somewhere else.

Since 1900, the square, like so many metropolitan districts, had been a shabby *entrepôt,* steadily declining as more and more shipments of people washed up in it for no special reason except that it was cheap and close to the centre of things. That was how I found myself there, too; I didn't feel I had to love it or be randy for its local colour . . . it was just a place to tie up until something better happened, it commanded no particular loyalty. But the conservation order changed that; it slapped a sudden value on all the fungoid stucco fronts, and young couples with a little money to put down on a deposit took to patrolling the square on Sunday afternoons. They stared at it squint-eyed and, after their first blank shock at the mean disorder of the place, they learned to look at it with affection. They saw a uniform line of white fronts, with brass knockers in place of the tangle of electric bells; they put leaves on the trees; they stripped the pavements of fish-and-chip papers; they looked at the people on the streets, thought for a while, and came up with the word cosmopolitan. Tennis in the evenings, dinner on the balcony in the sun . . . the rippling, laden branches of the elms . . . the clicking wheels of smart prams parading on the shady walk between the trees . . . this vision was at a long remove from what one could actually see, but the city is a stage for transformation scenes, and the square was a challenge to the imagination. It had sunk so low that it could only be rescued, restored like one of General Booth's street-harlots to rosy-cheeked prosperity by evangelism and a change of diet.

From then on, estate agents' boards began to sprout from the basements, and builders and interior decorators swarmed round the square, carrying whole walls away from inside houses, pointing the brickwork, painting the fronts, taking long speculative lunch hours in the pub, while Nigel and Pamela, Jeremy and Nicola, made flying spot-checks in their Renaults and Citroens. The leaves on the trees grew greener; old absentee landlords suddenly started to take an unprecedented interest in the lives of their tenants, shaking their heads gloomily at the absence of bathrooms and the damp patches and the jags of falling plaster, and suggesting that the tenant would be better off by far in a spick council flat in Finsbury Park. For every signboard advertising 'Vacant Possession' there had been a flyting game, alternately wheedling and vicious. Some landlords locked their tenants out of their lavatories; some hired thugs in pinstripe suits; some reported their own properties to the council as being unfit for habitation; many offered straight cash bribes – the going rate for eviction was £200, a large sum to tenants but one that was a fraction of the rising monthly value of the property. (In three years, a typical house on the terrace rose in price from £4000 to £26,000.) The tenants were winkled out; most of them were innocent of their rights, and those who tried to stay were subjected to long, elaborately-mounted campaigns of harassment. Alongside the builders' skips on the pavement, there were handcarts and aged minivans, with a transistor radio squawking pop tunes on top of the roped-together pile of tacky furniture. The local barber told me about the girl-graduates who came to sweet-talk him out of his flat, flashing their miniskirts and going on about vinyl bathrooms and 'conveniences'. He had already lost most of his customers, since the council was tearing down several acres of neighbouring streets to make way for glass-and-concrete apartment blocks.

It rained eviction notices, but the agents and landlords kept the slaughter out of sight of the prospective buyers, who were all people of principle, staunch Labour voters, dedicated lovers of the working class. They *wanted* the shawled Greek widows, the clowning blacks on the pavement outside the pub, the wise and melancholy Irish and the Cockney wits; they liked the square because it was real, and they found colour and charm where the landlords saw only dreck. And, as the tenants drifted unwillingly away, they left their familiars; lean mongrels and starved cats, who

roistered in the alleys and kept the square at night alive with
eldritch shrieks and desolated love-moans. There was an old
lady with a ruined pram who collected rags and discarded
clothes; her business thrived, and she trundled a mountain
of furs gone to verdigris and mothballs, and charred demob
suits, and plastic basketwork hats with bunches of artificial
cherries of an unlikely colour.

I was adopted by an abandoned cat, lean and black as an
old curate, with a voice that was uncannily guttural with
thirst and hunger. It tottered uncertainly about my flat,
took a snobbish shine to the central heating, and bedded
down gracelessly, like an evacuee. Pets are forbidden in
many council flats, and the ones left behind in the square led
a life of ingratiating atavism, battened on to the new wave
of middle-class immigrants, and developed sophisticated
cravings for cream and chicken livers. They were the real permanent residents of the square, these animals for whom the
rest of London, and the wheels of changing social fortune,
were not even rumours. The landlord could tear the cat's owner
away from the place he had lived in as long as he could
remember; but the cat stayed, like the name on the disconnected bell, and the dead-pigeon smell in the front-area—
mortal remains, of the kind preserved in old photographs
. . . things which survive, but only just long enough for the
collector of local colour to record them.

The people went, to Finsbury Park, the darker reaches
of Holloway Road, and brazen GLC estates on the Essex
border. The people who came in (a disproportionately small
number since a single middle class couple and their baby
can displace anything up to a dozen sitting tenants) were
from Kensington, or the northern outer suburbs, or the
Home Counties; and they settled avidly on the land, taking
over its shops and pubs, getting up little campaigns to preserve this and demolish that, starting playgroups, and giving
small intense dinner parties for other new pioneers. They
took tutorials in local gossip from their chars, and talked
knowledgeably about 'Ron' and 'Cliff' and 'Mrs H.' and

'Big Ted', as if the square and its history were their birth-right.

But it was by no means a complete takeover; people still repaired old cars from front rooms along the square, and on the unreclaimed east side, the houses seemed to actually swell with an influx of the displaced and the very poor. This part of London responds like a needle-gauge to disturbances across the world, and the expulsion of Asians from Kenya showed up on the square in a sprinkling of faces who looked bitterly unaccustomed to such want and cold, and were determined to move out before they got bogged down in the rising damp and learned to shiver with fortitude before the popping gas fire with half its plaster columns cracked or gone. On the far side, the sunny side, of the square, these unluckier migrants could see a future of a sort; a future of Japanese lampshades, *House and Garden*, French baby cars, white paint, asparagus tips, Earl Grey tea and stripped pine stereo systems – the reward of success is the freedom to choose a style of elegant austerity. It is hard to guess how such conspicuous rejection of the obvious fruits of wealth must have looked to the Asians, who had so recently been forcibly deprived of their money and its attendant powers. ('How much do you have now?' asked a radio interviewer of an expelled Asian businessman at Heathrow. 'Two hundred shillings,' said the man, speaking carefully, talking of the contents of his wallet like Mono-poly money.) They wandered glumly about in second-hand overcoats, glazedly detached from their own dereliction. When stray dogs snuffled at their feet, they kicked them, delicately and surreptitiously, in their bellies.

Both groups of immigrants were innocent of the impro-vised network of rules which had been evolved around the square. The smart young things trespassed casually, arro-gantly, secure in the conviction that the future of the square lay in their hands. The Asians were shy, beadily knowing, and usually wrong. Both groups made themselves unpopular.

On the nearby block of shops there were two opposite, nearly identical, grocery stores – one run by a Greek Cypriot,

and one by a family of African Asians who had come over
some years before. Each shop had its band of regular customers. The Cypriot was liked by the West Indian and
Irish women, and kept their local foods in stock. (I tried to
buy a loaf of bread there once. It looked ordinary enough.
An Irish lady made me put it back. 'You wouldn't want to
be eating that, it's blackie bread. You go black overnight,
if you eat that. Black as sin and too long and big for your
girlfriend too –' The shop was full of West Indians at the
time; I was the dupe and outsider, not they. They joined in,
threatening me with elephantine potency and body-hair if I
touched their wonder bread. Alas, I didn't.) The shop
opposite was mainly patronised by the respectable Cockney
working class; it was full of notices about not asking for
credit as a refusal might offend, and piled high with cans
of petfood. It was the chief gossip centre of the quarter, and
sent calendars and cards at Christmas to its regulars. Jokes
were the main currency of both shops; facetious insults,
usually of a bawdily intimate or racial kind, which buzzed
back and forth over the racks of breakfast cereals. These
jokes kept insiders in and outsiders out; they reflected –
harmlessly would not be strong enough, cathartically would
give them too importantly theatrical a function – the tensions
in the composition of the quarter. But the immigrants could
never get them quite right.

Both the Asians and the young pioneers wandered promiscuously into both shops. Once there they laughed too
loudly or not loudly enough at the ritual jokes; they asked
for foods which the shop they were in did not stock. When
they tried to initiate jokes themselves they were too elaborate,
too humorous – for humour was not the point at all – and
they were received with wary tolerance. Had they been able
to joke about their own peculiar tastes for white paint and
thrifty ecologism it might have been different; but they
presumed to a matey all-men-are-equal tone – and the visible
untruth of that ploy was all too clear to their auditors, whose
own lives were day-to-day struggles with a dramatic in-
equality (and that made harsher by the presence of these

well-heeled young couples), and hard-bitten compromises
with the other people in the quarter who were their territorial
competitors, if not their enemies.

The local pub was carefully demarcated into symbolic
territories. The public bar was the West Indian province,
with a smattering of white girls of catholic tastes and inclina-
tions. The saloon was for the Irish. There was one black, in a
shiny felt hat, who ambled leggily round the saloon bar
picking up empty glasses; and in the spade bar of the pub
there was a single, very sodden Irishman. These two hos-
tages strengthened the division. In the public bar, the juke
box hammered out Reggae records; in the saloon on Friday
nights Bridie the Singing Saxophonist carolled about the
Mountains of Mourne and the Rose of Tralee through an
amplifying system which made her sound like Frankenstein's
monster.

On Saturday mornings, the West Indians had the pavement
outside the pub to themselves, and called to the black girls
coming out of the service at the shout-and-holler gospel
tabernacle across the road, in their white dresses and tight
curls.

'Rosee!'
'Mary-*lyn*!'
'Gay-*lee*!'
'Oh, man.'

A sardonic toast, in rum and Guinness in the sun. Before
the pub opened in the morning, you could hear the singing
— 'Sweet *Jes*-us,' languorous and seductive, as if the Saviour
was being cajoled out of bed or bar — and the movement
of the bodies inside, pile drivers in muslin, stirring and
shaking in the thin walls. The Greek church, on the other side
of the block of shops, was more decorous, with a subdued
trickle of people in black leading pale scrubbed children. But
their priest rode like a gangster in a brand-new Ford Cortina;
fast, unsmiling, a pack of cigarettes open and spilling on the
dashboard like a fan of playing cards.

But the pioneers went everywhere regardless. They stood
on the pavement beside the West Indians, pretending they

were at a garden pub in Hampstead; they slummed in the
public bar, and put the occasional sixpence in the juke
box; they investigated the churches; they joined the villain-
ous Golden Star club, a black dive where you drank rum or beer
in paper cups and shuffled on the tiny dance floor to records
of amazing rhythmic crunch and volume. Wherever they
went, they spread money and principled amity. They were
interested in everybody, as temporary and ubiquitous as
secret policemen. The Polish tailor who had a workshop in
his front room in the block of shops grimaced at them as
they went by; he, presumably, had prior experience of
people who invade places armed with good intentions.

The local paper, the *Islington Gazette,* found its letter
columns filling with protests against 'the new Chelseaites',
with their one way traffic schemes (in Barnsbury, a few
blocks south of the square), and their cheque-book evictions.
The local Labour Party began to split down the middle,
between the soft-accented newcomers – all with honourable
theories of workers' control – and the old long-resident trades
unionist. It seemed like the beginning of a class war. But
the young couples had never conceived of themselves as a class
– they had rejected the bourgeois ethic, just as they had
rejected the florid display of Chelsea – and were strenuously,
idealistically individualist. They didn't see themselves in the
stereotypical portraits painted by the angry correspondents
in the paper; they were not like that, they *cared* and had
scruples. How could sincere socialists be accused of class-
exploitation? Or acres of white paint be construed as a vulgar
exhibition of financial power? Jeremy and Nicola, Pamela
and Nigel, were indignant and troubled; or they took the
vindictive portraits to refer to quite other people, and joined
in the chorus of execration.

All round the square, more working-class streets came
down. Windows were boarded up, and the London Electricity Board put LEB OFF in swathes of paint across the
front doors when it disconnected each house's supply. It
looked like a sign of a plague or a primitive curse. 'Leb
off!' As the demolition men moved in, a cloud of old brick-

dust hung over the streets, and more frightened cats migrated southwards into the square. Soon after I stopped living
there, Lesly Street residents refused to go; they barricaded
both ends of the road and tried to sit it out as the bulldozers
rumbled closer, taking down their garden walls and flattening
flower borders under their tracks. The residents were supported by some rebellious social workers and one sympathetic
Labour councillor, and their 'No Go Area' got into the national
newspapers. But Lesly Street has gone too, now. It wasn't
perhaps a class war, but there has certainly been something
suspiciously like a class victory.

In the converted house where I lived, privilege and choice,
like a thick belt of insulation, kept the destruction of the
surrounding streets to little more than an annoying noise that
interfered with one's reading. The garden in the centre
of the square was replanted; the trees, now we were in a smokeless zone, looked less sorry; the careening streams of after-
school kids thinned; the front area was easier to keep clean.
It was regarded as a small victory for conservation that the
wall at the back of the garden was kept high, so that the
tenants of the new council low-rise flats would not be able
to watch the sunbathing Brahmins leafing through the *New
York Review of Books* on their breakfast patios.

The off-licence which I used came down. The betting shop
was served with a surprise notice of demolition. Little back-
street businesses shifted or died. Every big city, even at times
of desperate property-shortage, has crannies into which the
feckless and the transient and some, at least, of the dis-
possessed, can lose themselves. No-one knows exactly where
everybody goes in these upheavals. Municipal housing helps
some; but the unlucky have to search out those remaining
areas which have not yet been picked out by the spotlight
of wealth and fashion or the dimmer beam, which often
accompanies it, of urban renewal. Ruinous terraces backing
on to the railway tracks in Camden . . . grim apartment houses
in east Holloway . . . derelict streets running alongside
disused wharves and warehouses south of the river . . .
There was a boy with a transistor radio and the scalp of a

clipped ferret who sold me a bargain Austin Sprite; by the
time the big-end went and the gearbox had exhausted the
sawdust he'd added, he had gone too — his house boarded
over, his business marked only by a long grease stain on
the pavement. He might crop up anywhere.

But the pioneers, the new Brahmins, are there to stay;
their money firmly invested, their place assured. The trees
grow greener for them; they outlive cats, charladies, sitting
tenants, they ride the tides of inflation and depression and
mobility just as their parents did. Though they have loftier
spirits than their parents, or more innocence. The square
is not — will not be — as 'real' as it was; but it is coming to be
a place of substance, which, on the economic scale of things,
is perhaps more important. If the frontier spirit with which
it was colonised is fading, it is being replaced by a sense of
imminent history — it is growing a pedigree from scratch . . .
as if the departed tenants had no more claim on it than the
delivery drivers who take cars out to their new owners and
put the clock back to zero. The tenants — 'temporary people'
in the words of a lady Brahmin — will always be on the road
somewhere, being passed by.

In its rehabilitation back into respectability, the Islington
square was recovered as property; for the middle-class residents it was *place* as something to purchase and own, where
for the departing tenants it had been a place to borrow,
squat on, or move through. North London is dull and upright
at heart; temporariness and mobility are frowned on, and
the signals of their existence — cafés, restaurants, bars as
meeting points rather than local pubs, take-away food stores,
boutiques, bedsitter agencies — are few and dingy. Tran-
sients there live a furtive and persecuted existence, regarded
as the flotsam of the city; and people hope that they will be
swept back to sea on the next tide. The most evident kind
of transience is the transience of failure — the shady car dealer,
the inept con man, the tramp dossing in the condemned
basement, the balding lodger who flits on rent day — and it
is against this that the white city of permanence, property,

thrift, and cleanliness is, in large part, a fortress. The exaggerated neighbourliness of the pioneers, their attempt to turn Islington into a cosy village of gossip, play groups, and intimate dinner parties, is a way of rejecting that other city of locomotion, dirt, discontinuity and failure.

I moved from Islington to Earl's Court, where motion and migration are the area's most constant, most evident features. It is under the flight-path to Heathrow and the pneumatic whoosh of low-flying jets punctuates the day at five-minute intervals. Container trucks speed north and south on either side of the square where I live, and the reverberation of a tube line somewhere nearby deep in the earth makes the top storey shudder on still evenings. Everyone is going somewhere. Even the area itself seems to float in a geographical vacuum: people call it, alternately 'Earl's Court', 'South Kensington', 'Chelsea', and 'Fulham', as if it too locomoted about the city, responsive to its inhabitants' self-images. But it is on the Earl's Court Road, that ravaged fiesta, where the directionless locomotion of the nomad turns into a sufficient way of life. People there have the isolated, depthless stare of returned transatlantic yachtsmen, not sure if this is land, or where the horizon ought to be. They carry most of what they own in grubby airline bags, and are blown about by the continuous eddies and tailwinds of the passing traffic. Earl's Court Road is a street of dreadful formica snackeries and chicken-and-chips takeaways. Its pubs have bloodstains on the lavatory walls; its pavements swirl with waste paper, and on Sunday mornings are streaked with thin, bilious vomit. Down narrow basements and tucked into alleys, there are dubious clubs where prostitutes lean in the hallways and boys with faces of corrupted cherubs smile winningly at fussy men of middle age who look like blackmail victims.

The quarter is temporarily coloured by a variety of tribal groups, and it changes according to the season and the time of day, for many of its most visible and vociferous inhabitants are here only for a few hours, weeks or days. In the evenings it belongs to the 'gays'; one of the few places in the city where men can fondle each other on the street. At weekends it is a meeting-point for West Indians; in summer, foreign students; Australians are always passing through – they come to Earl's Court when they first arrive in England, and put up in one of the hundreds of rank boarding houses and hotels; by day it is full of Italian waiters who work in restaurants all over London; in the small hours, it drifts into the hands of pimps, sharks and drunks, unsavoury men who watch from doorways or cruise slowly by in squashy American cars, their eyes alight for punters.

Time in Earl's Court is quite different from time in Islington. The north London square took its rhythms from the five-day week and the eight-to-six working day. Its shops opened at eight-thirty and closed at seven; and by day, women and children had the place to themselves. In Earl's Court, somewhere is open all the time; supermarkets do not close until midnight, and after that there are cafés, clubs and hot-dog stands. It does not feel strange to be an adult male on the street with nothing special to do except buy the papers at eleven in the morning – an activity that used to make me feel a bum in Islington. The only really dead time is the cold two-hour patch between 4 and 6 a.m.; an occasional London Transport worker in mittens on a bicycle, and the mechanical gurgle and squawk of a policeman's pocket radio. For the rest of the day and night, there is a continual tidal sweep of comers and goers, and they make their own suns and seasons, as if this was a completely synthesised underground city.

The square is big and grand; more than a quarter of a mile, all round, of importunate Victorian castles of yellow brick and stucco, with conservatories, slate-roofed penthouses with circular portholes, marble pillars and cream pilasters. Whenever there was an opportunity, its architects added a crazy dentistry of black spiked railings – on the ground, on balconies, or just as an ornamental frieze, to remind the lesser breeds of the teeth of nineteenth century capitalism. The pillars at each gate are square and solid enough to hold a drawbridge; and the designer of a medieval city transported

into the square might conclude that it was admirably fortified against an unspeakably barbaric and cunning enemy.
Only the flat roofs are open – attack from the air had not
been thought of – and people sunbathe there in the summer,
stuffing their ears with cotton wool to keep the noise of the
jets out of their heads.

It is a place of radical extremes. A tiny minority of its
inhabitants are very rich indeed, and live their fortified
anachronistic lives in houses so big that they hardly ever
need to leave them. Crates of wine and groceries go in to
their basement doors, green Harrods vans deliver parcelled
luxuries to flunkies, and the houses themselves seem to in-
hale these goods upwards to the double-glazed stratospheres
of their penthouses, where the only sounds, perhaps, are the
insipid rattle of the *Financial Times* and the tinkle of ice
against glass. But nearly every house was subdivided into
flats long ago, and each porch has an untidy rack of door-
bells: 'Clark', 'Kempinski', 'Durbridge', 'Mrs Andrewski',
'Plug & Rosie'. There are doorphones with buttons to press
to release the latch of the communal front door, and their
long buzz carries across to the pavements, along with the
distorted voices of the button-pushers interrogating their
callers like the furies of Gilbert Pinfold. Through some
basement windows, one can see palliasses laid on the floor,
side to side, end to end, as if this was a refugee camp
in some devastated city; so, in a sense, it is. Space is expensive, most of the young transient population cannot afford
more than a small share in a room, and property for them
means clothes, beads, records, not paint and furniture and a
private world.

Islington people live behind their housefronts, but many
of the houses on this square are just over-occupied dormi-
tories, places to doss down and brew coffee on the gas-ring.
The young here use cafés, bars, wide pavements and public
gardens as their living-room. They are improvising the
piazza life of the poor in an Italian renaissance city. The
dramatic seasonal population shift in Earl's Court runs
with the weather: in late spring, as soon as it is warm

enough to parade outdoors and sit on the pavements, the quarter swells with people. In midsummer, everywhere is a squash; there are long queues at the bank, especially around the foreign exchange desk, and you have to book in advance to get a table at a restaurant. In autumn, the streets empty and the squares are left to the pigeons and the tramps, the permanent and ubiquitous figures of urban survival in a cold climate.

The young migrants do not seek out privacy; they live on exhibition, a human counterpart to the boatshows and military tattoos which go on in the nearby concrete mausoleum of the Earl's Court Stadium. Their clothes and voices and hairstyles are garishly communicative; for in this maelstrom of tastes and conflicting identities, like has to spot like as speedily as one recognises a slogan or a poster. A girl is going by my window now; she is wearing a long, loose crushed velvet coat and octagonal spectacles with wire-thin gold rims, she carries a Red Indian bag. It is enough to go on: not my type.

Even the minority who own flats and houses, for whom the quarter is not merely a temporary stage on which to perform their brief act, go to bizarre lengths of exotic indulgence and display. Waiting for a taxi on the pavement one night, I saw a bow-windowed room full of humming birds. Lit from low down, they hovered brilliantly among the potted ferns and rubber plants, and I heard a Monteverdi record on the gramophone inside. In another house nearby, I saw a whole room converted into an aluminium cage for a monkey (and this in an area where human beings claw for a few square feet, enough to unroll a sleeping-bag in). The monkey's only companion was a huge stuffed ape in a glass case outside its cage. There are no stray cats here.

And for the very temporary, the commercial travellers and small businessmen here for one night, there are correspondingly bizarre entertainments. In the Austrian Bier-Keller, bored English girls in fishnet tights and peasant tops serve drinks at 75 pence a time with stale frankfurters (to beat the licensing regulations), while an elderly accordionist squeezes out old Beatles tunes. 'No touching, no dancing, no nothing,' says the girl, automatic as a speak-your-weight machine. By 2 a.m. the place has sucked in the overflow of drunks and scrubbers . . . 'On your own, dear? Mine's a scotch and soda – ' Men with paunches slouch about on the dance floor holding fluffy tarts in a bear-hug, and someone is noisily sick in the hallway. They have a brutish doorman to take care of that. A party of people who look suspiciously like schoolteachers sing 'Auf Wiedersehen' in Birmingham accents, and the accordionist puts on a face of ghastly jollity, exposing a jaw full of gold-capped teeth. Outside, there is a policeman, taking notes.

Earl's Court is a place where people come in order to be free of the sanctions which operate where they live; it is fiercely and commercially amoral, and utterly indifferent to the curious tastes of the temporary citizens who are out on its streets. There is a constant sexual electricity in the air, but it is sex to be bought and bargained over – everything has its price. Corner newsagents display advertising boards full of postcards : 'Exotic butterfly needs pinning', 'Intimate Swedish massage in your home or hotel,' 'Gentleman with extensive wardrobe', 'Lady gives riding lessons in private . . .', 'Beautiful cage-bird, in need of training . . .', 'Stocks and Bonds for sale . . .', 'Diving equipment . . .', 'Interesting position . . .'. Visiting cards from 'masseuses' turn up in the mail and are slipped under the back door along with appeals for jumble from the local church.

But most consistently visible of all Earl's Court people are the homosexuals. This is where the 'gay scene' is concentrated; and in the evenings, from all over London, by tube and car and motorbike, men come here dressed up in the varied uniforms of the gay ghetto : in their leathers, in peacock gear of wool and velvet, or, transformed for the night in drag, tiptupping on high heels in Jayne Mansfield shirtwaists, their faces looking like spoiled gouache paintings with rouged lips and powdered cheeks. They talk in the thieves' slang of Gayspeak – and many of their coterie

words, like *ecaf* and *riah,* are formed on exactly the same
backslang principle as Mayhew observed among East End
costermongers in 1860. They chatter loudly about 'duchesses'
and 'cottaging' (picking men up in public lavatories) and
'chicken' (under-age boys); it is a self-conscious code and is
used more boldly in Earl's Court than anywhere else in the
city.

I sometimes go to a gay club in the quarter. It is a pleasant,
civilised place with a restaurant and a dance floor, and
lighting which flatters the often middle aged faces of its
clientele. After heterosexual discotheques, what strikes one
first is the age range; the music is mainly acid rock, but
many of the men are in their fifties and sixties, cultivatedly,
rubicundly grey, like uncles. They have kept their figures,
and dance trimly with young men in French pullovers, all
snapping fingers and splayed calves. The uncles never look
tired or puffed; it is the young who are worn by fun and
end up puking in the discreetly cloistered lavatory. After
midnight, there is a drag cabaret. A fat man with henna
hair and rubber bosom obscenely mimes to a Doris Day
record, an accurate, satirical travesty of female mannerisms.
A young West Indian in the front row giggles hysterically at
the performance his head swinging from side to side, his
teeth enormously large and white under the stage lights.
The uncles smile indulgently, and pat the knees of their
companions, twinkling as uncles will.

The clubs are cosy places, out of the public eye, where the
homosexual coterie is the assured majority party and the
handful of 'straights' are a tolerated and untroublesome
minority. The pubs are different: sadder, more blatant,
bizarre. There are two large pubs just off the square; one
is a renowned meeting- and pickup-point for sado-maso-
chists, and one has a discotheque in an upper room which is
frequented by a number of transvestites as well as being a
centre of the 'teeny-bopper' sector of the gay scene. Both
are tainted with the hysterical edge of ghetto behaviour;
in them, clothes, voices, mannerisms are exaggerated and
extreme. For the pubs are both inside and outside 'straight'

society, and this marginal position forces an obsessive concern with signals and symbols, with self-announcement and ritual boundary-drawing.

Outside the sado-maso pub, twin Honda and Suzuki motorcycles are parked, leaning at a maritally identical angle. (Although many of the most conspicuous 'motorcyclists' actually arrive by tube, goggled and helmeted against the onrush of foetid air in the tunnels.) Inside, there are men zipped invisibly into one-piece black leather suits as thin as contraceptive sheaths. They wear peaked jockey caps, and their smooth figures are broken only by the bulges of their codpieces. Smart greying men cruise among them, buying drinks.

'I have some interesting colour slides of my body. I have been crucified three times, and the scars are very vivid . . .' The voice at my elbow is genteel and businesslike, the voice of an efficient tax-accountant. He skims through a Kodak wallet of slides.

'A view from the . . . rear –'

We peer together at the slide, holding it against the light over the dartboard.

'Very interesting.'

'That one came out particularly well.'

A pudgy yellow body, mottled by a sunray lamp; the scars and weals are exaggeratedly highlighted with cosmetics.

'Would you like to see some more?'

I am told that here you can employ a young man who will dress up in the costume of a Victorian chambermaid and do *petit-point* on your testicles . . . Or the 'chastity-belt' – a contraption into which you are locked by your partner and which prevents its wearer from urinating. After two days, people are said to howl with the pain. In this pub there are lounging Hell's Angels, six and a half feet tall, with a frogging of silver chains on their leather jackets and the jaws of rapacious imbeciles. Beside them stand small wiry men with pointed noses, narrow mouths and tinted spectacles; they look like artists with a razor or a dentist's drill.

These are, of course, only the outstandingly visible few; most of the people who come to the pub are shabby and unremarkable, but in the ghetto the tone is set by a florid minority of self-conscious symbolists. The rest of the inhabitants cluster round them, both protected and vicariously defined by a uniform which needs to be worn by only a few militant boundary-markers. Just as the leather men determine the character of one pub, so a few men in full drag dominate the other, whose upper room exudes a frumpish air of naughtiness. Besides the transvestites, it is full of boys with dyed blonde bouffant hair, sleeveless knitted pullovers, and adenoidal camp voices.

'Ooh! Never been felt up that way before. Ooh, both sides!'

Men dance with each other cheek to cheek, between groups of trim, over-youthful looking pickups, fresh from the gymnasium, who bay and squeal like goats. The transvestites go for a faded baby-doll look, all powder puffs and frilly petticoats; when they cross the floor, they travesty the bottom-wiggling, bust balancing shuffle of 1950s starlets. Everyone goes to the 'Ladies' lavatory, from which real women emerge in a state of evident shock. Here are the same cruising grey bachelors, shyly affable, reaching deep for drinks all round. They have cars and flats – 'my place, just round the corner' – and are solicitously interested in everybody.

'Been to sea again, Terry?'

'How's your mother, my dear?'

'How nasty for you . . .'

'Oh, dear.'

The bespectacled student who sells *Gay News* gets rapturously booed; there is a civil war in the homosexual world, and it is hard to tell who is on whose side. *Gay News* editorials adjure everyone to 'pull together', while the more sober *Lunch* presses for respectability and invisibility. While there is a certain amount of free flow between the two pubs, their hard-core customers are edgily hostile to each other. The Hell's Angels stare balefully across the road at the transvestites, and there is a bristling quarrelsomeness about which

shows up in brief, high-pitched arguments and quick scuffles.
When the pubs close, their separate clienteles spill out on
to the pavements, and police vans settle in the side-streets,
their lights off, their occupants attentive for trouble. There
are occasional arrests, and sometimes one hears screams,
and goes on reading.

Beneath this surface of flaunting self-advertisement and
baroque spectacle, there is a cowed indigenous life. Artfully
styled and hidden between the tall Victorian houses there
are blocks of council flats; and in the square itself many of
the shabbier flats are rent-controlled. For poor families, this
is a bad place to live; the local shops are expensive, the
streets are dangerous, and thieving and thuggery are part
of the essential pattern of life in the area. Elderly couples
hurry nervously arm in arm, keeping close in on the pavements. They chain their doors and answer with a single suspicious eye. They have good reason. There is a rising statistic
of pensioners who get battered in by strange young men;
the motiveless murder of old people is one of the most damn-
ing facts of city life — especially in areas like this, where
the young are in power and the old are frightened into making
themselves pitifully inconspicuous. Their church and church
hall are regularly vandalised. They seem to have resigned
themselves to having been left behind, while the quarter
changed from a dingily genteel place of lodging houses and
solid cheap flats to the freak show it often seems now.

By the 1920s, this had become an unfashionable suburb.
Middleton Murry had a flat just round the corner from
where I live now, and was thought to be very much out of
things, sequestered in a place where only thrifty maiden
aunts were supposed to live, neither Kensington nor Chelsea
solely distinguished by the long, crumbling gothic strip of
Brompton Cemetery. The quarter was characterless, com-
bining the worst and shoddiest elements of the more fashionable districts which abut on it. Now it is this very lack of a
fixed identity which has made Earl's Court so aggressively
metropolitan. It is changeable, corrupt and florid. It belongs
to no-one. Like a colonial state with a daily history of coups

and counter-coups, it goes through cycles of factional ascen-
dancies.

Everybody here is marginal – and to be old, or poor, or have
a regular job is to be both as odd and as ordinary as to
be a drag quean or a leather freak. In this part of the city,
no-one is normal, and each person is forced, by this condition of splintered isolation from the larger community, into
self-scrutiny and self-consciousness. There may be moments,
in the pub or club, or with one's neighbours, when one
seems to be comfortably entrenched in a group – but the
conviction easily dissolves during the course of a walk along
the block, and a succession of wary eye-encounters with
strangers who might as well be Eskimos or Hottentots for all
they appear to have in common with oneself.

Earl's Court people are distinguished by the way in which
the details of their lives do not match up. They are chame-
leons, and it is hard to guess how they must look when they
move outside this quarter. They are temporary; no-one asks
where they come from or go to; they leave no spaces behind
them when they move, only unpaid bills and unopened cir-
culars. For many of them, Earl's Court has been a place
to disappear into, and their brief showing here has left an
unexplained gap somewhere else.

To stay here is to be a rarity. I have lived on the square
for over a year now, and the milkman, the postman, and
some of the shopkeepers and restaurateurs know my name,
and they use it as if they and I were accomplices, sticking it
out while the rest of the world goes by. In most places, a
year is a very short time, but in Earl's Court it is an unusual
stretch of continuity, a hint of unaccustomed order. It often
seems that here all the divisive and fragmentary qualities,
intrinsic to the life of a metropolitan city, have come to a
pustular head: Earl's Court is the acid test – people who can
like it are true city-dwellers, I think.

It commands a form, a way of thinking and feeling, quite
different from that of Islington. It is possible to tell the
story of the square in north London; it has a history, and its
fortunes have been relatively consistent, just as they have

been wholly dependent on the manner in which the square has been regarded as property to be bought or leased. But the square in Earl's Court does not lend itself to narrative. Its history stopped when householders could no longer afford squads of servants – somewhere between 1920 and 1930. Now it needs a patchwork quilt of intrusions, guesses and observations to get anywhere near its truth. It is diverse, random, out of time, even out of place (it is too many different times and places). It is nearly all show, and it is impossible to root for the 'real' faces behind the carnival masks. Casual consumption and extravagance – the air of a perverted and garish resort – have endowed it with a deeply pervasive unreality. There are no community sanctions, except of the most official kind, and even formal agencies like the police seem lax and ready to turn a number of blind eyes. It is as easy to drown here unnoticed as it is to evade the law, the social authorities, or one's family. You are on your own, on your wits. Living here is lonely, potentially dangerous even. It is all possibility. In this quarter, one is plagued by the intuition that you are free to destroy yourself with your own fantasies, and that, in a large city, the most free of all communities, nobody – unless you fall grossly foul of the Inland Revenue or the Police – will do very much to rescue or deter you.

But this is always a necessary consequence of individual freedom; and people who hate cities (they would be certain to loathe Earl's Court and see it as living evidence of the dystopia they believe industrial cities are leading us towards) are surely right when they interpret them as the enemies of decent family life of community constraints, of 'public morals'. It is possible, however, to prefer the freedom of a place like this, with all its hazards, to the forced constrictions of the small town or organically conceived suburb. No-one in their right mind would see anything utopian in Earl's Court: its freedom is badly scarred, commercially exploited, licentious. It affords indifference not tolerance; it is a tribal wilderness not a community. On a summer night here you catch the rank stink of decadence – a combination of greasy banknotes, hasty expensive sex and stale whisky – a city smell, pungent and sweet, like the bad air of ancient Rome which Gibbon tasted as a prophecy. Yet here, for the lucky and the provident, a kind of private life is possible, a life of small freedoms away from curiosity and censure. That, given we have lost so much elsewhere, seems a good which should not be undervalued.

NINE

One American City

At ten o'clock on Saturday night, the old black man and his wife set up their piles of *Boston Sunday Herald-Americans* at the corner of Inman Square. But this is not a square; it's a deserted intersection, eerily darkened because of the Energy Crisis. The blacks, wrapped up like parcels against the December weather, have no customers. They flap their arms forlornly to keep warm, mooch five steps up the street, and five steps back. A big yellow car with a jagged fender skips the red light and heads towards whatever action there may be in downtown Boston. Crossing the road to get to the Gaslight Pub. I notice a laundry-bundle in a doorway which, seeing me, gets up and turns into the remains of a woman; a stunted thing with a big head and a frizzy mop of ochre-coloured hair. She starts singing gibberish first at me, then at her reflection in the glass of a shop door. Only the word 'babylove' is distinguishable.

'Babyloveshamingamingaliveaplingalove.' And cackles at me, her face as creased as Auden's. But something about the mouth is still only in its late teens or very early twenties; it has the raw-meat floppiness of adolescence.

'Is-scher-schplitzer-mishder-kwicks-a-schpearer-quarter.'

I hurry past.

'Fuck you!'

In the pub that is not a pub in the square that is not a square, there is an amiable seedy huddle around the bar. Plaid donkey jackets, a couple of tarts who look as though they've strayed in from the 1950s, one or two crimped under-fed faces from the Great Depression, and a man with a watch chain and hat from another era altogether. The rest of the place is laid out like a workman's café, in barren lines of tables and chairs. There's an unplayed-at club pool table with bald baize, a glass phone kiosk that looks as if it had been smuggled in off the street, and an electric tennis machine that has a cardiogram for a face and is hungry for quarters. Everything is out of kilter. Nothing in the room, except for the plaid jackets, comes together.

It takes a few minutes to notice the three men at separate tables, they are so still, so much a part of the bar furniture. Each one has his head sunk into his chest, an empty bottle of Schlitz on the table in front of him. Their coats trail in straight lines from shoulders to floor. Their eyes are closed tight as zip-fasteners. The man nearest to me seems to have forgotten his lips; they twitch and blink as if he were speaking in tongues. His thumb mashes what's left of a stale bagel to dust on the tabletop.

Outside on the street, the black couple are doing a joyless shuffle-dance on the sidewalk, like a lumpish parody of Fred Astaire and Ginger Rogers. Business is bad. They blow on their hands and gaze uptown for car lights. Nothing doing.

The Gaslight Pub, with its browbeaten collection of people and things in the wrong time and the wrong place, is true to the spirit of Boston as a city – a raw, dislocated place that never seems to quite come right. It is not even a city, exactly; rather, it is a shabby galaxy of more or less independent townships. Boston proper has less than three-quarters of a million inhabitants, but 'metropolitan Boston' is as big as Birmingham, swollen by more than a dozen separate 'communities' which have kept their autonomy ever since the Puritans settled in the area in the seventeenth century. They have their own town meetings, their own police forces, schools, courts, newspapers. Boston has a metropolitan economy and metropolitan-scale commuter routes – a gigantic tangle of expressways, subways and streetcar lines. But it has never coalesced into a metropolitan city. Its style is resolutely small-town — small-town emptiness, small-town sprawl, small-town isolation; it exudes the wet Sunday afternoon atmosphere of the dull province where there's no place to go, no big-city freedom, no glamour. Everything about Boston — its architecture and size, its strange concentration of eccentric talents — should have made it an exciting city. But no. That is not what Boston wanted. It craved discreet uneventfulness, the calm of a vast, woody suburb. Like so many American cities, it has succeeded in landing itself up in a terrible, anomalous mess.

When I first arrived here for a three-month stay, I was lost in a labyrinth of names and boundaries that were quite incomprehensible to an outsider. There was a fifteen-minute taxi ride from the airport on a looping expressway, through tunnels, on flyovers, past an architecture of ruddy brick, white-painted wood, sharp angles, bowfronts, balconies, pretty spires and small clusters of skyscrapers that looked as if they had been hired from New York for the day. There were changes of colour and texture in the journey, but were these the outskirts or the city centre? I couldn't tell. We crossed a river, and on all sides I saw the same jerky, up-and-down look. *There* must be the centre . . . no *there;* but there was no area of sufficient intensity on the skyline to be sure. We stopped at the great redbrick shoebox of an apartment house where I was to be living. This was . . . Boston? No, Cambridge. But isn't Cambridge a part of Boston? No, Cambridge is Cambridge. A few days before, I'd read in the English papers of the murder of a woman by immolation on a vacant lot in Boston. Was that near here? No, that was in Roxbury. Is Roxbury part of Boston? Well, sort of . . . yes, you could say Roxbury is a part of Boston. How far from here? About, oh, three miles. My second night, still giddy with these names, there was a huge fire in Chelsea; we could see the flames from the top of our block. But Chelsea, of course, is not in Boston, and it's not even next door to Cambridge, so the fire was none of our business : it was an interesting blaze in another country, to hear about on the radio.

Never have I been so confined to quarters. It was like

being back at boarding school, for nearly everywhere turned
out to be out of bounds. The newcomer to the American
city finds himself being constantly buttonholed by his acquaintances. 'How well do you actually *know* Boston?' they
inquire, as if you were not to be trusted with your frivolous
European idea of the freedom of the city. Then come the
warnings. 'You mustn't think it's like London, you know.' By
the end of the first day, I had learned that I was not to
cross the river, go on to or beyond the Cambridge Common;
that I could go to Harvard Square, but not as far as Central
Square, a mile further down. Somerville, the neighbouring
'community' was unsafe. I must not take taxis, they were
much too expensive, and I mustn't ride on the subway because
a lot of people were getting mugged there. I found that
I was stuck, and that during daylight hours only, with an
area of about a square mile; a small, frustrating cell of city
space, beset by phantoms on every side.

Within a few days, these boundaries had become as real
and oppressive as the walls of a ghetto. They enclosed
Harvard University and a few leafy suburban streets of
wooden mansions, their fronts as full of rigging, balconies
and quarter-decks as Mississippi steamboats. There were lots
of nice old ladies who got blown along the sidewalks with
the fall leaves, their voices dry and querulous – the characteristic note of the old Boston accent, genteel as an embroidery
needle stitching a sampler. There were rangy students, and
triumphantly androgynous young women, and squat European
sages in berets and mufflers, but there was no sense at all of
a city. Here was 'The Square', 'The Yard'; one department
store, two cinemas, a clutch of second-rate restaurants . . .
enough, perhaps, to make a life, but the life would have the
small, defensive certitude of a scholarly village parson's.
You could enclose it in a little glass dome, adding water and
a snowstorm of plastic chips, then sell it in the gift shop on
Brattle Street: 'A Souvenir from Harvard College.'

It is a pretty toy ghetto. Like a nanny's frightening stories
of the outside world, designed to keep the children safe
inside the nursery, there are scary rumours about the rest of

the city. Everywhere else in Greater Boston, so it would seem,
is the exclusive territory of some group, patrolled by vigilantes
on the lookout for strangers like you. Never go to Roxbury or
Dorchester, or you will be murdered by 'the blacks' . . . in
the North End, the Italians will get you . . . in Somerville,
the poor whites . . . in Chelsea, the poor Jews . . . in Brookline, the rich Jews . . . on the back of Beacon Hill, the
junkies . . . on the front of Beacon Hill, the Brahmins . . .
and if you go near water, you will be bitten by the snapping
turtles. A graduate student, who had displayed no other
signs of insane paranoia, solemnly asserted that the Back
Bay 'had been taken over by the Jews'. From the perspective
of Cambridge, Boston is a chequerboard of enemy camps, and
anyone who moves from his square is taking his life in his
hands.

Yet, looking over the city from the safe vantage point of the
restaurant on the fifty-second floor of the Prudential Center,
all I could see was miles and miles of the same, infinitely
extended small town – low, bricky, sprouting elms and maples
in every available gap between the buildings. The two tallest
blocks in Boston are owned by rival insurance companies –
the stockily provincial Prudential building and the rakish,
slender, very New York, John Hancock Tower – and that
seems appropriate for the city, with its detached suburban
spaciousness, its deceptive owner-occupier air. Dogs . . .
year-old cars . . . the funny-sections of the Sunday *Globe* . . .
a night out at a family movie, followed by the weary exotica
of sweet-and-sour pork and chicken chop suey. I went underground, to Filene's basement, where women squabble over
cut-price frocks, upending themselves in floral heaps of mark
downs. It all seemed a long way from the nightmare city
I had been warned of by experienced Bostonians; a place
where, I would have thought, one was more likely to die
from dullness than from gunshot wounds.

Crime figures, of all statistics, are the most misusable; but
Boston's do raise an ugly question mark over my innocent
perception of the city's tedious homeliness. There were 136
murders here in 1973, a number that climbs appallingly

close to the annual death toll in the Ulster war (something over 200). Even inside Cambridge's glass globe, with the snow settling prettily over the Colonial churches, the nightmare was coming real. Across the street from Longfellow's house with its elegant pilasters, a Harvard professor's wife was dragged screaming into a park and shot. Another woman was blinded when a man rammed a broken brick into her face. On Thanksgiving Day, a robber with a gun was threatening people in the apartment house where I was staying; he rode away with his loot on a yellow ten-speed bicycle, a travelling man, from another part of town. In November, the fire-raisers were on our avenue, setting light to heaps of gasoline-soaked newspapers in garages.

As the catalogue of these events, some tragic, others merely ominous and dispiriting, grew longer, so they seemed to thicken the brickwork of the walls of our ghetto. Illogically, they made the boundaries even tighter. They did not so much make Cambridge a bad place, as strengthen our terrors of Roxbury and Dorchester and Somerville. Evil deeds were attributed to outsiders; they were taken as signs of what happens when the rottenness of the city beyond the walls reaches into the protected Eden of 'our neighbourhood'. They just went to show that Nanny was right. As the fall wore on, we huddled closer to each other, telling bloodcurdling stories at dinner parties, praying that the phantoms of the city at large would withdraw to their proper quarters and leave us safe inside our globe.

With a borrowed car, all windows up and doors securely locked from the inside, I did some timid trespassing. I crossed the river into a scrawny landscape of marsh, abandoned gas stations, and craven redbrick public housing projects that looked like vandalised urinals. Wire-mesh fencing bulged and tottered; the sidewalks were cracked and broken, and the roads seemed subject to a continuous, mild volcanic action — a subterranean bubbling of earth and water which might at any moment simply swallow what little human life was left. The people I saw looked too vanquished for violence. A great deal of English poverty is borne amiably, with the air of long, tolerant habituation. No London slum has the raw, exposed, beaten appearance of these sinks of American urban poverty. Nobody was making an attempt to keep up, to put on their best face; there were no lone geraniums, no flowers of any kind. Broken glass lay where it had fallen out of windows, half-covered with straggling tendrils of tangle-weed. Black women were leading their children to an evangelist's shack (it was a Sunday afternoon); their faces had gone to the livid purple of a bruise in the cold.

But this was not a place in Boston's mythology; it was a nowhere, a bit of seedy emptiness in the shadow of an expressway, too dead and desolate to warrant a name. An American woman was scornful of my shock. 'It's just a public housing project; you've seen nothing. They're all like that. That's not *Roxbury*.' I had thought it was – at least, I wanted to go nowhere that was worse. I like cities on principle; but in America, my liking was rapidly turning sour, my enthusiasm was beginning to seem to me glib and blinkered.

Roxbury – real Roxbury – shocks in the most unexpected way of all. I knew exactly what a 'black ghetto' was. It was the steep scabrous tenements of Harlem, the intense, murky street-life, as thick with infection and activity as a slide of pond mud under a microscope. It was close clumps of grey concrete high rises, built on the ash-and-brick ruins of older slums. I was not prepared for a ghetto that was a precise mirror image of the ghetto from which I had come – another dainty suburb fresh from the gift shop in the December sun.

Roxbury was the first and the sweetest of the nineteenth-century 'streetcar suburbs' of Boston. Every wooden cottage had a baby country estate for its backyard; its whiteness shone through a tangle of greenery, and, rocking on the balconied porch with the *Evening Transcript,* one would have looked out over a dreamland where all the nicest people lived in the nicest possible American way. This was the garden where Adam could buy a tidy lot with a gabled doll's house set square in its centre. He could fall asleep with green shutters murmuring in a country breeze and, in the

morning, ride the car into town. To his ear, 'Roxbury' and
'rus in urbe' ran tranquilly into a single word. The com-
manding spires of the Unitarian churches, with their genial
ethical theology of God, Man and Nature all in harmony,
were fitting landmarks in this innocently prelapsarian quarter of the city.

The churches, the houses, the tall trees on the streets, are
there still. The paint is pocky, much of the wood is rotten,
and slats of shingling have fallen away exposing the skeletal
frames, but the basic lineaments of the old dream are clear
enough even now. It takes a few minutes before you notice
that the windows are mostly gone and only a few shutters
are left. Each house stares blindly through eyes of cardboard
and torn newspaper. Burn marks run in tongues up their
sides, and on most blocks there is a gutted shell, sinking
onto its knees in a flapping ruin of blackened lath and tar-
paper. Our own century has added rows of single-storey
brick shacks, where bail-bondsmen and pawnbrokers do their
business. What were once front lawns are now oily patches
of bare earth. The carcases of wrecked Buicks, Chevrolets
and Fords are jacked up on bricks, their hoods open like
mouths, their guts looted. No-one is white. Stopped at the
lights, I am inspected blankly by the drivers alongside me.
A kid on the sidewalk yells 'Honky! . . . Hey, Honky!'

It is hard not to feel both scared and guilty. One should
not trespass, and this is no place for tourists. This is not my
country, my city, or my quarter; probably the most one can
learn from a voyeuristic trip like this is that there are parts
of other people's cities that are as inhospitable and remote
as moon-craters. If I had believed before in a city-freedom
that permits everyone to roam into other social worlds, here
was proof of the reality of those boundaries about which
I'd been so sceptical. I was in the wrong place and anxious
to get out.

Yet Roxbury was like an optical maladjustment, a troubling
double image; each time one looked at it one saw a pretty
tranquil suburb and an angry wound – each image stubbornly
refused to take precedence. Its prettiness turned into an

insult, its anger into an irony. Much of its incongruity seemed perversely deliberate. The word *KILL* spray-gunned on a wall had been executed with a sign-painter's shapely precision. A family on the sidewalk arranged itself as formally as a portrait-group in an early American painting. The speed of the traffic was slow and stately in comparison to the precipitate, shoving style of most Boston driving. A very slight blurring of vision, and one might be in that ideal pastoral place which Cambridge has tried so hard to be and failed.

I got back to our apartment block. The air in the corridors is thick, burnt and biscuity; the walls are thin, the lifts shudder and creak. With the mythological arbitrariness that is Boston's special gift, it has been consecrated as a respectable middle-class place in a 'good area'. But were a blind-folded man to be driven to it, and allowed to look only when he was inside the hall, he would say with some certainty that he was in a ruinous tenement. It might just as well be a den of thieves living off welfare and plunder as a den of teachers, psychoanalysts, secretaries and small-businessmen. What counts here, though, is the mythology. There is a logic that dictates why rich Bostonians should cluster in the splendid Georgian houses round Louisberg Square on Beacon Hill. But why should the Italians all cram themselves behind the expressway in the North End? Why should Negroes live in Roxbury, and Jews in Chelsea? By what law do Boston suburbs turn into rigidly circumscribed ghettoes, when they look so much alike, so quaintly attractive, so prim, so dull? For it is as if someone had taken a map of the city and, resolutely blind to its topography, had coloured in irregularly shaped lumps labelled 'Blacks', 'Jews', 'Irish', 'Academics', 'Gentry', 'Italians', 'Chinese', 'Assorted Others'.

Clearly the civic authorities are very keen on ghettoes. On the Fitzgerald Expressway, there is an exit sign marked 'To Chinatown'. One then has to weave through a sign-posted maze, one's expectations rising as the trip to this obviously important place lengthens. Just off Washington Street, there are a few Chinese restaurants, oriental groceries and Hong Kong kitsch shops. They are dwarfed by looming warehouses, and one would barely notice them if one had not been alerted by the string of signs. The Bell Telephone Company has chipped in with phone boxes rigged out as pagodas, and the National Shawmut Bank advertises itself with illuminated Mandarin characters. 'Chinatown' is a fake ghetto, an exercise in official image-projection. But in a city that has so many real ghettoes, why should it have seemed desirable to fabricate one?

There are some answers to these questions to be sniffed out in the ghetto in which I was staying. All Cambridge academic life bears down on Harvard Square, a queer grey tangle of spotlights, kiosks, pretentious neo-Georgian architecture and telegraph wires. Winds collect here, laden with garbage; so do automobiles, hippie-entrepreneurs selling political stick-ons, candles, pottery and fortunes, Salvation Army bands, boys waiting for their girls, and sandwich-board men grim with cold, deep in conversation with topknotted religious fanatics. Here all routes collide, and one might on first glance mistake the square for the local version of Piccadilly Circus. But it is not. Rather it is Cambridge's village green. Here one bumps into the people one was having dinner with last night; the phrase 'Oh, *hi'* whines and tinkles all round. In the tobacconist's, a drink is fixed, at the subway entrance, a supper-date for next week.

For the first few days, this smallness seems delightful, then it starts to suffocate. For Cambridge, with its intense, pressured containedness, repeats itself like a mouse's wheel. At dinner after dinner, the same knot of intelligent, ironic faces; the same topics of conversation; the same wry jokes. There are half a dozen celebrities held in common by the village, and in gossip they loom infinitely larger than life; practice and study have made their every twitch and gesture famous, so that stories about them hinge on the teller's discovery of a new tiny detail that will become public and accrete to the myth. On those rare occasions when the celebrities are actually present (they are heavily in demand, greedily hoarded, and unwillingly shared around among the villagers), there is a breathless unease: with X leaning heavily over the claret at the far end of the table, Jack has to be kicked by his wife before he stops telling his great story about X which went down so well at the Herzbergers last week. The famous village dead still live on in gossip, like the ancestors who brood over conversations in the bars of Irish hamlets. Professor Perry Miller stalks by candlelight nightly, at a score of Harvard parties. Every inflection of his has been perfected and preserved in mimicry; and the manner of his dying is told, again and again, with a reverent Shakespearian regard for irony, narrative and pathos. As Longfellow knew, there are great consolations for the man who dies popular at Harvard; one kind of immortality, at least, is guaranteed for him.

The tightly circumscribed limits of conversation correspond exactly to those limits which forbade me to travel to Somerville and Roxbury. They stake out Cambridge and its confines against the rest of Boston. But I was not at Harvard, I was a visitor on its fringes and lacked the anchor of a position to keep me safe inside the walls. I made a point of breaking bounds, lunching several days a week in Boston proper. 'You go to lunch in *Boston?*' I might as well have said that I was going to a favourite Howard Johnson's in Woonsocket. The journey takes twelve minutes, and costs a dime, on the subway – about half the cost and half the time of a trip from where I live in England to a lunch-date in London.

But there is a deep suspicion in Cambridge that the name of Perry Miller might lose some of its shine at the wrong end of the subway – that in Boston certain persons might not even have *heard* of Professor Miller.

Indeed, in Boston, Cambridge does seem to recede into a far, upriver distance. Sometimes I lunched at the Tavern Club, a generous, genial, timbered place in a secret alley off Boston Common. Its members are lawyers, painters, publishers, newspapermen; its tone is worldly and jovial. Under a chandelier at a huge round table, it is easy to slide crabwise back into the old, compact, genteel city of the nineteenth century. Talk here is much more rangy and unbuttoned than in Cambridge; appetites, of every kind, are more expansive. Yet there is still a curious sense that one is somehow living in miniature. Across the Common, with its frozen, greying turf and modest statuary, lie the State House, law courts, and Athenaeum Library. The offices of the two major Boston publishers, Little, Brown and Houghton Mifflin, are close by; so are the headquarters of the Boston *Globe* and *Christian Science Monitor*. For most of the men at lunch, work is only a digestive stroll away. Many of them now live in the country or the outer suburbs, but a good number still have houses on Beacon Hill, or, another short step across the public Gardens, in Back Bay. 'Oh, you've come in from *Cambridge?*' The candles flicker on the chandelier; the wine passes round the table. I feel like a traveller, short of suitable tales about the land from which I've come; perhaps a remark or two about how the weather was when I left Cambridge would be in order.

In London, villaging is an expensive game, played self-consciously, with a constant sense that it is an enjoyable indulgence, that it goes against the grain of the city. In Canonbury and Camden Town, it's largely an evening hobby valued precisely because most people spend most of the day trekking through areas of the city far from their own quarter. But the Boston 'village' is stiflingly real – and the word *village,* fitting enough, perhaps, for privileged places like Harvard and the Tavern Club, turns into a bleak irony when tagged to Roxbury, Dorchester or Somerville. One man's village is another's ghetto, and both proceed from a single vision of what the city ought to be.

During the 1860s and 1870s there was real local pride in Boston's success as a metropolis. The suburbs of Roxbury and Dorchester voted to annex themselves to the central city, to share its bigness and bustle, to help pay for the new civic amenities – the concert halls, monuments, transit systems. But the 'annexation movement' soon wore through.

Brookline voted to stay separate, so did Cambridge, Somerville and the others. Enthusiasm for the city is not an American weakness. The independent township, 'the small, self-contained center of life' (in the words of the southern agrarian manifesto *I'll Take My Stand*) is where most Americans would prefer to stake out the perimeters of their backyards. They may need the enlarged economy and technology of the big city to earn their living, but, by hook or crook, they'll sleep where the grass and the trees are. The *neighbourhood* is all-important; the city is a mere abstraction – vague, threatening, impersonal. The crazy-quilt of town-lines that enmeshes Greater Boston flies in the face of visible fact. But the further the city spreads and congeals, the more passionately do people cling to 'communities' which are really only nostalgic dreams and historical relics.

By sheer force of will, Bostonians have made these ancient cartographers' divisions real, mythologising them into actuality by a massive conspiracy of Cartesian concentration. They have had local taxes to help them, so that Brookline, for instance, was able to spend $1,470 per pupil in its schools in 1970-71, while Somerville only managed $756. There were comparable inequalities of expenditure on policing, streetlighting, garbage disposal and fire services. Taxes diverted in the interests of an ideology are powerful weapons. As one stands on Beacon Street, midway between Cambridge and Somerville, one is suspended between two quite different worlds. Behind one, there are shady avenues and handsome houses; new cars, faces bathed in all the creams that keep skin soft and youthful, an air of proper and discreet prosperity. In front, the streets narrow to alleys, the temperature is colder, rubbish skids across soiled sidewalks, and people have the bent, furtive look of habitual scurriers, always on the lookout for trouble. To a European, these sudden abrupt transitions within the city are amazing; he can measure to the inch where poverty stops and starts, and soon learns to translate these maplike lines into other, more subtle divisions of race and nationality. It takes much longer to realise that these boundaries are simply and effectively enforced by a mad system of tax differentials.

Yet behind the madness lies a dream of an independent life away from the destructive abstraction of the city. The ghettoes – or villages – are real because Boston, in common with the majority of American cities, feared the unmanageable bigness of New York or London. It has tried to remain a little city on a hill, surrounded by a pretty cluster of small towns and villages. To do so, it has had, like the city-elders in Plato's Republic, to conscientiously fake its history, its geography, its economy, even the individual memories of its citizens. A painter in Cambridge, whom I spoke to because he was mounting a campaign to shift the Kennedy Memorial Library to the far side of the river Charles (where it would turn into Boston's problem), said sadly : 'Ten years ago, Cambridge was a village. Everybody knew each other. Now look at it.' *Ten* years? That was not true fifty years ago, or even a hundred years ago, when W. D. Howells used the place as a setting for his *Suburban Sketches*. Mythological taboos and hectic rounds of dinner parties make ghettoes, not villages.

Nor am I using 'ghetto' lightly. The preserved, exemplary lives of Cambridge and Beacon Hill have been instrumental in making Roxbury what it is. And Roxbury is a real ghetto. Brookline, Cambridge, and the rich end of Boston have dug a deep moat around it, isolating it with fear and rumour. The constituent parts of Boston are now so separated, and so inequitably served, that it is almost impossible to imagine the place ever coming together again as a city. Expressways and rapid transit systems will not connect it up when the Bostonian's whole habit of mind is superstitiously bent on staying out, on sticking to his village, on loathing what 'the city' stands for in America at present. Ironically, Boston has succeeded in attracting big-city problems to itself like flies, while it lacks nearly all of the big-city virtues. There is no freedom of movement in it; socially, it is as tight as three separate drawing-rooms with a warren of unspeakable quarters below stairs. It has no flair, and its surprises are nearly always unpleasant ones. In Harvard and MIT it has two of the best universities in the country, it has a superb symphony orchestra, some of the finest libraries, a marvellously varied architectural texture in its individual buildings (though they, too, never cohere into a recognisable city). Yet it stays stubbornly beset by the conviction that it is better not to be a city; it is a great, sluggardly, anomalous Peter Pan of a place, which has preferred never to grow up.

If one belongs somewhere in it, one is very lucky. The people in the Gaslight Pub had the weary, peculiarly Boston look of those who fit nowhere. They too were on the boundary line between Cambridge and Somerville, but they had fallen through. Without a village, without even a ghetto, they were people of the gaps between, with little more than their dislocation in common. That may be the hardest of all Boston fates, even, perhaps the most frequent, certainly the strongest charge with which the place might be indicted – to be a citizen without a city.

TEN

The Foreign Girl

Can I say my thinkings now?

I wouldn't like in your story a unhappy, a misery girl, a sad girl.

Because London can give to a clever girl lots and lots of things to make up. Loud voices, noices, and that terrible crowd (able to make me headache) walking along the streets.

Why not a girl with feelings-melange?

Just like a Gainsborough's landscape. With shadows and lights in the same time.

Just too, like this Covent Garden's market and a smart hotel restaurant where a man play piano wonderfully.

But in this case is difficult to know which of the both is the light.

The girl must ask to herself this question living in a town so extravagant and changeable.

It's the first letter I write in your language.

Why to believe so much in words?

Letter from Mayte

She trailed a silver bag with the name of the Sweet Sixteen Boutique picked out on it in black art-deco letters, and her *A-Z of London and Suburbs* was always open, bulging over the hump of her thumb. Some places she knew : Piccadilly, Trafalgar Square, Oxford Circus . . . the rest was a labyrinth, this city that spread beyond the final termini of the underground railways like a vast grey slurry of lava. She would come up escalators out of the earth, stunned : each station that she stopped at broke open on the same dull sun, the same vegetable odour of diesel and sweat, the same cramped and blackened houses abutting on 24-hour launderettes. On

the Northern and Piccadilly lines, she would make abruptly
for the exit doors as another name stopped in the frame of
the carriage window. TUFNELL PARK, ARNOS GROVE,
MORNINGTON   CRESCENT,   ARSENAL,   EAST
FINCHLEY, BRENT . . . but they were all the same. Stepping
into the amazing patch of sunlight on concrete, past the
nigger who took tickets and the posters that told how many
pence you could earn if you worked for the railway company,
she would see that this was not the place. But she no longer
felt the heavy sag of disappointment. Her ascents were now
formal, mechanical : she would start to puzzle over the tube
map on the back of her *A-Z* even before the sun showed up on
the identical, appalling street, full of the old and ugly jab-
bering at each other in a language that sounded as if they were
chewing over mouthfuls of broken glass.

On her first day in London, she asked newsagents for
papers in her own language.

'*Die Welt?*'

'No, no, not that a-one.'

Osservatore Romano, Der Spiegel, Paris Match, Pravda . . .
they flashed by, quicker and quicker at each showing, a
waterfall of languages. Then came ones in characters she
only dimly recognised – Arabic, Greek, even Chinese.

'No. Is not the one.'

'It'd be a blackie lingo, then? Or one of them middle
eastern tongues?'

'Pardon?'

'We have them regularly on order for the Persians and the
Paki Stans.'

She listened carefully, trying the sounds out again in her
head, but they didn't seem to make sense. The man looked
pleased with himself in the sun. He had a tattoo. A low-class
man.

'I . . .' he pointed to himself, 'no . . .' he shook his head,
'help . . .' he paused, thought, and just repeated the word,
but more loudly, 'you . . .' and he stabbed his forefinger at
her, grinned at his performance, hawking around the passers-
by for an audience.

'Is okay. Thank you.'

On the down-escalator of Queensway station, she had to dab at her eyes with a used Kleenex. It came away carboned with mascara. She rode to Marble Arch and looked up the name in her dictionary. An *axtl* made of *chzlim*. And then, in the sun again, across a smoky ravine of automobiles, she saw the *axtl chzlimbo* by itself on an island, like an illustration of a word in an elementary schoolbook. It was lovely. It had no reasons attached to it: nothing went through it, it wasn't a gate to anywhere . . . it was just there, solid, sunlit, a marvel. She leaned on the railing, took out her notebook from the Sweet Sixteen bag, and wrote carefully: MARBLF ARCH AXTL CHZLIMBO. She would come here again.

In the wide street of shops, there were many windows. She passed rich ladies stepping out of limousines, youths with rucksacks stuck over with flags, men in livery, a state politzer who smiled and did not show his gun. At Bourne and Hollingsworths, she saw a belt of pigskin with a silver buckle. It winked at her. She wanted it. Behind the glass, the furry surface of the suede looked as supple, soft and breathing as a living animal. Already she could feel it, tightening around her own waist. But the distance between her and the belt was enormous; a scrubland of mines and tripwires. There would be escalators, commissionaires, words with arrows telling you to go here and there and down and up, shrugs, shouts, gibbering.

'BELT' it said in the dictionary.

'Blut,' she said. 'Beelet.' But every time she said the word, it went as shapeless and rubbery as a lump of bubble-gum in her mouth. 'Lt!' she stammered aloud on the pavement, 'Lt! Lt! Lt! Lt! Lt!'

A scented, waxy shopwalker peered at the word in her dictionary.

'Accessories, third floor.'

'Pardon?'

He pointed at the signboard. The white letters bobbed in front of her eyes like a regatta. 'Accessories,' he said. She wanted to cover her ears with her hands. He was going to shout.

'*Sorries?*'

'Ack,' he said, 'Ack-sess-*sorries*,' and the last syllables blew out of his mouth with a loose explosive crump.

She found the belt. It was lovely, dark, chocolatty.

The salesgirl jabbered at her, her face a great bright lamp that swayed on its stalk above the till, fingers rapping on the glass counter beside the spike of impaled bills.

Then they were fighting for the belt, the salesgirl jerking at its buckle, the foreign girl clinging to its soft tongue.

'You don't want it wrapped?' the salesgirl was doing eye-semaphore with her colleague in Handbags.

'I wear. I wear.'

'You'll need a receipt.'

'Pardon?'

Handbags signalled *Screw the lot of them — Yanks, Frogs, You-name-its* as she filled out a Diner's Club cheque for a Nebraskan piston-ring heiress. Belts passed the foreign girl a paper slip with a frozen shrug, and spiked its duplicate on her prong.

The belt lapped her, deep and comforting. Its buckle, a flaring silver sun, shone from the wide Vee of her groin. Suddenly private in the stew of the escalator, she touched the corrugations of the metal, felt the rough point of a sun's ray. It left a milled white mark on her fingertip. Around her bags, umbrellas, small pale children, and the heavy smell of sandalwood, air-conditioning and cologne congealed with the murmur of the machine as it took them down towards the street. The crowd was whispering in her language. *Alaxm mashook vilimbabo cosconzilim.*

She stayed in the north with the old lady and her Spainish. 'Is rich?' 'One is moderately well to do,' said the old lady, smoothing out the *Telegraph* gardening page, making the paper shriek. The lady's husband, Mr Phillips, had done

business with the girl's father. 'Flips,' her father called him.
'Tomflips.' '*Fill*-ipz, say *Fill*-ipz,' said the old lady.

'Is hard to me, Mizflips. Feel-ipz.'

'Good girl,' And the old lady pegged the bell for the
Spainish.

When Mr Phillips died of an undetected cancer in a hotel
room in West Berlin, the girl's father got the translator at
his firm to write a letter of condolence to the widow. He
whom God requireth for his great harvest . . . He whom the
thunderbolt shall strike down . . . the good die young . . .
greatest happiness in the overworld of the immortal spirits
. . . It was a fine letter, and had a rich black border. Everyone saw it before it was sent off, sprinkled on each corner
with holy water that smeared a few words into indecipherable
inky trails. The old lady wrote that she was much comforted
in her bereavement, and the girl's father, who loved dramatic
gestures, and sometimes wept in his box at the opera, had
despatched his daughter to London. The arrangements had
been intricate, and had taken nearly a week of trips to em-
bassies and tranquil, Madonnalike pauses before Polaroid
cameras. She'd needed seven different visas. Jetl, her father's
private secretary, was sent with her, and filled in all the forms,
leaving only the space for her signature. On the third day, in
the incense-smelling, tapestry-hung vestibule of the Maranian
embassy, he'd kissed her, and the twin oiled points of his beard
had stung her neck like mosquitoes. Then she'd giggled and
pulled away; he tasted of liquorice and menthol gum-re-
freshers. Now she daydreamed of Jetl and his purple cloak,
of hiding, crooked in its folds with his ringed fingers winking
in her hair . . . and of her father who called her his rabbit.
A lovely, stupid rabbit. She liked him saying that, and cut
his cigars for him with a penknife, and laid them in a neat
row for him on the table of the morning-room. Eight delicately
circumcised cigars, each showing a soft, damp tip of tobacco at
its head.

The *Telegraph* rattled. The Spainish had come in with
letters on a tray. The girl did not like the Spainish. She had
pale eyes flecked with blue like ovoids of gorgonzola, and

her skin was as dark as a nigger's. She was a common Spainish. You could see she'd been left too long in the sun. The Spainish arranged a clutch of letters above Mrs Phillips's plate of toast, paused, and insolently flipped a blue aerogramme to within three feet of the girl's plate. She had to reach for it, the sleeve of her dress ruckling above the elbow, under the slow cheesy eye of the Spainish.

The girl dropped her lids at the maid, waited, and raised them, expecting her to be gone. But she was still there, lolling, watching the blue aerogramme with the contemptuous sly greed of an alley cat.

'Uxtl,' said the girl. 'You go.' The Spainish didn't move; just swung her head away towards the old lady.

Mrs Phillips cracked her paper on its fold and stared for a moment at the foreign girl. 'Thank you, Andresa,' she said, and the Spainish, rolling her pupils up into her bronzed skull as she looked at the girl, left the room, the starched strings of her apron dancing on her rump.

'I will tell the girl when to go, dear,' said the old lady, with the exaggerated lip-movements that people use to talk to the deaf and the gaga.

'Pardon?'

But the old lady had begun to slit open her letters with an ivory rule.

'Spainishes not good. Frenches good, Swedishes . . . no Spainish. Never. Thiefs.'

The rule stopped in mid-slit above the jar of Cooper's Oxford Marmalade. There was a silence, a thin, stringy asthmatic sigh, and the rule finished its slice, very slowly and deliberately.

The girl took the rule from the table and opened her own letter. It was like a badly-managed rape. The paper tore in wrinkled jags around its seams, and the short letter, in her mother's baby-round writing, fell in two pieces on her plate. She fitted them together, matching the top and bottom halves of a line of words.

'May I have the knife, dear?'

Mudji. The aerogramme had trapped a little of her dust:

jasmine . . . the creamy colour of a full brocade dress . . . the taste, winy and sharp, of lipstick at the end of the evening when her parents came back in the Cadillac chauffeured by Jetl.

Dezne . . .

'The paper-knife—' The old lady reached for her; the girl thought she was after Mudji's letter and whipped back in her chair, but the old lady only pulled the ivory rule from between her fingers.

Dezne,

Z pzlm y caroo dy szlimp fazlim! Chzta fxam poolmx ty fanzia occherinzo mo puci. Dizikaps cantonas libikazzi fik, lamacchozonni gembria oozot kyroks — saglio maschtaps dimi-krave imbilbo, avele!!! Tescotta lasko ponvi encielda ombi. Dembo, demba . . . Piraxa chelui concosdat silba — ombilevi automobila casca cogenzi — oops!!!! Tomrava anhali disco Nancy Sinatra cali frenzo! Pocharta condifizzim poscamjat caselni intendlam flozm — Coogi jambi i posclui poribom ino hospringa!! Uxjo — onbozma — drivalgo comitzalna dig — Derimicso flom camriche goolap — floridabbo milesli Sv. Phillips caffervo sipsas!

Lervoji micsam—
Mudjier
XXXXXXXXXX

Z.M. *'Loodob?' cor 'Moxl?' phipso lervoji!!!*

Her mother had a wonderful sense of humour, everybody said so. She always made animals and children sound really comical, calling them by funny names and making them get up to all sorts of whimsical capers. She read her letter again and laughed aloud at the bit about Tescotta and Tom-rava—how she wished she could have seen that, it would have been a scream. Her eyes began to bulge, bcvine with self-pity.

'Good letter, dear?'

'Is humour. My mother. Makes to laughs of everythings.'

'Oh, good. It's so nice to get letters when one's abroad,

isn't it? One simply hangs on the post—'

But the girl was hearing the Nancy Sinatra record, and seeing Tescotta and Tomrava, five and six, dancing to the wind-up gramophone in the patio under the shade of the pink flowering vine. She saw the dark knots of the branches, the jug of iced water on its stand, heard, beyond the crumbling stucco of the high wall, with its intrepid Alpine blossoms breaking from every cranny and loose brick, the regular lap-lap of the tideless sea.

When she went to her room, the Spainish was there, folding back the coverlet. The girl, holding her letter, inched past the big, black-clad bottom of the maid. It didn't shrink for her. The Spainish stayed bent over the bed as if the foreign girl didn't exist. She walked stiffly, watching herself, to the dressing-table; things were not as they'd been before. The Spainish had been at her compact: she saw a dark smudge, a deeper furrow, in her foundation cream. The mirror, when she gazed in, held the imprint of a coarse Mediterranean face. The girl folded her letter into a tight, stamp-sized rectangle, and locked it into her trinket box with the key she kept on a chain around her neck.

The Spainish slowly unbent. She put her finger and thumb over her nose as she tapped with her other hand on the pillow.

'Phoo!' she said, sniffing so that you could hear the mucus bubbling in her sinuses.

'Uxtl! Uxtl! Go! Spainish! Pig! Spainish pig!'

She chased her, shouting, words in English and her own language breaking in her, painfully slowly, like airbubbles in oil. On the landing, the Spainish leaned on the banister, going 'Phoo! Phoo!', and holding her nose, and gibbering like a Rhesus monkey. When she went down the stairs she was still snorting, full of herself; the girl hung in her doorway and cried, a quiet hiccuping that took her body and rattled it like an empty can on a paved court in a wind.

But the Spanish hadn't got to her relics. When she opened the narrow drawer beneath the mirror, they were as she'd left them : the opals and garnets, the bead string of polished seeds, the silver mandala – she kissed the delicately tooled and beaten juncture of its snake's head and tail.

'Ansalvo corzimla Anvilvi condilmo . . .'

The Spanish would be a Catholic – Catlicis, gorgers of body and blood. The President had got rid of the Catlicis in his ordinance of 1968. They had put poison in the rivers and were, as the President said over the radio in a voice that rippled and throbbed like a harp, the swollen maggots of the economy – technicians, small shopkeepers, pay-clerks. After the edict, they huddled at the airport and on the dock side with bulging fibre suitcases that were patchworks of stamps and dockets. Catlicis. They smelled of garlic and rank velvet. They lived in shacks between clumps of bougainvillea, and bred prolifically, and were cruel to animals. On the day they left (a few had been hung and quartered in the villages, in what the Minister of Justice later called an outbreak of over-enthusiasm) the air had tasted cleaner, the vine-blossom had gained in brilliance.

Now she had the stink of the Catlico in her things. Everywhere she moved in the room, the spoor of the Spainish was there. Her phrasebooks and guides were piled in a brisk tidy column; her silver Sweet Sixteen bag was squashed under the sidetable; her hairbrushes were arranged like the hands of a clock at ten to two, or two crossed knives. She heard the slippered shuffle of the Spainish's feet along the landing. It stopped at her door. A rustle, the push of paper under the jamb, and the Spainish's laugh, a mad giggle, like the song of a demented thrush. A folded note, blue, scented, was on the floor.

In the old lady's writing.

Go to SOUTH KENSINGTON (Piccadilly Line)
1. Victoria and Albert Museum. (Costumes, furniture, Eng-

lish portrait miniatures. Look out for NICHOLAS HILLIARD – very pretty.)

2. Science Museum, across the road. Machines, telescopes, working models, etc. Interesting if you are mechanically minded.

3. Natural History Museum. Birds, animals, some prehistoric. My favourite. You will find directions to all of these in the tube station. I hope you have an enjoyable day. Dinner will be at 7.30 SHARP.

B.P.

She found most of these words in her dictionary. She wondered why the old lady thought she had a brain like a machine; nobody had ever said anything like that to her before. In her country, no one had ever thought she was clever. It wasn't polite for a girl to be clever, you got called 'spectacle face' and 'broken reed shoulder'. But perhaps in England it was a sort of compliment. She scrutinised the phrase again. It was a little gauche, maybe, but probably not intentionally malicious.

She sat down in front of the mirror. Was she changing? She stared, first at her chin, then tipped her forehead to the glass. She showed her cheeks in turn, wiping the skin over her cheekbones with her middle finger. Teeth . . . gums . . . the soft crannies where her nostrils folded back into her face. She found a fine spray of heat spots on her right cheek. She'd never had those before. It must be the air; greasy, mortal, London air that corroded the flesh as it bit into the brickwork and left the stucco stained with tonguelike tidemarks. She plucked her lashes, touched the rash of heat-spots with the loaded tip of a tiny brush like a painter putting in his final highlights, and watched her eyes turning in her head as she searched the reflection of the room in the glass. They looked like fish, like the black, glistening backs of trout hanging in the pool below the bridge at home. In the evenings, when the sun left the water, these trout would break the surface, twisting and diving, ringing the pool with splashes like giant raindrops. But her eyes were as distant, as shy, as subaqueous, as fish in the dead heat of summer. She could scatter them with a footfall.

For good luck, she avoided the cracks between the paving stones, counting off her steps in units of seven. She burned her finger along the nape of bristles on someone's close-pruned privet hedge. She ran down the escalator so fast that the posters on the side went into a liquid blur, their words skeetering like the pages of a thumbed book. Underground, she felt exhilarated, part of the secret circulation of the city. In a long porcelain tunnel, her shoes clicking with the crowd so that she couldn't tell which footsteps were her own, a hippie was singing to a guitar, squatting over its empty case.

'Love is just like a merry-go-round . . .' But the lines of the song and the metallic chords of the guitar rolled round and round inside the porcelain tube until they had the melancholy, tuneless resonance of a distant wind-harp. *Wuh-wuh wuh-wuh-wuh-wuh-bil-a-bah*. She liked it, and stopped, and dropped some shillings into the hippie's guitar case. *Thank-you-wuh-bil-a-bah*. When the train came, driving a column of hot stale air before it that stung her face like a hair-dryer at full blast, she could still hear the hippie and his guitar, sad, vague, remote, over the rattle of the doors and the electric rumble of the stopped engine.

Today, the names of the stations might as well have been in Cyrillic script. They stopped halfway in the carriage window, they held out no promises. She was more interested in a man in an electric blue suit who sat sucking the handle of his telescopic umbrella like a banana. Every so often, his eyes would travel swiftly from one end of the carriage to the other, return to centre, and drop over his umbrella as if he was saying prayers. Once he stared at the shining sun-buckle of her belt, and his big lips quivered, pouted, whispered something into the wet plastic handle. She covered her buckle with her *A-Z*.

Once her father had taken her to the pithead of one of his

mines. There'd been an explosion, and gangs of women in shawls muttered among the parked ambulances on the mauve asphalted hilltop. She had seen the wounded men winched up to the daylight in stretchers, had imagined how they must have seen that dim patch of sun growing and growing on their closed lids until it blinded them. Now it was as if she too was being cranked up a long dripping shaft, leaving the terrors and explosions of language behind. Out of words, out of reason, out of time, she came up and up on her stretcher, hearing the dull creak of the winch and the wordless muttering of the crowd in the sun up above.

She was at a formica Sandwich Bar; her coffee cup was enormous, big as a burial urn. Men spoke to her, and she went *yeh-yeh-yeh,* crooning to herself, gentling, not knowing what they said. The soft mush of identical green notes in her wallet thinned, as she scattered them on baubles. A wooden toy seen in a window, a little stick man with rubber joints and a perspex tube for a nose; a pair of sandals with cork soles awkward and thick as stilts; a thumb-size guardsman in a busby; a ticket for a competition; a deflated balloon; a matchbox full of tiny coloured bricks to make things with; a rippling, concertina string of postcard views of London; two paper stickers that said WHITEHALL and CARNABY STREET; a football scarf; a mock-brass alarm clock with a bright Union Jack on its face. Her Sweet Sixteen bag grew as lumpy with surprises as a Christmas stocking.

She found she was on a plunging Big Dipper of feelings. One moment she was singing in her head at the amazing dazzle of sun over Brompton Oratory, a giant, illuminated piece of master confectionery. The next, she imagined her body tossed and smashed in a red blur among the traffic of the Cromwell Road. Her body turned into a blown sheet of crepe paper, harmlessly dancing between the wheels of a column of taxis. She saw, on the back of a man's neck, as he teetered on the pavement waiting to cross, an egg-shaped growth that looked as if it was wrapped in turkey skin. The growth swelled to the size of Brompton Oratory. She saw herself, dwarfed to the height of her guardsman, picking her way through its repulsive folds.

At a corner chemists she bought a camera, grinning and pointing.

'Yeh, yeh, yeh. Is that one.'

The man put a film in for her. She scattered more bank-notes, and snapped the man.

'You'd need a flash for indoor shots.'

'Pardon?'

But she was gone. She photographed a policeman, a street scene, the front of the V & A (it leaned precipitously backwards in the viewfinder as she tried to get the top pinnacle into the frame), an episcopally purple taxi, a pale adolescent Buddhist with a shaven head and saffron robe, and a dog on a step with a tongue like a length of rubber hose. Then, suddenly depressed, she stuffed the camera into her bag beside the football scarf.

She ate a puffy pastry at a patisserie, and thought of her body thickening and swelling, the stretched skin of her stomach tight as a guitar string, pulling around the sag weight of flesh and guts. Her legs would turn to bloated stumps; she would waddle, hopeless as a terrapin on wet sand.

In the cathedral cool of the Victoria and Albert Museum, she dressed herself in all the costumes in the glass cases. She was in crinoline, in hoops, she dragged long velvet trains, she felt the dry crackle of a ruff tickling the soft gland beneath her jawbone. Around her, platoons of methodical Americanos quacked attentively through their adenoids. Weak sunlight filtered through windows of stained glass and made the polished tops of antique tables look as if they were swilling with a wet film. Everywhere she caught her own reflection, all mouth and eyes, a fish that swam to meet her against the invisible wall of an aquarium.

Twice she came up against the same man. His lugubrious, guilty face sprouted like an inverted root-vegetable from a suit of white denim. He reminded her of the colonial English in tropical kit who got gored by the clockwork tiger in the Indian Gallery.

The second time, he said, 'Hullo,' and looked ashamed.

''Allo,' she said, drifting past him in an eighteenth-century wedding dress. She could smell the musk of it clinging to her. She heard the squelch of the man's crepe soles behind her for a while, but they stopped at the William Morris Room.

In the dark grotto where the miniatures were lit like glowing icons, she found the Hilliard portrait of a sad Elizabethan gentleman. Leaning against a tree, framed by pale dogroses, every thorn picked out with a brushstroke, on the vellum, the young man stared, preoccupied, past her left shoulder, his black cloak slipping unnoticed from his back.

Dat poenas laudata fides, she read in letters of tiny gothic gold leaf over his head, but she couldn't puzzle its meaning out. She'd liked doing Latin with her tutor; he'd had the same feathery moustache as Hilliard's gentleman. But she was never very clever at it. In Latin, people were always having wars and laying siege to cities. French was nicer; it was about furniture and meals and aunts and uncles. But she would have liked to have known what the young man was saying. Perhaps he had just come back from a war. It looked as if he was in love. It would be easy to tear your dress on those dogroses: he was lucky not to have got holes in his tights. But then it was only a picture. Perhaps he wasn't really a misery man at all, and cracked jokes like her tutor, sly puns that she giggled over, then tried to work out later. The delicate shading where the young man's narrow white thighs joined under his doublet seemed to shimmer and widen, as if he was stepping towards her from his thicket of thorns.

Some girls, foreigns from the sound of them, were jostling against her in front of the glass. She spread her feet wide and stuck out her elbows like a peasant. They shuffled off, whispering. Then, in the dead silence of the grotto, she heard the apologetic squelch of crepe soles.

The man in the white denim suit pulled a face at her, a sick grin.

'Hilliard . . .' he said, and coughed, and turned away.

'Pardon?'

'Ah . . . admire . . . marvellous brushwork . . . eloquent sense of setting . . . fine . . . love miniatures . . . don't you?' She watched his tongue working away in his mouth as if it was busy putting things in drawers. She shrugged amiably. She would like to take a picture of that tongue making its noises. They sounded arbitrary, yet urgent, strings and dollops of sound that piled on top of each other; the man might have been trying to fill up a deep hole with them.

'I say,' he said when she started to move out of the grotto. 'I say . . .' and squelched behind her, slapping his rolled-up catalogue on the back of his wrist.

He bought her set-tea in the tea room, still tapping, stammering, hang-dog. 'Do you see what I mean?' He tried French on her : 'yeh, yeh, yeh', and she sank her fork into a squashy lemon-coloured gateau. He hissed the word *relationship* over and over again, and she thought of this boat with the man in the white suit in it drifting over a mirror sea above acres of pink coral.

Wherever she was, he was there too. On the steps of the museum, she photographed him. He turned into a little red and white homunculus in the viewfinder. Then, when she put the camera down, he was there, huge, close beside her, with the long face of an aardvark.

'I find it so easy to talk to you, you know? You understand?'

She handed the camera to him. He fussed with the knobs. 'You've run out of film.'

'Me,' she said. 'Photo me.'

He showed her the red window at the back. She wanted to be distant and small in the glass. He was talking technicalities to her.

'No worry,' she said, and stuffed the camera back into the Sweet Sixteen bag, her mouth creasing with impatience.

'All I want is to be your friend.' They were in a restaurant with chandeliers, and the empty circular face of the waiter hung between them like a low moon. The foreign girl coaxed a snail from its shell, as the man wooed her across the table with the guttural murmur of a sinner in a confessional box. He wrote words for her on slips of paper torn from his napkin. She looked at them and smiled; his handwriting looked like knotted balls of wool. 'You understand?'

'Is nice.'

'What would you like to do?'

'Discotheque,' she said, tired of all that language issuing from the man's mouth like ectoplasm. In her mother's dressing-room there were brown photographs of men in high collars and moustaches, their hair plastered back across their skulls in bangs. They were, said her mother, men of great spirituality, always in contact with the Other Side. They could make things materialise. In their photos, they looked as if they were swallowing dirty sheets.

'Spiritualismo?' she asked in a taxi as they sped round the darkening rim of the park.

He took her hand. His own felt like a clammy flannel.

'Yes,' he said, squeezing his grateful eyes, bland and serious as a marmoset. 'One does feel things with people sometimes that go beyond, I don't know, beyond . . . words.' His head swivelled back and forth. She imagined him coated in fur, his neck muscles bunching in the fur. They were travelling in parallel with another taxi; a man's face stared out from behind the glass. He wore a turban. She smiled at him. His taxi accelerated and he was pulled slowly, unevenly ahead of them. The last she saw of him, he was craning for a sight of her, his hand brushing at the foggy glass.

'What are you smiling at?'

'Pardon.'

Then they were in a big noise. 'Lulu's,' said the man, 'Oh, I know you'll like Lulu's.' It was a cave of pebbled walls and lights the colour of redcurrants. A young man with a wig drank Coca-Cola through a straw and put records on the gramophone. He stood behind the windshield of the severed front half of an old Austin car. Its headlamps winked on and off to the beat of the music, dizzy flashes of electric blue. In these stroboscopic pulses, the white denim suit took amazing leave of its owner: she saw it frozen, in rigid gesture after rigid gesture, unearthly, illuminated, like a saint falling out of the sky in an old picture.

The man bought her Campari and, fascinated, she watched the ice lumps in her glass leap into brilliance, their veins outlined in dazzling blue, then die. The music went *bang-bang-bang-bang*; it filled her cranium, as if the whole city was gathering itself up into a concerted heart and thumping in her head, *bang-bang-bang-bang*. The disc jockey's melon-slice smile hung disembodied over the bonnet of his car.

'I like,' she said.

When she came back from the Ladies, past the makeshift bamboo bar, she saw that the whole room was lined at its edges with bodies. They leaned and lay against each other on upholstered benches like so many uncollected parcels. She saw one stir, and in a strobe flash saw its bespectacled half-caste face. It looked like a face on a newsreel, surprised to be there, bathed in a sudden unasked-for celebrity. At the end of the record there was a general swelling and sighing amongst the bodies; the shaking out of a girl's hair, an up-raised ringed finger, a mouth in bulbous silhouette, an ankle bare between trouser leg and sock, a cigarette sharp and white in the flame of a silver lighter. She found the man in the white suit, absurdly upright, running his forefinger around the lip of his glass, making the glass squeal.

'Is funny,' she said.

In the middle of 'Brown Sugar' she found herself pulled into the flashing folds of the denim. A pocket slid by, and her head came to a stop beside a button. She took it between her lips. In the corner of her eye, she saw the bodies; they had the aquatic exhaling motion of the elastic skin of a toad. Above her the man was mumbling, questioning; his voice kept on rising in little breathy squeaks, but she was safe from it, cocooned in the terrific amplified crash of the record. The denim tasted dry, crackly; she could feel it printing its close weave on her cheek. When the man's lips trailed wetly over her forehead and through her hair she thought of glistening horned slugs, but did not mind.

'You like it, Brown Sugar!'

She liked it, turned her face, and licked the twin slugs of the man's lips with a butterfly-flicker of her tongue.

In another taxi, with the lights going out all over the streets, she thought she was on the pitching deck of a boat. 'Is asleep,' she said, and clung to the man, seeing him, white-suited, alone and drifting on his relation-ship. She found one of his hands around her left breast, deferential, apologetic. It was a guilty hand, and she took it away without rancour; it just seemed the wrong place for a hand to be.

He woke her at the house number she had given, and when the driver switched on the light in the cab, she saw his face, stretched, earnest, the colour of faded wallpaper. He was on a spree of words. She had forgotten something: for a moment she stared at the man trying to remember what it was — some feeling, some dim, generous turning of the heart. But, wherever it was, it wouldn't come. She settled gravely for a rubbery kiss.

'Bye-bye,' she said. 'Bye-bye.'

The taxi driver switched him off. One moment he was there, white, gesticulating, boiling with his speech; the next he was darkened, drowned by the starting motor. The taxi carried him off and she thought of the pictures of tumbrils in her history book.

Only the kitchen light was on in the house. When she opened the door, she saw the Spainish sitting at the oilcloth-covered table with a man. A chair skreaked as she came in, and the Spanish looked bad; her whole body had a fishy droop. Between the Spanish and her man was a half-empty bottle of dry sherry and two blue and white striped mugs. The man, Spainish too by the look of him, wore the servile smirk of a born waiter. His clip-on bow tie had come undone on one side, and dangled from his collar. He watched the girl as she snapped down the latch on the lock. His eyes, black and creamy as molten tar, were fixed on the flaring sun of her buckle.

She walked past them, through the far door, and into the darkened carpeted hall. The Spainish caught her at the foot of the stairs with the shy *pluck-pluck* of a trout going for an artificial fly.

'No tell?' said the Spainish, her head a featureless silhouette in the light from the kitchen. 'No tell lady?'

She had her foot on the first stair. 'No tell. I no tell.' And she laughed at the Spainish, a brisk dismissive snicker that left the maid still teetering nervously, still plucking at her. She climbed the stairs to her room.

She lay in bed in the dark, feeling the starched sheets heavy on her. The slightest movement made them screech like cicadas. She listened.

Through the open window of a distant room, she could hear the Spainish and her man. Their words had stopped. She listened to the mean, methodical thump of their bodies in the dark, like the *chop-chunk* of a woodcutter in the glade beyond the paddock. Then the thin, prolonged squeal of the Spainish, amazed and gratified, and the sobbing grunt of her man. The girl smiled and whispered to herself, her own company.

She would go to other cities, Rome, Paris, New York, Amsterdam; they stretched away in a haze of lights and taxis, of people murmuring in all their languages, of curtained rooms, of rivers that made buildings twice as tall, and dark places, and the corners of streets where strangers collided and separated, and long connecting tunnels where sounds softened to a low animal hum. Her sheets creaked round her as she turned in bed. She felt her cheek, touched the faint, corrugated imprint of denim. She could feel it fading under her finger. By morning, it would be quite gone.

Open-eyed, she lay absolutely still, listening to her city like a lover, hearing it wheeze and mumble in its sleep, waiting for the turquoise stir of sunrise and for the monotonous gobble of the pigeons on the lawn.

ELEVEN

A City Man

For eight months, the manuscript of this book has come with me wherever I have gone. In orange ring-bound note-books, growing increasingly pulpy and dog-eared, it has bounced, locked in my briefcase, between my knees in tubes and taxis. This exploration of the discontinuities of city life has provided a steady line of continuity for me – a plot for my own personal scenario. For the city and the book are opposed forms: to force the city's spread, contingency, and aimless motion into the tight progression of a narrative is to risk a total falsehood. There is no single point of view from which one can grasp the city as a whole. That, indeed, is the central distinction between the city and the small town. For each citizen, the city is a unique and private reality; and the novelist, planner or sociologist (whose aims have more in common than each is often willing to admit) finds himself dealing with an impossibly intricate tessellation of personal routes, spoors and histories within the labyrinth of the city. A good working definition of metropolitan life would centre on its intrinsic illegibility: most people are hidden most of the time, their appearances are brief and controlled, their movements secret, the outlines of their lives obscure. Writing a book one pretends to an omniscience and a command of logic which the experience of living in a city continuously con-tradicts. The truest city is the most private, and autobiography is the kind of writing which is least likely to muddy the city with the small untruths of seeming to know and deduce much more about its life than is really possible.

I came to London late, and its dazzle has not yet worn off. I still wake in the mornings glad to be here, reassured even by the irritations – the pounding of the traffic, the hangover look of the morning streets, the crush of ashen faces at the entrance to the tube. I grew up, and later worked, in places where strangers were stared at, and certain kinds of behaviour were not tolerated. Upright and censorious, these villages and small towns bred an ethic of knowing yourself, your limits, your station. Being conceited, getting above yourself, were cardinal sins against the community. The local mental hospitals were full of people whose identities had gone soft on them, or who had failed to measure up to the rigorous standards exacted by the community – raggy cadaverous men and bloated women who poked aimlessly about behind high railings, 'inadequates', in the awful word used by the jolly female social workers who came to tea at my family vicarage. 'He's in Knowle,' my father would say of yet another pale parishioner, and the hospital was a terminus for villagers who were not up to the strenuous moral art of villaging. Yet as an adolescent, I felt as mad as them, as unbounded, unsure and unfitted. With each job I took, the new town seemed to settle round me, a source of mild paranoia as soon as it was known. There are two hills, one above Aberystwyth, one above Norwich, and from them you can see the entire town ringed by green, a natural tourniquet on the social life inside, a limit to anonymity and privacy. I could not stand those views. One needs to live in a very large city indeed if one is not to be aware of its boundaries and controls; the rings of green hem in the self just as much as they circumscribe the factories and houses. In central London or New York, one cannot see or feel its limits – the city is boundless, perfectly labyrinthine. From here in Earl's Court, there is no horizon except that provided by distant squares full of houses exactly like one's own. The sky is streaked pink and lemon like the dyed backcloth in a theatre, and the noise of brakes and engines is a continuous swirl which penetrates every last still corner. One is hardly aware of the changing of the seasons, and the only stir of wildlife is among the pigeons, a scraggy, corrupted, urbanised lot who pester old ladies and live off *Swoop* birdfood, and loiter, gobbling and lurching like meths drinkers, on pavements whitened with their excrement. This is a place where everything is fabricated; much of it is shabby and jerry-built, but there isn't an inch which doesn't bear the imprint of someone's attempt to make something of himself and his landscape. The failures are endearing in themselves. Earl's Court is a living tribute to the fact that most of what we try is spoiled, ugly, done on the cheap, doomed to look tired and ripe for demolition almost as soon as it is completed. It does not set impossibly high standards for human conduct. It even makes virtue look easy by its own default. It is hard to be an 'inadequate' in Earl's Court.

I live here on a corner of the square in a borrowed flat, without property, at haphazard. By comparison with the tight family and neighbourhood life of the small town, I have few attachments or continuities. My existence is lax and unshaven. I have no proper job, just an irregular series of commissions and assignments, the chores and errands of a middle-class hobo. My occupation is characteristically metropolitan, dependent on those rarefied entrepreneurs which only an extremely complex urban industrial economy can support – agents, publishers, editors, producers of radio and TV programmes. In 1903, Georg Simmel observed:

> Cities are, first of all, seats of the highest economic division of labour. They produce thereby such extreme phenomena as in Paris the remunerative occupation of the *quatorzième*. They are persons who identify themselves by signs on their residences and who are ready at the dinner hour in correct attire, so that they can be quickly called upon if a dinner party should consist of thirteen persons.

Freelance writers, like professional diners-out, live off the slack in the metropolitan economy; their uses are etiolated and hard to define, and they tend to drift to the peripheral fringe of things, habitual onlookers and overhearers. My flat is pitched on the western edge of my private version of London, a place to make forays from, scavenging east-

wards for material and odd jobs. I am on the rim, both geographically and socially, and this marginal position suits me
very well. The villager who drifts to the outskirts of his
society soon finds himself the target for a hail of small
sharp stones; there marginality is mistrusted and derided as
a destructive anti-social force. It is different in cities. Nearly
everyone feels himself to be marginal in a metropolis, and
he is inclined to be indifferent to the eccentricities of other
people. That is something to be grateful for. My friends are
mostly expatriates and anomalies, people who have come
unstuck from their original countries and communities, for
whom the city is benign because it makes no special demands
on their loyalties. Me too. I find it hard to think of myself
as 'a citizen', but I belong to the city in a way that I have
been able to belong to very little else. I respect its rules
and special skills. Competence in the uniquely imaginative
and creative life of a big city is something to be proud of,
and even the oddest, most ramshackle characters can possess
it. More than anything else, I would like, sometime, to be
a capable citizen.

It is an ambition few people ever realise. Cities are scary
and impersonal, and the best most of us can manage is a
fragile hold on our route through the streets. We cling to
friends and institutions, exaggerate the importance of belonging, fear being alone too much. The freedom of the city is
enormous. Here one can choose and invent one's society, and
live more deliberately than anywhere else. Nothing is fixed,
the possibilities of personal change and renewal are endless
and open. But it is hard to learn to live as generously as
real citizenship demands. I spot in others the same mouse-
like caution which keeps me hugging the edge of the pavement, running from bolthole to bolthole, unequipped to
embrace that spaciousness and privacy of city life which so
often presents itself as mere emptiness and fog.

For me, a city day is a succession of guarded moves, as if
one was crossing a peat bog. Today I have a morning re-
cording at the BBC, and take the District Line east across
the city. Between tunnels there are stunted trees growing

out of the crumbling brickwork of the cuttings, and short stretches of greasy sky. On this line, one keeps a tenuous contact with the city up above, a stronger sense of direction, a feeling that there is some connection between the different locations which one turns up at then disappears from. South Kensington goes by, a derelict skeleton of Victorian railway whimsy, then Chelsea, and Victoria where I change for Oxford Circus. On tube stations one sees the really mad and abandoned. Astraddle an iron flight of steps, her cotton dress blowing in the draught from the trains, a drunken woman croons about religion. 'Jesus hasn't forgotten you,' she slurs at the quickening back of an embarrassed accountant. But I have a purpose in view, am going somewhere, and push past her with the rest of the crowd. We haven't come to that, yet.

Up from underground, on the jam of Regent Street, the crowd changes from workers to shoppers, a fair field of carrier bags crammed with blouses, lingerie and gew-gaws. Carried away on the tide of middle-aged women, past Peter Robinson's and the Lyons snack bar, I go soggy with sweat and scent. People on a crowded street create their own climate and season – this has the high temperature and smelly, feverish sirocco of a subtropical swamp. One looks up to the sky to discover with surprise that it is April; a weak, misty lozenge of sun over All Souls, Langham Place barely lights the street. A single abstracted face from the crowd : a woman with a raspberry patch spreading from nose to ear, with a quiff of dyed flaxen hair pulled half over it in an ashamed, ineffective gesture of concealment. Few details reach one while one is on the move through the crowd, and those which do are extreme and cruel. One remembers the grotesques, ranged along one's route like waxworks. In a crowd, Rowlandson turns into a realist, the caricature a measure of the sated urban perception which is woken only by deformity and gross extravagance. Even teashops here are neon-lighted, painted scarlet, and thick with stereo tapes of acid rock. The Russian travel agency is lost completely in the crowd; too ideologically pure to condescend

to the city knack of self advertisement and bizarre display.
It needs a flashing troika, ten feet tall, or Lenin's tomb is
luminous coloured perspex. The bored women, plunging
among the latest dress materials and Mickey Mouse clocks,
shove at each other, all mottled elbows and ringed fingers.
Not much more than a century ago, they might have been able
to round off their day with a good public hanging. I push
through them, a tired swimmer, my head filling with noise
and nonsense, going soft.

Broadcasting House is safe ground: John Reith dedicated
this 'temple of the arts and sciences' to Almighty God, no
less; and its severe wedge front looks down Regent Street
like a long, disapproving Presbyterian nose. One can sit
here in the lobby watching people come in out of the crowd.
Past the swing doors, they turn into somebodies; persons of
opinion and authority, with gestures and expressions that
will make secretaries remember them. This is a place for
christian names and gossip, for talking of people one hardly
knows with people one knows even less. In front of the
microphone, one's identity is magically enhanced, cushioned on
drink and recognition. Here the shyest and dullest men turn
waggish; their recorded laughter chortles portily on discussion programmes, while their long jokes are mostly edited
out. Out of the crowd, we double in size, figures of carnival,
bursting with impressions of the latest experimental novel
and the newest piece of Hungarian *cinema verité*.

But the street is a great leveller, and, returned to the
crowd, one shrinks back to normal. This is the time to seek
out phone boxes, to set oneself up with some immediate
destinations. Pubs and sandwich bars soon make one fizzle
out to nothing in the crush, and I run to ground, nosing
acquaintances from out of the woodwork. A drinking club in
Greek Street, a billiards club in Frith Street, the Savile Club
on Brook Street, are my corners-off from the city, sanctuaries
to head for when I feel myself going soft. They hold friends
and, with friends, the assurance that one belongs, not just
to the club, but to the city.

The drinking club is a long dim room which always has

its curtains drawn against the public world beyond. A trades-union leader, his face familiar from the TV screen, is at the bar telling a long dirty story. On TV, he always wears an expression of unnatural sententious sobriety and moral in-dignation – he looks as unionists are expected to look, and his cover is a good and practised one. But here, a step away from the street and the screen, his old actor's face lets go. 'Then it's the Greek's turn. Well the Greek, he goes up there, and there's a hell of a banging . . . furniture falling, legs off the bed . . .' A far cry from parity and exploitation, but truer, in its fashion. My friend is slopping beer in a corner under a scarlet bulb; a private person in black, another escapee. Meetings in the city, even when you have arranged them beforehand, are always small coincidences to be glad of and surprised about.

But on the far edge of each engagement there is always the unfathomed area of panic, when you know that you have to flop back again into the crowd. These moments of privacy and recognition and intense communicativeness are delicate bubbles, and in time they burst. You sustain your conversation, or the perfect angle of the cue ball on the black against the city. I keep most things going too long, am reluctant to leave. Back among strangers – the essential con-dition of metropolitan life – straphanging in a rush hour tube, everyone avoids each other's eyes. I lurch between an Indian with perfectly pared fingernails and a straw-hatted lady with a Harrods green plastic bag. Who belong to what? Guesses do not take one far. Yet each city-life is an intricate pattern of belonging interspersed with these stretches of locomotion when one is stripped of credentials and credibility, when one sees oneself as just another moon-face in the crowd.

It is surely because of this that the city exaggerates our sexuality. In the crowd, I catch the eyes of girls – that rapid, casual, essentially urban interrogation : a glance held between a man and a woman fixes each for a moment, gives them back at least the minimal identity of their sex. The train pulls away from the platform, and she too, behind the double

glass of the carriage window, but we have made each other
exist for an instant; another belonging, of a kind. A big
city is an encyclopedia of sexual possibility, and the eye-
language of the crowd asserts this possibility without the
risk of real encounters. It happens best at a distance – when
you are on an up-escalator while the girl is travelling down;
through carriage windows; across streets thick with traffic.
These are not invitations to an assignation. They are simply
the small, reassuring services which men and women can
render for each other, and they are particularly precious
when we are sucked in and reduced by the crowd.

Home, alone, is a place for picking thorns out of one's
skin, for finding oneself again. My old chair, the shelves of
books, the scatter of weekly magazines, cigarette butts and
unanswered mail – these are what we always come back to in
the end after the choppy crossings of the city. They survive
after most of the people one has met have been swallowed by
the fog. And in the other flats in the house, the crash of a
door, the distant buzz of a bell, a record put on the gramophone, isolate this room. The crowd starts in the communal
hall and its noise is always there to remind me of this small
patch of space which is my exclusive corner of the city.
I've never in the past been so territorially possessive, so
conscious of walls and boundaries. It is not just that city
life hems us in so closely together that we develop the
aggressive animal's protective instincts towards our own scraps
of space; it is rather that the stranger in one's hall or on
the pavement outside is *so* strange, so culturally different
from oneself, so much a member of clubs and castes to which
one has no access, that his presence continually forces one
to question one's own identity. Sometimes one treats oneself
as one might another stranger in the crowd – in one's own
head, the language of the Personal Column . . . '*New Statesman*-reader, 30, separated, interested in books and the country
. . .' A curious, egoistic way of going on, but, I think, a
characteristically metropolitan one. We are on the brink of
being strangers to ourselves in the city.

Blown up one moment, punctured and shrivelled the next

we need to hold on tight to avoid going completely soft in a soft city. So much of metropolitan life is just the show-ing of symptoms of fright. In the city one clings to nostalgic and unreal signs of community, takes forced refuge in codes, badges and coteries; the city's life, of surfaces and locomo-tion, usually seems too dangerous and demanding to live through with any confidence. The mad egotism of the man who stops you in Soho Square to tell you he is John the Baptist, or the weird rural delusions of another tramp nearby who fishes hopefully through a grating at the corner of Old Compton Street ('Caught anything?' 'I had some good bites.'), seem not unlikely consequences of the exercise of the free-dom of the city. Its discontinuities give one vertigo; few people who aren't criminals or psychopaths will risk themselves on the rollercoaster ride of change and incongruity which the city offers. So much of city life is an elaborate process of building up defences against the city – the self a fortified town raised against the stranger. We hedge ourselves in behind dreams and illusions, construct make-believe villages and make-believe families. It could perhaps be otherwise; but we shall need more daring, more cool understanding than we are displaying at present. We live in cities badly; we have built them up in culpable innocence and now fret helplessly in a synthetic wilderness of our own construction. We need – more urgently than architectural utopias, ingenious traffic disposal systems, or ecological programmes – to comprehend the nature of citizenship, to make a serious imaginative assess-ment of that special relationship between the self and the city; its unique plasticity, its privacy and freedom.

Harvill Paperbacks are published by Collins Harvill,
a Division of the Collins Group.